DANCING
AT THE
EDGE
OF THE
WORLD

BOOKS BY URSULA K. LE GUIN

NOVELS

Always Coming Home
The Eye of the Heron
The Beginning Place
Malafrena
Very Far Away from Anywhere Else
The Word for World Is Forest
The Dispossessed
The Lathe of Heaven
The Farthest Shore
The Tombs of Atuan
A Wizard of Earthsea
The Left Hand of Darkness
City of Illusions
Planet of Exile
Rocannon's World

SHORT STORIES

Buffalo Gals and Other Animal Presences
The Compass Rose
Orsinian Tales
The Wind's Twelve Quarters

FOR CHILDREN

Catwings
Solomon Leviathan's 931st Trip Around the World
A Visit from Dr. Katz
Leese Webster

POETRY AND CRITICISM

Wild Oats and Fireweed
Hard Words
The Language of the Night
From Elfland to Poughkeepsie
Wild Angels

DANCING
AT THE
EDGE
OF THE
WORLD

THOUGHTS ON WORDS, WOMEN, PLACES

Ursula K. Le Guin

GROVE PRESS

New York

Published by Grove Press
a division of Wheatland Corporation
841 Broadway
New York, N.Y. 10003

Library of Congress Cataloging-in-Publication Data

Le Guin, Ursula K., 1929–
Dancing at the edge of the world: thoughts on words, women, places/
by Ursula K. Le Guin.
p.   cm.
ISBN 0-8021-1105-X
I. Title.
PS3562.E42D36   1988
814'.54—dc 19   88-11266
                              CIP

Designed by Irving Perkins Associates
Manufactured in the United States of America
This book is printed on acid-free paper.
First Edition 1989

10 9 8 7 6 5 4 3 2 1

CONTENTS

REVIEWS

KEY: ♀ Feminism   ○ Social Responsibility   □ Literature   → Travel

INTRODUCTORY NOTE

This is a collection of talks, essays, occasional pieces, and reviews from the past ten years. An earlier book of my nonfictional writings, *The Language of the Night,* edited by my friend Susan Wood, has been in print during this same decade. I have decided that the trouble with print is, it never changes its mind.

The pieces are arranged in chronological order (except for the reviews, which are all together at the end). This may be a rather simplistic arrangement, but it does provide a sort of mental biography, a record of responses to ethical and political climates, of the transforming effect of certain literary ideas, and of the changes of a mind.

Writers get asked to make speeches on all kinds of topics. Being sometimes weak of will, I sometimes agree to speak. Being a writer but not a speaker, I have to write out what I'm going to say, if it's longer than eight words. Thus I have the texts of talks that might otherwise (mercifully?) have passed with the occasion. These "public" pieces reflect matters personally important to me, in that I agreed to talk about them. Other pieces, such as the commencement addresses, the travel diaries, and the essays, reflect my own interests more directly.

Writing is the only thing besides housework that I really know much about; therefore it is the only thing I feel competent to teach. When asked to be didactic in public, I try to limit myself to topics on which, without claiming expertise or wisdom, an effort to think honestly and feelingly might do some good, or matters on which I think I ought to stand up and be counted, lest silence collude with injustice. A number of such pieces are in this book, and they are going to bother people who are able, as I am not, to make clear distinctions between Art and Politics, between High Art and low stuff, between being a woman and being a feminist, and so on. My goal always being to subvert as much as possible without hurting anybody's feelings, I have devised a system whereby readers may find what they want and avoid what they don't. In the Table of

Contents, small symbols will be seen to follow the titles—as in the *Guide Michelin* or AAA handbooks, where little knives and forks and beds and wineglasses tell you what to expect. The *Guide Ursuline* has four symbols indicating the principal character or bent of each piece:

     ♀ (a woman):   feminism
     ○ (the world):   social responsibility
     □ (a book):   literature, writing
     → (a direction):   travel

I hope these are useful, as indicating which way or ways a piece tends, and so steering readers unsympathetic to that tendency away from it—unless, of course, they're willing to take whatever the landlady offers.

Brief introductory notes of time and place are provided where needed; footnotes, mostly rather erratic, I fear, will be found at the end of the piece they belong to. The date at the head of each piece is the year it was written (sometimes different from the year of publication, which can be found in the Acknowledgments). Where the text differs from a published text, it is usually because I follow my manuscript, not the edited version; occasionally because I emended a fault or patched a glitch while preparing this book.

TALKS AND ESSAYS

1976–1988

THE SPACE CRONE

(1976)

The menopause is probably the least glamorous topic imaginable; and this is interesting, because it is one of the very few topics to which cling some shreds and remnants of taboo. A serious mention of menopause is usually met with uneasy silence; a sneering reference to it is usually met with relieved sniggers. Both the silence and the sniggering are pretty sure indications of taboo.

Most people would consider the old phrase "change of life" a euphemism for the medical term "menopause," but I, who am now going through the change, begin to wonder if it isn't the other way round. "Change of life" is too blunt a phrase, too factual. "Menopause," with its chime-suggestion of a mere pause after which things go on as before, is reassuringly trivial.

But the change is not trivial, and I wonder how many women are brave enough to carry it out wholeheartedly. They give up their reproductive capacity with more or less of a struggle, and when it's gone they think that's all there is to it. Well, at least I don't get the Curse any more, they say, and the only reason I felt so depressed sometimes was hormones. Now I'm myself again. But this is to evade the real challenge, and to lose, not only the capacity to ovulate, but the opportunity to become a Crone.

In the old days women who survived long enough to attain the menopause more often accepted the challenge. They had, after all, had practice. They had already changed their life radically once before, when they ceased to be virgins and became mature women/wives/matrons/mothers/mistresses/whores/etc. This change involved not only the physiological alterations of puberty— the shift from barren childhood to fruitful maturity— but a socially recognized alteration of being: a change of condition from the sacred to the profane.

3

With the secularization of virginity now complete, so that the once awesome term "virgin" is now a sneer or at best a slightly dated word for a person who hasn't copulated yet, the opportunity of gaining or regaining the dangerous/sacred condition of being at the Second Change has ceased to be apparent.

Virginity is now a mere preamble or waiting room to be got out of as soon as possible; it is without significance. Old age is similarly a waiting room, where you go after life's over and wait for cancer or a stroke. The years before and after the menstrual years are vestigial: the only meaningful condition left to women is that of fruitfulness. Curiously, this restriction of significance coincided with the development of chemicals and instruments that make fertility itself a meaningless or at least secondary characteristic of female maturity. The significance of maturity now is not the capacity to conceive but the mere ability to have sex. As this ability is shared by pubescents and by postclimacterics, the blurring of distinctions and elimination of opportunities is almost complete. There are no rites of passage because there is no significant change. The Triple Goddess has only one face: Marilyn Monroe's, maybe. The entire life of a woman from ten or twelve through seventy or eighty has become secular, uniform, changeless. As there is no longer any virtue in virginity, so there is no longer any meaning in menopause. It requires fanatical determination now to become a Crone.

Women have thus, by imitating the life condition of men, surrendered a very strong position of their own. Men are afraid of virgins, but they have a cure for their own fear and the virgin's virginity: fucking. Men are afraid of crones, so afraid of them that their cure for virginity fails them; they know it won't work. Faced with the fulfilled Crone, all but the bravest men wilt and retreat, crestfallen and cockadroop.

Menopause Manor is not merely a defensive stronghold, however. It is a house or household, fully furnished with the necessities of life. In abandoning it, women have narrowed their domain and impoverished their souls. There are things the Old Woman can do, say, and think that the Woman cannot do, say, or think. The Woman has to give up more than her menstrual periods before she can do, say, or think them. She has got to change her life.

The nature of that change is now clearer than it used to be. Old age is not virginity but a third and new condition; the virgin must be celibate, but the crone need not. There was a confusion there, which the separation of female sexuality from reproductive capacity, via modern contraceptives, has cleared up. Loss of fertility does not mean loss of desire and fulfillment. But it does entail a change, a change involving matters even more important—if I may venture a heresy—than sex.

The woman who is willing to make that change must become pregnant with herself, at last. She must bear herself, her third self, her old age, with travail and alone. Not many will help her with that birth. Certainly no male obstetrician will time her contractions, inject her with sedatives, stand ready with forceps, and neatly stitch up the torn membranes. It's hard even to find an old-fashioned midwife, these days. That pregnancy is long, that labor is hard. Only one is harder, and that's the final one, the one that men also must suffer and perform.

It may well be easier to die if you have already given birth to others or yourself, at least once before. This would be an argument for going through all the discomfort and embarrassment of becoming a Crone. Anyhow it seems a pity to have a built-in rite of passage and to dodge it, evade it, and pretend nothing has changed. That is to dodge and evade one's womanhood, to pretend one's like a man. Men, once initiated, never get the second chance. They never change again. That's their loss, not ours. Why borrow poverty?

Certainly the effort to remain unchanged, young, when the body gives so impressive a signal of change as the menopause, is gallant; but it is a stupid, self-sacrificial gallantry, better befitting a boy of twenty than a woman of forty-five or fifty. Let the athletes die young and laurel-crowned. Let the soldiers earn the Purple Hearts. Let women die old, white-crowned, with human hearts.

If a space ship came by from the friendly natives of the fourth planet of Altair, and the polite captain of the space ship said, "We have room for one passenger; will you spare us a single human being, so that we may converse at leisure during the long trip back to Altair and learn from an exemplary person the nature of the race?"—I suppose what most people would want to do is provide them with a fine, bright, brave young man, highly educated and in peak physical condition. A Russian cosmonaut would be ideal (American astronauts are mostly too old). There would surely be hundreds, thousands of volunteers, just such young men, all worthy. But I would not pick any of them. Nor would I pick any of the young women who would volunteer, some out of magnanimity and intellectual courage, others out of a profound conviction that Altair couldn't possibly be any worse for a woman than Earth is.

What I would do is go down to the local Woolworth's, or the local village marketplace, and pick an old woman, over sixty, from behind the costume jewelry counter or the betel-nut booth. Her hair would not be red or blonde or lustrous dark, her skin would not be dewy fresh, she would not have the secret of eternal youth. She might, however, show you a small snapshot of her grandson, who is working in Nairobi. She is a bit vague about where Nairobi is, but extremely proud of the grandson. She has worked hard at small, unimportant jobs all her life, jobs like cooking, cleaning, bringing up kids, selling little objects of adornment or pleasure to other people. She was a virgin once, a long time ago, and then a sexually potent fertile female, and then went through menopause. She has given birth several times and faced death several times—the same times. She is facing the final birth/death a little more nearly and clearly every day now. Sometimes her feet hurt something terrible. She never was educated to anything like her capacity, and that is a shameful waste and a crime against humanity, but so common a crime should not and cannot be hidden from Altair. And anyhow she's not dumb. She has a stock of sense, wit, patience, and experiential shrewdness, which the Altaireans might, or might not, perceive as wisdom. If they are wiser than we, then of course we don't know how they'd perceive it. But if they are wiser than we, they may know how to perceive that inmost mind and heart which we, working on mere guess and hope, proclaim to be humane. In any case, since they are curious and kindly, let's give them the best we have to give.

The trouble is, she will be very reluctant to volunteer. "What would an old woman like me do on Altair?" she'll say. "You ought to send one of those scientist men, they can talk to those funny-looking green people. Maybe Dr. Kissinger should go. What about sending the Shaman?" It will be very hard to explain to her that we want her to go because only a person who has experienced, accepted, and acted the entire human condition—the essential quality of which is Change—can fairly represent humanity. "Me?" she'll say, just a trifle slyly. "But I never did anything."

But it won't wash. She knows, though she won't admit it, that Dr. Kissinger has not gone and will never go where she has gone, that the scientists and the shamans have not done what she has done. Into the space ship, Granny.

IS GENDER
NECESSARY?
REDUX

(1976/1987)

"Is Gender Necessary?" first appeared in Aurora, *that splendid first anthology of science fiction written by women, edited by Susan Anderson and Vonda N. McIntyre. It was later included in* The Language of the Night. *Even then I was getting uncomfortable with some of the statements I made in it, and the discomfort soon became plain disagreement. But those were just the bits that people kept quoting with cries of joy.*

It doesn't seem right or wise to revise an old text severely, as if trying to obliterate it, hiding the evidence that one had to go there to get here. It is rather in the feminist mode to let one's changes of mind, and the processes of change, stand as evidence—and perhaps to remind people that minds that don't change are like clams that don't open. So I here reprint the original essay entire, with a running commentary in bracketed italics. I request and entreat anyone who wishes to quote from this piece henceforth to use or at least include these reconsiderations. And I do very much hope that I don't have to print re-reconsiderations in 1997, since I'm a bit tired of chastising myself.

In the mid-1960s the women's movement was just beginning to move again, after a fifty-year halt. There was a groundswell gathering. I felt it, but I didn't know it was a groundswell; I just thought it was something wrong with me. I considered myself a feminist; I didn't see how you could be a thinking woman and not be a femi-

7

nist; but I had never taken a step beyond the ground gained for us by Emmeline Pankhurst and Virginia Woolf.

[Feminism has enlarged its ground and strengthened its theory and practice immensely, and enduringly, in these past twenty years; but has anyone actually taken a step "beyond" Virginia Woolf? The image, implying an ideal of "progress," is not one I would use now.]

Along about 1967, I began to feel a certain unease, a need to step on a little farther, perhaps, on my own. I began to want to define and understand the meaning of sexuality and the meaning of gender, in my life and in our society. Much had gathered in the unconscious— both personal and collective—which must either be brought up into consciousness or else turn destructive. It was that same need, I think, that had led Beauvoir to write *The Second Sex,* and Friedan to write *The Feminine Mystique,* and that was, at the same time, leading Kate Millett and others to write their books, and to create the new feminism. But I was not a theoretician, a political thinker or activist, or a sociologist. I was and am a fiction writer. The way I did my thinking was to write a novel. That novel, *The Left Hand of Darkness,* is the record of my consciousness, the process of my thinking.

Perhaps, now that we have all *[well, quite a lot of us, anyhow]* moved on to a plane of heightened consciousness about these matters, it might be of some interest to look back on the book, to see what it did, what it tried to do, and what it might have done, insofar as it is a "feminist" *[strike the quotation marks, please]* book. (Let me repeat that last qualification, once. The fact is that the real subject of the book is not feminism or sex or gender or anything of the sort; as far as I can see, it is a book about betrayal and fidelity. That is why one of its two dominant sets of symbols is an extended metaphor of winter, of ice, snow, cold: the winter journey. The rest of this discussion will concern only half, the lesser half, of the book.)

[This parenthesis is overstated; I was feeling defensive, and resentful that critics of the book insisted upon talking only about its "gender problems," as if it were an essay not a novel. "The fact is that the real *subject of the book is . . ." This is bluster. I had opened a can of worms and was trying hard to shut it. "The fact is," however, that there are other aspects to the book, which are involved with its sex/gender aspects quite inextricably.]*

It takes place on a planet called Gethen, whose human inhabitants differ from us in their sexual physiology. Instead of our continuous sexuality, the Gethenians have an oestrus period, called *kemmer.* When they are not in kemmer, they are sexually inactive and impotent; they are also androgynous. An observer in the book describes the cycle:

In the first phase of kemmer [the individual] remains completely androgynous. Gender, and potency, are not attained in
isolation. . . . Yet the sexual impulse is tremendously strong in
this phase, controlling the entire personality. . . . When the individual finds a partner in kemmer, hormonal secretion is further
stimulated (most importantly by touch—secretion? scent?) until
in one partner either a male or female hormonal dominance is
established. The genitals engorge or shrink accordingly, foreplay
intensifies, and the partner, triggered by the change, takes on
the other sexual role (apparently without exception). . . . Normal
individuals have no predisposition to either sexual role in kemmer; they do not know whether they will be the male or the
female, and have no choice in the matter. . . .The culminant
phase of kemmer lasts from two to five days, during which
sexual drive and capacity are at maximum. It ends fairly
abruptly, and if conception has not taken place, the individual
returns to the latent phase and the cycle begins anew. If the
individual was in the female role and was impregnated, hormonal activity of course continues, and for the gestation and
lactation periods this individual remains female. . . .With the
cessation of lactation the female becomes once more a perfect
androgyne. No physiological habit is established, and the
mother of several children may be the father of several more.

Why did I invent these peculiar people? Not just so that the book
could contain, halfway through it, the sentence "The king was
pregnant"—though I admit that I am fond of that sentence. Not,
certainly not, to propose Gethen as a model for humanity. I am not
in favor of genetic alteration of the human organism—not at our
present level of understanding. I was not recommending the Gethenian sexual setup: I was using it. It was a heuristic device, a thought-
experiment. Physicists often do thought-experiments. Einstein
shoots a light ray through a moving elevator; Schrödinger puts a cat
in a box. There is no elevator, no cat, no box. The experiment is
performed, the question is asked, in the mind. Einstein's elevator,
Schrödinger's cat, my Gethenians, are simply a way of thinking.
They are questions, not answers; process, not stasis. One of the
essential functions of science fiction, I think, is precisely this kind of
question-asking: reversals of a habitual way of thinking, metaphors
for what our language has no words for as yet, experiments in
imagination.

The subject of my experiment, then, was something like this:
Because of our lifelong social conditioning, it is hard for us to see
clearly what, besides purely physiological form and function, truly

differentiates men and women. Are there real differences in temperament, capacity, talent, psychic processes, etc.? If so, what are
they? Only comparative ethnology offers, so far, any solid evidence
on the matter, and the evidence is incomplete and often contradic-
tory. The only going social experiments that are truly relevant are
the kibbutzim and the Chinese communes, and they too are inconclusive—and hard to get unbiased information about. How to find
out? Well, one can always put a cat in a box. One can send an imaginary, but conventional, indeed rather stuffy, young man from Earth
into an imaginary culture which is totally free of sex roles because
there is no, absolutely no, physiological sex distinction. I eliminated
gender, to find out what was left. Whatever was left would be,
presumably, simply human. It would define the area that is shared
by men and women alike.

I still think that this was a rather neat idea. But as an experiment,
it was messy. All results were uncertain; a repetition of the experiment by someone else, or by myself seven years later, would probably give quite different results. *[Strike the word "probably" and replace it
with "certainly."]* Scientifically, this is most disreputable. That's all
right; I am not a scientist. I play the game where the rules keep
changing.

Among these dubious and uncertain results, achieved as I
thought, and wrote, and wrote, and thought, about my imaginary
people, three appear rather interesting to me.

First: the absence of war. In the thirteen thousand years of
recorded history on Gethen, there has not been a war. The people
seem to be as quarrelsome, competitive, and aggressive as we are;
they have fights, murders, assassinations, feuds, forays, and so on.
But there have been no great invasions by peoples on the move, like
the Mongols in Asia or the Whites in the New World: partly because
Gethenian populations seem to remain stable in size, they do not
move in large masses, or rapidly. Their migrations have been slow,
no one generation going very far. They have no nomadic peoples,
and no societies that live by expansion and aggression against other
societies. Nor have they formed large, hierarchically governed
nation-states, the mobilizable entity that is the essential factor in
modern war. The basic social unit all over the planet is a group of
two hundred to eight hundred people, called a *hearth,* a structure
founded less on economic convenience than on sexual necessity
(there must be others in kemmer at the same time), and therefore
more tribal than urban in nature, though overlaid and interwoven
with a later urban pattern. The hearth tends to be communal,

independent, and somewhat introverted. Rivalries between hearths, as between individuals, are channeled into a socially approved form of aggression called *shifgrethor*, a conflict without physical violence, involving one-upsmanship, the saving and losing of face—conflict ritualized, stylized, controlled. When shifgrethor breaks down there may be physical violence, but it does not become mass violence, remaining limited, personal. The active group remains small. The dispersive trend is as strong as the cohesive. Historically, when hearths gathered into a nation for economic reasons, the cellular pattern still dominated the centralized one. There might be a king and a parliament, but authority was not enforced so much by might as by the use of shifgrethor and intrigue, and was accepted as custom, without appeal to patriarchal ideals of divine right, patriotic duty, etc. Ritual and parade were far more effective agents of order than armies or police. Class structure was flexible and open; the value of the social hierarchy was less economic than aesthetic, and there was no great gap between rich and poor. There was no slavery or servitude. Nobody owned anybody. There were no chattels. Economic organization was rather communistic or syndicalistic than capitalistic, and was seldom highly centralized.

During the time span of the novel, however, all this is changing. One of the two large nations of the planet is becoming a genuine nation-state, complete with patriotism and bureaucracy. It has achieved state capitalism and the centralization of power, authoritarian government, and a secret police; and it is on the verge of achieving the world's first war.

Why did I present the first picture, and show it in the process of changing to a different one? I am not sure. I think it is because I was trying to show a balance—and the delicacy of a balance. To me the "female principle" is, or at least historically has been, basically anarchic. It values order without constraint, rule by custom not by force. It has been the male who enforces order, who constructs power structures, who makes, enforces, and breaks laws. On Gethen, these two principles are in balance: the decentralizing against the centralizing, the flexible against the rigid, the circular against the linear. But balance is a precarious state, and at the moment of the novel the balance, which had leaned toward the "feminine," is tipping the other way.

[At the very inception of the whole book, I was interested in writing a novel about people in a society that had never had a war. That came first. The androgyny came second. (Cause and effect? Effect and cause?)

I would now write this paragraph this way: . . . The "female principle" has historically been anarchic; that is, anarchy has historically been identified as female. The domain allotted to women—"the family," for example— is the area of order without coercion, rule by custom not by force. Men have reserved the structures of social power to themselves (and those few women whom they admit to it on male terms, such as queens, prime ministers); men make the wars and peaces, men make, enforce, and break the laws. On Gethen, the two polarities we perceive through our cultural conditioning as male and female are neither, and are in balance: consensus with authority, decentralizing with centralizing, flexible with rigid, circular with linear, hierarchy with network. But it is not a motionless balance, there being no such thing in life, and at the moment of the novel, it is wobbling perilously.]

Second: the absence of exploitation. The Gethenians do not rape their world. They have developed a high technology, heavy industry, automobiles, radios, explosives, etc., but they have done so very slowly, absorbing their technology rather than letting it overwhelm them. They have no myth of Progress at all. Their calendar calls the current year always the Year One, and they count backward and forward from that.

In this, it seems that what I was after again was a balance: the driving linearity of the "male," the pushing forward to the limit, the logicality that admits no boundary—and the circularity of the "female," the valuing of patience, ripeness, practicality, livableness. A model for this balance, of course, exists on Earth: Chinese civilization over the past six millennia. (I did not know when I wrote the book that the parallel extends even to the calendar; the Chinese historically never had a linear dating system such as the one that starts with the birth of Christ.)

[A better model might be some of the pre-Conquest cultures of the Americas, though not those hierarchical and imperialistic ones approvingly termed, by our hierarchical and imperialistic standards, "high." The trouble with the Chinese model is that their civilization instituted and practiced male domination as thoroughly as the other "high" civilizations. I was thinking of a Taoist ideal, not of such practices as bride-selling and foot-binding, which we are trained to consider unimportant, nor of the deep misogyny of Chinese culture, which we are trained to consider normal.]

Third: the absence of sexuality as a continuous social factor. For four-fifths of the month, a Gethenian's sexuality plays no part at all in his social life (unless he's pregnant); for the other one-fifth, it dominates him absolutely. In kemmer, one must have a partner, it is imperative. (Have you ever lived in a small apartment with a tabby-cat in heat?) Gethenian society fully accepts this imperative. When a

Gethenian has to make love, he does make love, and everybody expects him to, and approves of it.

[I would now write this paragraph this way: . . . For four-fifths of the month, sexuality plays no part at all in a Gethenian's social behavior; for the other one-fifth, it controls behavior absolutely. In kemmer, one must have a partner, it is imperative. (Have you ever lived in a small apartment with a tabby-cat in heat?) Gethenian society fully accepts this imperative. When Gethenians have to make love, they do make love, and everybody else expects it and approves of it.]

But still, human beings are human beings, not cats. Despite our continuous sexuality and our intense self-domestication (domesticated animals tend to be promiscuous, wild animals pair-bonding, familial, or tribal in their mating), we are very seldom truly promiscuous. We do have rape, to be sure—no other animal has equaled us there. We have mass rape, when an army (male, of course) invades; we have prostitution, promiscuity controlled by economics; and sometimes ritual abreactive promiscuity controlled by religion; but in general we seem to avoid genuine license. At most we award it as a prize to the Alpha Male, in certain situations; it is scarcely ever permitted to the female without social penalty. It would seem, perhaps, that the mature human being, male or female, is not satisfied by sexual gratification without psychic involvement, and in fact may be *afraid of it,* to judge by the tremendous variety of social, legal, and religious controls and sanctions exerted over it in all human societies. Sex is a great mana, and therefore the immature society, or psyche, sets great taboos about it. The maturer culture, or psyche, can integrate these taboos or laws into an internal ethical code, which, while allowing great freedom, does not permit the treatment of another person as an object. But, however irrational or rational, there is always a code.

Because the Gethenians cannot have sexual intercourse unless both partners are willing, because they cannot rape or be raped, I figured that they would have less fear and guilt about sex than we tend to have; but still it is a problem for them, in some ways more than for us, because of the extreme, explosive, imperative quality of the oestrous phase. Their society would have to control it, though it might move more easily than we from the taboo stage to the ethical stage. So the basic arrangement, I found, in every Gethenian community, is that of the kemmerhouse, which is open to anyone in kemmer, native or stranger, so that he can find a partner *[read: so that they can find sexual partners]*. Then there are various customary (not legal) institutions, such as the kemmering group, a group who choose to come together during kemmer as a regular thing; this is like the primate tribe, or group marriage. Or there is the possibility of vowing kemmering, which is marriage, pair-bonding for life, a personal commitment without legal sanction. Such commitments have intense moral and psychic significance, but they are not controlled by Church or State. Finally, there are two forbidden acts, which might be taboo or illegal or simply considered contemptible, depending on which of the regions of Gethen you are in: first, you don't pair off with a relative of a different generation (one who might be your own parent or child); second, you may mate, but not vow kemmering, with your own sibling. These are the old incest prohibitions. They are so general among us—and with good cause, I think, not so much genetic as psychological—that they seemed likely to be equally valid on Gethen.

These three "results," then, of my experiment, I feel were fairly clearly and successfully worked out, though there is nothing definitive about them.

In other areas where I might have pressed for at least such plausible results, I see now a failure to think things through, or to express them clearly. For example, I think I took the easy way in using such familiar governmental structures as a feudal monarchy and a modern-style bureaucracy for the two Gethenian countries that are the scene of the novel. I doubt that Gethenian governments, rising out of the cellular hearth, would resemble any of our own so closely. They might be better, they might be worse, but they would certainly be different.

I regret even more certain timidities or ineptnesses I showed in following up the psychic implications of Gethenian physiology. Just for example, I wish I had known Jung's work when I wrote the book: so that I could have decided whether a Gethenian had *no* animus or anima, or *both*, or an animum.... *[For another example (and Jung wouldn't have helped with this, more likely hindered) I quite unnecessarily locked the Gethenians into heterosexuality. It is a naively pragmatic view of sex that insists that sexual partners must be of opposite sex! In any kemmerhouse homosexual practice would, of course, be possible and acceptable and welcomed—but I never thought to explore this option; and the omission, alas, implies that sexuality is heterosexuality. I regret this very much.]* But the central failure in this area comes up in the frequent criticism I receive, that the Gethenians seem like *men*, instead of menwomen.

This rises in part from the choice of pronoun. I call Gethenians "he" because I utterly refuse to mangle English by inventing a pronoun for "he/she." *[This "utter refusal" of 1968 restated in 1976 collapsed, utterly, within a couple of years more. I still dislike invented pronouns, but I now dislike them less than the so-called generic pronoun he/him/his, which does in fact exclude women from discourse; and which was an invention of male grammarians, for until the sixteenth century the English generic singular pronoun was they/them/their, as it still is in English and American colloquial speech. It should be restored to the written language, and let the pedants and pundits squeak and gibber in the streets. In a screenplay of* The Left Hand of Darkness *written in 1985, I referred to Gethenians not pregnant or in kemmer by the invented pronouns a/un/a's, modeled on a British dialect. These would drive the reader mad in print, I suppose; but I have read parts of the book aloud using them, and the audience was perfectly happy, except that they pointed out that the subject pronoun, "a" pronounced "uh" [ə], sounds too much like "I" said with a Southern accent.]* "He" is the generic pronoun, damn it, in English. (I envy the Japanese, who, I am told, do have a he/she pronoun.) But I do not consider this really very important. *[I now consider it very important.]* The pronouns wouldn't matter at all if I had been cleverer at *showing* the "female" component of the Gethenian characters in *action. [If I had realized how the pronouns I used shaped, directed, controlled my own thinking, I might have been "cleverer."]* Unfortunately, the plot and structure that arose as I worked the book out cast the Gethenian protagonist, Estraven, almost exclusively in roles that we are culturally conditioned to perceive as "male"—a prime minister (it takes more than even Golda Meir and Indira Gandhi to break a stereotype), a political schemer, a fugitive, a prison-breaker, a sledge-hauler. . . . I think I did this because I was privately delighted at watching, not a man, but a manwoman, do all these things, and do them with considerable skill and flair. But, for the reader, I left out too much. One does not see Estraven as a mother, with his children *[strike "his"]*, in any role that we automatically perceive as "female": and therefore, we tend to see him as a man *[place "him" in quotation marks, please]*. This is a real flaw in the book, and I can only be very grateful to those readers, men and women, whose willingness to participate in the experiment led them to fill in that omission with the work of their own imagination, and to see Estraven as I saw him *[read: as I did]*, as man and woman, familiar and different, alien and utterly human.

It seems to be men, more often than women, who thus complete my work for me: I think because men are often more willing to identify as they read with poor, confused, defensive Genly, the Earthman, and therefore to participate in his painful and gradual discovery of love.

[I now see it thus: Men were inclined to be satisfied with the book, which allowed them a safe trip into androgyny and back, from a conventionally male viewpoint. But many women wanted it to go further, to dare more, to explore androgyny from a woman's point of view as well as a man's. In fact, it does so, in that it was written by a woman. But this is admitted directly only in the chapter "The Question of Sex," the only voice of a woman in the book. I think women were justified in asking more courage of me and a more rigorous thinking-through of implications.]

Finally, the question arises, Is the book a Utopia? It seems to me that it is quite clearly not; it poses no *practicable* alternative to contemporary society, since it is based on an imaginary, radical change in human anatomy. All it tries to do is open up an alternative viewpoint, to widen the imagination, without making any very definite suggestions as to what might be seen from that new viewpoint. The most it says is, I think, something like this: If we were socially ambisexual, if men and women were completely and genuinely equal in their social roles, equal legally and economically, equal in freedom, in responsibility, and in self-esteem, then society would be a very different thing. What our problems might be, God knows; I only know we would have them. But it seems likely that our central problem would not be the one it is now: the problem of exploitation—exploitation of the woman, of the weak, of the earth. Our curse is alienation, the separation of yang from yin *[and the moralization of yang as good, of yin as bad]*. Instead of a search for balance and integration, there is a struggle for dominance. Divisions are insisted upon, interdependence is denied. The dualism of value that destroys us, the dualism of superior/inferior, ruler/ruled, owner/owned, user/used, might give way to what seems to me, from here, a much healthier, sounder, more promising modality of integration and integrity.

"MORAL AND ETHICAL IMPLICATIONS OF FAMILY PLANNING"

(1978)

This talk was read to a Planned Parenthood symposium in Portland in March 1978. The quotations—somewhat abridged and manipulated for oral presentation—are from the chapter "The Second Apple" in Irene Claremont de Castillejo's Knowing Woman (*Harper & Row, Colophon Books, 1974*), *pp. 93–94.*

I wondered how the Moral Implications and the Ethical Implications in our title actually differed, so I looked in my *Shorter Oxford Dictionary,* and it told me: Ethics, the Ethical, is "the science of morals" (1602), "the science of human duty . . . including the science of law . . ." (1690), and "rules of conduct" (1789). The Moral, Morals, are "of or pertaining to character or disposition; of or pertaining to the distinction between right and wrong, or good and evil," and that usage is from Middle English, so you see that English morals are four or five hundred years older than English ethics.

Now, when I was trying to think what to say to this meeting, every woman friend I talked to, when I said, "What am I going to say, I am in the Planned Parenthood discussion about the Ethics of Family Planning"—every single woman said, with indignation, "What has it got to do with *ethics?*"

I think they were afraid, as I am afraid, that because ethics is a set of rules or rational theories, it will lead us straight into the same old arguments, the same sterile discussions, where people say, "This is right" and "That is wrong," and don't listen to anybody else. Abstractions about right and wrong, whether they are as old as Thou Shalt Not Kill or as modern as Do Your Own Thing, very often serve only to confuse and weaken genuine moral decision.

The dictionary's primary meaning of "moral" refers to character, to the person; and a moral choice is, I believe, an act performed by one person. It may or may not conform to law. It may or may not coincide with the edicts or advice of a government, a church, or a body of concerned people like us.

A moral choice in its basic terms appears to be a choice that favors survival: a choice made in favor of life.

This arises, surely, from the biological, but we are not biological beings only, and "survival" does not necessarily mean the personal, physical survival of the individual. Death may be chosen, for the sake of moral survival as opposed to moral destruction, or for the sake of what is perceived as spiritual value or the undying soul. Death may be chosen for the sake of the survival of the clan, the nation, the species, or life itself.

The survival of our species and of all higher forms of life on the planet now depends primarily and, as I understand it, very urgently upon the limitation of the human population. It appears that we really have only three options: strict family planning to reach zero population growth and then a decline until we get back into ecological balance; or plague and/or famine; or World War III.

I don't include as an option the scenario of Science saving us with miracle soybeans or artificial asteroids to migrate to, or anything of that kind, because unfortunately all that is—as of now—science fiction.

So there seem to be only three options; and the trouble with using ethics to tell us which one to choose is, it doesn't work: the rules are out of date, they were not made for this situation. We can sit around arguing with the Right-to-Life people, and trying to get fundamentalists to use their minds, and trying to overcome all the huge machinery of antiquated law with arguments and reasons, until Doomsday; which won't be long in coming. We are in a bind. Our reasons are good, but they are not enough. We need an appropriate morality. We need people who are able to make the choice in favor of life.

I think one place we have to look for such people is among women.

After all, almost all the rules, laws, codes, and commandments we have—all our ethics—were made by men: by men and for men. Until just a generation or two ago, this was entirely and literally true. Women had no voice, no vote. We let the men make all the choices. There are reasons why we did so; they seemed adequate. They no longer seem adequate. Our survival, and our children's survival, is on the line.

Where man-made ethics differ most radically from female morality, from what women think and feel to be right and wrong, is precisely in this area where we need a new morality: the area in which men and women differ: the area of sexuality, of conception, pregnancy, childbirth, and the responsibility for children. I must admit that to me personally most of the rules men have made on these matters seem, if not simply irrelevant, disastrous. And yet we are still pretending that it's a "man's world," still letting that myth run us. And it's going to run us right into the ground.

I suppose a morality that arises from and includes the feminine will have to be invented as we go along. Rigidity and codification are exactly what we want to get away from, after all. But here—for it's so easy to talk about things like "a new morality" and so hard to show what one means—here, perhaps, is a suggestion of the kind of thing I and many, many others are groping towards. In her book *Knowing Woman*, Irene Claremont de Castillejo writes:

> Woman, who is so intimately and profoundly concerned with life, takes death in her stride. For her, to rid herself of an unwanted foetus is as much in accord with nature as for a cat to refuse milk to a weakling kitten. It is man who has evolved principles about the sacredness of life . . . and women have passionately adopted them as their own. But principles are abstract. . . . Woman's basic instinct is not concerned with the *idea* of life, but with the *fact* of life. The ruthlessness of nature which discards unwanted life is deeply ingrained in her.

You see, she is trying to show how a woman's desire to have children, and to love and care for them, can be twisted all out of shape by ethical coercion, until it becomes a bondage, a hideous sentimental trap. Here she offers an example of natural, unperverted feminine morality:

> I have been struck with the spontaneous reaction of many women and girls to the thalidomide tragedies. So often they

exclaim with absolute conviction, "Of course they should be aborted! It is criminal to make a woman carry a deformed child." [And pressed further, they say,] "It is monstrous that men should decide whether a woman should or should not have her own baby."

That is not ethics. But it is morality.

If we can get that realistic feminine morality working for us, if we can trust in ourselves and so let women think and feel that an unwanted child or an oversize family is wrong—not ethically wrong, not against the rules, but morally wrong, all wrong, wrong like a thalidomide birth, wrong like taking a wrong step that will break your neck—if we can get feminine and human morality out from under the yoke of a dead ethic, then maybe we'll begin to get somewhere on the road that leads to survival.

Note (1988): Castillejo's statements still seem as strong as any I have read on this subject, but they do, in equating woman-mother with cat-mother, run the risk of implying that women are "natural," that their morality is "natural" or "instinctive" (and hence "lower" than that of "civilization," i.e., male-dominated society). I have found Carol Gilligan's *In a Different Voice* (Cambridge: Harvard University Press, 1982) one of the most useful guides into the difficult area of the cultural determination and enforcement of differences between male and female moral perception.

IT WAS A DARK
AND STORMY NIGHT; OR,
WHY ARE WE HUDDLING
ABOUT THE CAMPFIRE?

(1979)

This talk was the last paper read at a three-day symposium on narrative held at the University of Chicago in 1979. Some of the obscurer bits of it are incorporations of and jokes about things read or said by other participants in the conference, the proceedings of which may be found in Critical Inquiry (*vol. 7, no. 1, Autumn 1980). I had bought my first and only pair of two-inch-heeled shoes, black French ones, to wear there, but I never dared put them on; there were so many Big Guns shooting at one another that it seemed unwise to try to increase my stature.*

It was a dark and stormy night
and Brigham Young and Brigham Old
sat around the campfire.
Tell us a story, old man!
And this is the story he told:

It was a dark and stormy night
and Brigham Young and Brigham Old
sat around the campfire.
Tell us a story, old man!
And this is the story he told:

21

It was a dark and stormy night
and Brigham Young and Pierre Menard, author of
   the *Quixote,*
sat around the campfire,
which is not quite the way my Great-Aunt Betsy
   told it
when we said Tell us another story!
Tell us, *au juste,* what happened!
And this is the story she told:

It was a dark and stormy night, in the otherwise unnoteworthy
year 711 E.C. (Eskimo Calendar), and the great-aunt sat
crouched at her typewriter, holding his hands out to it from time
to time as if for warmth and swinging on a swing. He was a
handsome boy of about eighteen, one of those men who suddenly excite your desire when you meet them in the street, and
who leave you with a vague feeling of uneasiness and excited
senses. On a plate beside the typewriter lay a slice of tomato. It
was a flawless slice. It was a perfect slice of a perfect tomato. It is
perfectly boring. I hold out my hands to the typewriter again,
while swinging and showing my delicate limbs, and observe that
the rows of keys are marked with all the letters of the English
alphabet, and all the letters of the French alphabet minus accent
marks, and all the letters of the Polish alphabet except the dark
L. By striking these keys with the ends of my fingers or, conceivably, a small blunt instrument, the aging woman can create a flaw
in the tomato. She did so at once. It was then a seriously, indeed a
disgustingly flawed tomato, but it continued to be perfectly
boring until eaten. She expires instantly in awful agony, of
snakebite, flinging the window wide to get air. It is a dark and
stormy night and the rain falling in on the typewriter keys writes
a story in German about a great-aunt who went to a symposium
on narrative and got eaten in the forest by a metabear. She writes
the story while reading it with close attention, not sure what to
expect, but collaborating hard, as if that was anything new; and
this is the story I wrote:

It was a dark and stormy night
and Brigham al-Rashid sat around the campfire
   with his wife
who was telling him a story in order to keep her head
   on her shoulders,
and this is the story she told:

The *histoire* is the what
and the *discours* is the how
but what I want to know, Brigham,
is *le pourquoi.*
Why are we sitting here around the campfire?

Tell me a story, great-aunt,
so that I can sleep.
Tell me a story, Scheherazade,
so that you can live.
Tell me a story, my soul, animula, vagula, blandula,
little Being-Towards-Death,
for the word's the beginning of being
if not the middle or the end.

"A beginning is that which is not itself necessarily after any-thing else, and which has naturally something else after it; an end, that which is naturally after something else, either as its necessary or usual consequent, and with nothing else after it; and a middle, that which is by nature after one thing and has also another after it."[1]

But sequence grows difficult in the ignorance of what comes after the necessary or at least the usual consequent of living, that is, dying,

and also when the soul is confused by not unreasonable doubts of what comes after the next thing that happens, what-ever that may be.

It gets dark and stormy when you look away from the camp-fire.

Tell me what you see in the fire, Lizzie, Lizzie Hexam,
down in the hollow by the flare!
I see storm and darkness, brother.
I see death and running water, brother.
I see loving-kindness, brother.
Is it all right to see that, teacher?
What would Alain Robbe-Grillet say?

Never mind what he says, Lizzie.
Frogs have a lot of trouble with the novel,
even though kissed right at the beginning by the
    Princesse de Clèves;
maybe they do not want to look down and see Victor
    Hugo glimmering *au fond du puits.*

Brigham, this is stupid stuff!
Tell us a story, old man,
or old woman as the case may be,
or old Tiresias, chirping like a cricket,
tell us a story with a proper end to it
instead of beginning again and again like this
and thereby achieving a muddle
which is not by nature after anything in particular
nor does it have anything consequent to it
but it just hangs there
placidly eating its tail.

In the Far West, where Brigham Young ended up and I started from, they tell stories about hoop snakes. When a hoop snake wants to get somewhere—whether because the hoop snake is after something, or because something is after the hoop snake—it takes its tail (which may or may not have rattles on it) into its mouth, thus forming itself into a hoop, and rolls. Jehovah enjoined snakes to crawl on their belly in the dust, but Jehovah was an Easterner. Rolling along, bowling along, is a lot quicker and more satisfying than crawling. But, for the hoop snakes with rattles, there is a drawback. They are venomous snakes, and when they bite their own tail they die, in awful agony, of snakebite. All progress has these hitches. I don't know what the moral is. It may be in the end safest to lie perfectly still without even crawling. Indeed it's certain that we shall all do so in the end, which has nothing else after it. But then no tracks are left in the dust, no lines drawn; the dark and stormy nights are all one with the sweet bright days, this moment of June— and you might as well never have lived at all. And the moral of *that* is, you have to form a circle to escape from the circle. Draw in a little closer around the campfire. If we could truly form a circle, joining the beginning and the end, we would, as another Greek remarked, not die. But never fear. We can't manage it no matter how we try. But still, very few things come nearer the real Hoop Trick than a good story.

There was a man who practiced at the Hoop Trick named Aneirin.

But let us have the footnotes first.

"We have to bear in mind that the *Gododdin* [and its associated lays] are not narrative poems. . . . Nowhere is there any attempt to give an account of what it was really all about."[2] I disagree with this comment and agree with the next one, which points out that the work goes rolling and bowling all about what it is all about. "While some of these [early Welsh poems] will 'progress' in expected fashion from a beginning through a middle to an end, the normal structure is 'radial,' circling about, repeating and elaborating the central theme. It is all 'middle.' "[3]

This is the Gododdin; Aneirin sang it. [I]

Men went to Catraeth, keen their war-band. [VIII]
Pale mead their portion, it was poison.
Three hundred under orders to fight.
And after celebration, silence.

Men went to Catraeth at dawn: [X]
All their fears had been put to flight.
Three hundred clashed with ten thousand.

Men went to Catraeth at dawn: [XI]
Their high spirits lessened their lifespans.
They drank mead, gold and sweet, ensnaring;
For a year the minstrels were merry.

Three spears stain with blood [XVIII]
Fifty, five hundred.
Three hounds, three hundred:
Three stallions of war
From golden Eidin,
Three mailclad war-bands,
Three gold-collared kings.

Men went to Catraeth, they were renowned, [XXI]
Wine and mead from gold cups was their drink,
A year in noble ceremonial,
Three hundred and sixty-three gold-torqued men.
Of all those who charged, after too much drink,
But three won free through courage in strife:
Aeron's two warhounds and tough Cynan,
And myself, soaked in blood, for my song's sake.

My legs at full length [XLVIII]
In a house of earth.
A chain of iron
About both ankles,
Caused by mead, by horn,
By Catraeth's raiders.
I, not I, Aneirin,
Taliesin knows it,

Master of wordcraft,
Sang to Gododdin
Before the day dawned.

None walk the earth, no mother has borne   [XLIX]
One so fair and strong, dark as iron.
From a war-band his bright blade saved me,
From a fell cell of earth he bore me,
From a place of death, from a harsh land,
Cenan fab Llywarch, bold, undaunted.

Many I lost of my true comrades.   [LXI]
Of three hundred champions who charged to Catraeth,
It is tragic, but one man came back.

On Tuesday they donned their dark armour,   [LXIX]
On Wednesday, bitter their meeting,
On Thursday, terms were agreed on,
On Friday, dead men without number,
On Saturday, fearless, they worked as one,
On Sunday, crimson blades were their lot,
On Monday, men were seen waist-deep in blood.
After defeat, the Gododdin say,
Before Madawg's tent on his return
There came but one man in a hundred.

Three hundred, gold-torqued,   [XCI]
Warlike, well-trained,
Three hundred, haughty,
In harmony, armed.
Three hundred fierce steeds
Bore them to battle.
Three hounds, three hundred:
Tragic, no return.[4]

"I, not I, Aneirin"—"won free"—"for my song's sake." What is
Aneirin telling us? Whether or not we allow that a story so muddled
or all middle can be a narrative, or must be lyric or elegiac, but do
classic Greek definitions fit Welsh Dark Ages traditions?—so, as
Barbara Myerhoff pleaded, in all courtesy let us not argue about it
at this point, only perhaps admitting that the spiral is probably the
shortest way of getting through spacetime and is certainly an effective way to recount the *loss* of a battle—in any case, what is Aneirin
trying to tell us? For all we know or shall ever know of the Battle of

Catraeth is what he tells us; and there is no doubt that he very much wanted us to know about it, to remember it. He says that he won free for his song's sake. He says that he survived, alone, or with Cynan and two others, or with Cenan—he seems to have survived in several different ways, also, which is very Welsh of him—he says that he survived in order to tell us about his friends who did not survive. But I am not sure whether he means by this that he must tell the story because he alone survived; or that he survived because he had the story to tell.

And now for quite another war. I am going to speak in many voices for a while. Novelists have this habit of ventriloquy.[5]

"The SS guards took pleasure in telling us that we had no chance of coming out alive, a point they emphasized with particular relish by insisting that after the war the rest of the world would not believe what had happened; there would be . . . no clear evidence" (a survivor of Dachau).

"Those caught were shot, but that did not keep Ringelblum and his friends from organizing a clandestine group whose job was to gather information for deposit in a secret archive (much of which survived). Here . . . survival and bearing witness become reciprocal acts" (Des Pres).

"[In Treblinka] the dead were being unearthed and burned [by work squads], and soon the work squads too would go up in smoke. If that had come to pass, Treblinka would never have existed. The aim of the revolt was to ensure the memory of that place, and we know the story of Treblinka because forty survived" (Des Pres).

"I found it most difficult to stay alive, but I had to live, to give the world the story" (Glatstein, from Treblinka).

"Even in this place one can survive, and therefore one must want to survive, to tell the story, to bear witness" (Primo Levi, from Auschwitz).

"It is a man's way of leaving a trace, of telling people how he lived and died. . . . If nothing else is left, one must scream. Silence is the real crime against humanity" (Nadyezhda Mandelshtam).

"Conscience . . . is a social achievement. . . . on its historical level, it is the collective effort to come to terms with evil, to distill a moral knowledge equal to the problems at hand. . . . Existence at its boundary is intrinsically significant. . . . the struggle to live—merely surviving—is rooted in, and a manifestation of, the form-conferring potency of life itself" (Des Pres).

"We may at least speculate that . . . survival depends upon life [considered] as a set of activities evolved through time in successful response to crises, the sole purpose of which is to keep going" (Des Pres).

"Living things act as they do because they are so organized as to take actions that prevent their dissolution into the surroundings" (J. Z. Young).

"It seems as if Western culture were making a prodigious effort of historiographic *anamnesis*. . . . We may say . . . this *anamnesis* continues the religious evaluation of memory and forgetfulness. To be sure, neither myths nor religious practices are any longer involved. But there is this common element: the importance of precise and total recollection. . . . The prose narrative, especially the novel, has taken the place of the recitation of myths. . . . The tale takes up and continues 'initiation' on the level of the imaginary. . . . Believing that he is merely amusing himself or escaping, the man of the modern societies still benefits from the imaginary initiation supplied by tales. . . . Today we are beginning to realize that what is called 'initiation' coexists with the human condition, that every existence is made up of an unbroken series of 'ordeals,' 'deaths,' and 'resurrections.' . . . Whatever the gravity of the present crisis of the novel, it is nonetheless true that the need to find one's way into 'foreign' universes and to follow the complications of a 'story' seems to be consubstantial with the human condition."[6]

"For Heaven only knows why one loves it so, how one sees it so, making it up, building it round one, tumbling it, creating it every moment afresh. . . . In people's eyes, in the swing, tramp, and trudge; in the bellow and the uproar; the carriages, motor cars, omnibuses, vans, sandwich men shuffling and swinging; brass bands; barrel organs; in the triumph and the jingle and the strange high singing of some aeroplane overhead was what she loved; life; London; this moment of June."[7]

Why are we huddling about the campfire? Why do we tell tales, or tales about tales—why do we bear witness, true or false? We may ask Aneirin or Primo Levi, we may ask Scheherazade or Virginia Woolf. Is it because we are so organized as to take actions that prevent our dissolution into the surroundings? I know a very short story that might illustrate this hypothesis. You will find it carved into a stone about three feet up from the floor of the north transept of Carlisle Cathedral in the north of England, not all that far from Catterick, which may have been Catraeth. It was carved in runes, one line of

runes, laboriously carved into the stone. A translation into English
is posted up nearby in typescript under glass. Here is the whole
story:

Tolfink carved these runes in this stone.

Well, this is pretty close to Barbara Herrnstein Smith's earliest
form of historiography—notch-cutting. As a story, it does not really
meet the requirement of Minimal Connexity. It doesn't have much
beginning or end. The material was obdurate, and life is short. Yet I
would say Tolfink was a reliable narrator. Tolfink bore witness at
least to the existence of Tolfink, a human being unwilling to dissolve
entirely into his surroundings.

It is time to end, an appropriate time for a ghost story. It was a dark
and stormy night, and the man and the woman sat around the
campfire in their tent out on the plains. They had killed the woman's
husband and run away together. They had been going north across
the plains for three days now. The man said, "We must be safe. There
is no way the people of the tribe can track us." The woman said,
"What's that noise?" They listened, and they both heard a scratching
noise on the outside of the tent, low down, near the ground. "It's the
wind blowing," the man said. The woman said, "It doesn't sound like
the wind." They listened and heard the sound again, a scraping,
louder, and higher up on the wall of the tent. The woman said, "Go
and see what it is. It must be some animal." The man didn't want to
go out. She said, "Are you afraid?" Now the scraping sound had got
very loud, up almost over their heads. The man jumped up and went
outside to look. There was enough light from the fire inside the tent
that he could see what it was. It was a skull. It was rolling up the
outside of the tent so that it could get in at the smokehole at the top. It
was the skull of the man they had killed, the husband, but it had
grown very big. It had been rolling after them over the plains all
along and growing bigger as it rolled. The man shouted to the
woman, and she came out of the tent, and they caught each other by
the hand and ran. They ran into the darkness, and the skull rolled
down the tent and rolled after them. It came faster and faster. They
ran until they fell down in the darkness, and the skull caught up with
them there. That was the end of them.

There may be some truth in that story, that tale, that discourse,
that narrative, but there is no reliability in the telling of it. It was
told you forty years later by the ten-year-old who heard it, along

with her great-aunt, by the campfire, on a dark and starry night in California; and though it is, I believe, a Plains Indian story, she heard it told in English by an anthropologist of German anteced-ents. But by remembering it he had made the story his; and insofar as I have remembered it, it is mine; and now, if you like it, it's yours. In the tale, in the telling, we are all one blood. Take the tale in your teeth, then, and bite till the blood runs, hoping it's not poison; and we will all come to the end together, and even to the beginning: living, as we do, in the middle.

Notes

1. Aristotle, *On the Art of Poetry,* trans. Ingram Bywater (Oxford: Oxford Univer-sity Press, 1920), p. 40.

2. K. H. Jackson, *The Gododdin: The Oldest Scottish Poem* (Edinburgh: Edinburgh University Press, 1969), pp. 3–4.

3. Joseph P. Clancy, introduction to *The Earliest Welsh Poetry* (London: Macmillan, 1970).

4. Clancy's translation of the text of the *Goddodin,* in ibid.

5. The following citations appear in Terence Des Pres, *The Survivor: An Anatomy of Life in the Death Camps* (New York: Oxford University Press, 1976).

6. Mircea Eliade, *Myth and Reality,* trans. Willard R. Trask (New York: Harper & Row, 1963), pp. 136, 138, 202.

7. Virginia Woolf, *Mrs. Dalloway* (New York: Harcourt, Brace & Co., 1925), p. 5.

WORKING ON
"THE LATHE"

(1979)

In January of 1980, the stations of the Public Broadcasting Service first showed the film based on my novel The Lathe of Heaven. *The magazine* Horizon *asked me for a piece to accompany release, and so I wrote this fragmentary memoir of my first involvement in film-making.*

To answer a question I am often asked: No, I didn't write the script. I worked on it, though, and learned a good deal about scripting, and about film-making, as "creative consultant," with far more real consulting and creative power than usual in that position.

The other question is usually "Do you like the movie?" And I say, Well, we sure could have used another quarter of a million bucks, but I think we turned a shoestring into a pretty good silk purse. Since the tight budget forced us to shoot in a few weeks, without retakes, in Dallas not Portland, we couldn't get the close, gritty, local texture of life I longed for. And though Ed Emshwiller's war in space—using, I believe, Frisbees for flying saucers—is a delight, our Alien is a disaster: stiff and mechanical instead of beautiful and strange and sea-turtlish. But not only is the film faithful to the sense of the book; the acting, the directing, the camera work, the music, all of very high quality, integrate and work together to make a strong, vivid film, quite independent of the book. Yes, I like it.

PORTLAND

"Hello," said this voice, "I'm David Loxton of the TV Lab at WNET, and I want to come talk to you about making a TV film of one of your novels."

"No, you don't," I said, terrified.

"Well, actually I do," said the voice in a mild, astonished tone.

I could not say that the only thing I dread more than phone calls from strangers is visits from strangers, because that's not the sort of thing you can say to strangers.

"I'm sorry I have this English sort of accent," said the voice. "It's because I'm English, but I live in New York. Would it be all right if I came on Wednesday?"

He said it "Weddnsdy"; there was no doubt he was English.

"You can't come all the way to *Oregon*," I said desperately, but it was no use. He came. He conquered. We made a TV movie out of one of my novels.

David wanted me to choose which novel. I picked *The Lathe of Heaven* because it's the only one of my books that I ever enjoyed imagining as a film. When I began imagining it as a TV film I enjoyed it still more and very soon had dropped my novelist's suspicions and skittishness and was taking the project seriously; because, as I listened to David, I began to understand the possibilities. In television there's no need for the spectacular; in fact the medium rather leads away from it—inward; in science-fiction terms, from outer to inner space. And *The Lathe of Heaven* is about dreams and dreaming—what Dr. Haber, the dream specialist in the novel, calls "the all-night show on Channel One." There's a good deal in common between the mind's eye and the TV screen, and though the TV set has all too often been the boobtube, it could be, it can be, the box of dreams.

Then also *Lathe* had the virtue—given a Public Broadcasting Service budget—of being set on Earth in the very near future and having a small and almost entirely human cast. There was really only one Alien Being to worry about, and it could wear a space suit or shell, which would help. But what about melting Portland? "No trouble," David said grandly. "We can quite easily melt Portland. Especially if we film that bit in Dallas."

David Loxton is a large man, with large dreams.

NEW YORK

First Read-Through with the Actors

Thursday morning we all meet in the ballroom of a truly weird hotel on West End Avenue, with plastic azaleas and ancient ladies also partly plastic, I believe, and you have to get the key to the toilet from the caterer, who looks like a native of some perhaps ammonia-atmosphere planet. The ballroom is hung with dusty chandeliers all smearily ablaze, and set about at intervals with phthisical chairs and a white piano with a hernia. Here we will rehearse, because the director can mark out the floor with tape to the size of the shooting area of each scene, and move chairs about to represent sets, and so on. I don't suppose anything he did would matter much to the management of this hotel.

Enter our "Heather," Margaret Avery, incredibly elegant, quiet, fierce, fragile. Enter our "George," Bruce Davison, blue jeans and thick, fair hair and clear, complicated eyes. Enter our "Dr. Haber," Kevin Conway, red Irishman, erect, intense, intelligent, formidable. Enter into the increasingly complex mixture of personalities Fred Barzyk, the director, who always seemed such a calm quiet fellow. One must see the beast in its native habitat. . . .

Rehearsals

Fred's copy of the script is the thickness of the Manhattan phone book. It's interleaved, many extra pages for each page of script: sketches of the set or location, where the camera can be or must be, what kind of light at what time of day, what's outside the windows, what movements are possible—endless information; and all this he, with the most self-effacing, easygoing courtesy, tells the actors as they begin to walk through the scene; and he moves around and among them with his hands up before his face forming a square: the camera eye, to which they play. It sounds awkward, but it's lovely to watch. It is choreography at the moment of creation. What I see is that the stage, fixed and oriented in one direction, audience-ward, becomes infinite. The orientation can be to any side, at any height, any distance, and so the actors' "dance" is, by so much, more complex and subtle. In this enlargement of possibility, this openness, film is surely more of our time than regular theater (and theater in the round is a sorry compromise, to my taste). I had to see how it's done before I could realize that. I wonder if when I watch the actual filming I will still be able to see what's really going on; probably I'll be confused by mere machinery, the cameras and lights and booms and so on. But here I did see how it's done, and it's beautiful.

DALLAS

The Man with the Boom

We got here on Tuesday at four in the afternoon. They were taking the Alien apart. They had just finished that day's shooting, which had begun at one in the morning. That was an uncommonly long day (they'd been shooting in the Hyatt Hotel and had done as much as possible in the dead of night so as not to disturb the hotel's routine, especially since this was the scene where everybody is grey), but all their days are twelve hours at least—8:00 a.m. to 8:00 p.m., six days a week.

A domestic touch: in the hall there's a huge coffee urn, a carton of apples and bananas, and various great boxes of doughnuts and cookies and other innocent victuals, and the crewpeople, most of whom are pretty young, eat like the orangs and the elephants in the zoo; they just sort of vacuum-clean their way through twenty dozen doughnuts, *schloop,* gone. . . .

The Damned Augmentor

We're shooting with one camera, which is, I am told, the classy way, but also the hard way. It means essentially that each scene, each take, is shot first as wide as possible, the whole scene, and then up close. If it's a dialogue, in the close take the camera stays on George throughout the scene, then it goes around to the other side and takes Haber throughout the same scene. And each of these angles is usually shot twice, and possibly five or six times if anything goes wrong, and there are a lot of things that can go wrong. Especially the Augmentor—Dr. Haber's dream machine. I truly wish Dr. Haber and I had never invented the damned thing. The different takes will be spliced when the film is edited—a bit from this take and a bit from that, George's face while he talks and Haber's while he answers and then a cut to the Augmentor showing George's brain scan—and so each take has to be like all the other takes in every detail. So that while George is saying a certain line of dialogue, the exact same bit of electronic jiggery-pokery has to be running on the various readout screens of the Augmentor every time he says that line, in each retake of the scene. All the same, that was simple compared to the mashed potatoes.

The Mashed Potatoes, or, The Glamorous Life of the Film Star

Hey, baby, you wanna be in the movies?

Imagine yourself sitting in a crowded cafeteria in Dallas, Texas. You are wearing kind of funny clothes and transparent plastic shoes that don't fit, but so is everybody else. Two people jammed against your back at the next table are muttering, "What is the name of thisyere movie? *The Way to Heaven?*" "No, it's *The Lake of Heaven,* but Ah sure's hell can't figure what it's about." To your right is your fifteen-year-old son; across from him your husband; next to your husband is his eighty-year-old aunt Ruby, who lives in Dallas and decided to come help us shoot the movie. Husband looks like lemme-out-of-here, but Ruby is as merry as a grig. At the end of the table is a beautiful Black woman deep in conversation with a fair-haired man. In front of each of them, in front of everybody in the whole cafeteria, is a tray, and everybody's tray is exactly the same: on it is a pile of old, cold mashed potatoes, a pile of old, cold boiled carrots, and a cup of something that once might have been tea. Now imagine that you are a movie star, well anyhow an extra, and you are eating your old, cold mashed potatoes and talking and smiling while you do so. O.K.? You can do that, sure. It's easy to be an actor. Yes, but that was Take 1. Now we have to do Take 2. And if you ate some mashed potatoes in Take 1, you have to eat some mashed potatoes in Take 2, don't you, because the action has to be the same so they can splice shots. So a sadist comes and puts a nice new pile of old mashed potatoes on your tray. And then there's Take 3 . . . and Take 4 . . . and Take 10. . . . Actually we extras were only in a few shots and only got slightly sick, and Ruby insisted she liked the carrots. Margaret was clever and only toyed with her food; but Bruce sat there for three mortal hours re-eating stale mashed potatoes and laughing. If the life of the film stars is glamorous, believe me, they earn it!

I sure hope they don't cut Aunt Ruby.

THE MUSIC OF THIS WORK

The filming took a few weeks; the editing, months. At last the edited film went in cassette form to the composer. And a couple of months after that, we find the composer, Michael Small, standing pipe in mouth behind a drafting table amidst a storm-tossed sea of score, conducting. Some thirty musicians sit among trains, trails, endless entrails of electric cord; shadows of microphone booms stand angular and elegant on the fibrous walls of the recording studio. On a small TV set facing Michael a scene of the film runs in silence, subtitle numbers ticking off hour/minute/second/frame. Crescendo: a subtle theme I have learned to listen for emerges, changes, returns, and fades.

"O.K.," says Michael. "Could you violins sound a little more other-worldly in bar fifteen?"

"No sweat," says an altogether this-worldly Violin.

"Hey," says the Trumpet to the Synthesizer, snidely, "you still plugged in over there?"

Ian the Synthesizer, knowing that he's the one who's really going to melt Portland, smiles, serene.

"Seymour," says Michael to the Cello, whose part has one of those eerie tweedling passages strings can do, "how long can you go on playing those sixteenth notes?"

"Till Tuesday, if you want me to," says the Cello. I believe him.

"Rosin!"—a strangled cry from the Percussion enclosure, also known as the Jungle, where the percussionist is bowing temple bells.

"That last note you have," Michael says to the Oboe, "that was beautiful, could you hold it a while?"

"A while," the Oboe says modestly. I believe him.

"O.K., let's make it," says Michael, raising his baton.

Guinness Book of Records please note: the longest sustained note ever held by a human oboist was played at the National Recording Studio on West Forty-seventh Street on September 13, 1979, by Henry Schuman during the taping of *The Lathe of Heaven* score. These guys can do anything.

And the music is beautiful. The rawboned beast of a movie we have worked on so long is transformed, transfigured, by the music; the music for this scene, this moment; the music of this work. It comes together, now, at last. All the months; all the money; all the machinery; all the many people. It comes together. We have made it.

SOME THOUGHTS
ON NARRATIVE

(1980)

This paper incorporates parts of the Nina Mae Kellogg Lecture given at Portland State University in the spring of 1980.

Recently, at a three-day-long symposium on narrative, I learned that it's unsafe to say anything much about narrative, because if a poststructuralist doesn't get you a deconstructionist will. This is a pity, because the subject is an interesting one to those outside the armed camps of literary theory. As one who spends a good deal of her time telling stories, I should like to know, in the first place, why I tell stories, and in the second place, why you listen to them; and vice versa.

Through long practice I know how to tell a story, but I'm not sure I know what a story is; and I have not found much patience with the question among those better qualified to answer it. To literary theorists it is evidently too primitive, to linguists it is not primitive enough; and among psychologists I know of only one, Simon Lesser, who has tried seriously to explain narration as a psychic process. There is, however, always Aristotle.

Aristotle says that the essential element of drama and epic is "the arrangement of the incidents." And he goes on to make the famous and endearing remark that this narrative or plotly element consists of a beginning, a middle, and an end:

> A beginning is that which is not itself necessarily after anything else, and which has naturally something else after it; an end, that which is naturally after something else, either as its neces-

37

sary or usual consequent, and with nothing else after it; and a middle, that which is by nature after one thing and has also another after it.

According to Aristotle, then, narrative connects events, "arranges incidents," in a directional temporal order analogous to a directional spatial order. Causality is implied but not exactly stated (in the word "consequent," which could mean "result" or merely "what follows"); the principal linkage as I understand it is temporal (E. M. Forster's story sequence, "and then . . . and then . . . and then . . ."). So narrative is language used to connect events in time. The connection, whether conceived as a closed pattern, beginning-middle-end, or an open one, past-present-future, whether seen as lineal or spiral or recursive, involves a movement "through" time for which spatial metaphor is adequate. Narrative makes a journey. It goes from A to Z, from then to then-prime.

This might be why narrative does not normally use the present tense except for special effect or out of affectation. It locates itself in the past (whether the real or an imagined, fictional past) in order to allow itself forward movement. The present not only competes against the story with a vastly superior weight of reality, but limits it to the pace of watch hand or heartbeat. Only by locating itself in the "other country" of the past is the narrative free to move towards its future, the present.

The present tense, which some writers of narrative fiction currently employ because it is supposed to make the telling "more actual," actually distances the story (and some very sophisticated writers of narrative fiction use it for that purpose). The present tense takes the story out of time. Anthropological reports concerning people who died decades ago, whose societies no longer exist, are written in the present tense; this paper is written in the present tense. Physics is normally written in the present tense, in part because it *generalizes,* as I am doing now, but also because it deals so much with nondirectional time.

Time for a physicist is quite likely to be reversible. It doesn't matter whether you read an equation forwards or backwards—unlike a sentence. On the subatomic level directionality is altogether lost. You cannot write the history of a photon; narration is irrelevant; all you can say of it is that it might be, or, otherwise stated, if you can say where it is you can't say when and if you can say when it is you can't say where.

Even of an entity relatively so immense and biologically so complex as a gene, the little packet of instructions that tells us what to be, there is no story to be told; because the gene, barring accident, is immortal. All you can say of it is that it is, and it is, and it is. No beginning, no end. All middle.

The past and future tenses become useful to science when it gets involved in irreversible events, when beginning, middle, and end will run only in that order. What happened two seconds after the Big Bang? What happened when Male Beta took Male Alpha's banana? What will happen if I add this hydrochloric acid? These are events that made, or will make, a difference. The existence of a future—a time different from now, a then-prime—depends on the irreversibility of time; in human terms, upon mortality. In Eternity there is nothing novel, and there are no novels.

So when the storyteller by the hearth starts out, "Once upon a time, a long way from here, lived a king who had three sons," that story will be telling us that things change; that events have consequences; that choices are to be made; that the king does not live forever.

Narrative is a stratagem of mortality. It is a means, a way of living. It does not seek immortality; it does not seek to triumph over or escape from time (as lyric poetry does). It asserts, affirms, participates in directional time, time experienced, time as meaningful. If the human mind had a temporal spectrum, the nirvana of the physicist or the mystic would be way over in the ultraviolet, and at the opposite end, in the infrared, would be *Wuthering Heights.*

To put it another way: Narrative is a central function of language. Not, in origin, an artifact of culture, an art, but a fundamental operation of the normal mind functioning in society. To learn to speak is to learn to tell a story.

I would guess that preverbal narration takes place almost continuously on the unconscious level, but pre- or nonverbal mental operations are very hard to talk about. Dreams might help.

It has been found that during REM (rapid eye movement) sleep, the recurrent phase of sleep during which we dream abundantly, the movement of the eyes is intermittent. If you wake the dreamer while the eyes are flickering, the dreams reported are disconnected, jumbled, snatches and flashes of imagery; but, awakened during a quiet-eye period, the dreamer reports a "proper dream," a *story.*

Researchers call the image-jumble "primary visual experience" and the other "secondary cognitive elaboration."

Concerning this, Liam Hudson wrote (in the *Times Literary Supplement* of January 25, 1980):

> While asleep, then, we experience arbitrary images, and we also tell ourselves stories. The likelihood is that we weave the second around the first, embedding images that we perceive as bizarre in a fabric that seems to us more reasonable. If I confront myself, while asleep, with the image of a crocodile on the roof of a German *Schloss*, and then, while still fast asleep, create for myself some plausible account of how this implausible event has occurred, I am engaged in the manoeuvre of rationalisation— of rendering sensible-seeming something that is not sensible in the least. In the course of this manoeuvre, the character of the original image is falsified. . . .
>
> The thinking we do without thinking about it consists in the translation of our experience to narrative, irrespective of whether our experience fits the narrative form or not. . . . Asleep and awake it is just the same: we are telling ourselves stories all the time, . . . tidier stories than the evidence warrants.

Mr. Hudson's summary of the material is elegant, and his interpretation of it is, I take it, Freudian. Dreamwork is *rationalization,* therefore it is *falsification:* a cover-up. The mind is an endless Watergate. Some primitive "reality" or "truth" is forever being distorted, lied about, tidied up.

But what if we have no means of access to this truth or reality except through the process of "lying," except through the narrative? Where are we supposed to be standing in order to judge what "the evidence warrants"?

Take Mr. Hudson's crocodile on the roof of a German castle (it is certainly more interesting than what I dreamed last night). We can all make that image into a story. Some of us will protest, No no I can't, I can't tell stories, etc., having been terrorized by our civilization into believing that we are, or have to be, "rational." But all of us can make that image into some kind of story, and if it came into our head while we were asleep, no doubt we would do so without a qualm, without giving it a second thought. As I have methodically practiced irrational behavior for many years, I can turn it into a story almost as easily waking as asleep. What has happened is that Prince Metternich was keeping a crocodile to frighten his aunt with, and the crocodile has escaped through a skylight onto the curious, steep, leaden roofs of the castle, and is clambering, in the present tense because it is a dream and outside time, towards a machico-lated nook in which lies, in a stork's nest, but the stork is in Africa, an egg, a wonderful, magical Easter egg of sugar containing a tiny window through which you look and you see— But the dreamer is awakened here. And if there is any "message" to the dream, the dreamer is not aware of it; the dream with its "message" has gone from the unconscious to the unconscious, like most dreams, without any processing describable as "rationalization," and without ever being verbalized (unless and until the dreamer, in some kind of therapy, has learned laboriously to retrieve and hold and verbalize dreams). In this case all the dreamer—we need a name for this character, let us call her Edith Driemer—all Edith remembers, fleetingly, is something about a roof, a crocodile, Germany, Easter, and while thinking dimly about her great-aunt Esther in Munich, she is presented with further "primary visual (or sensory) experi-ences" running in this temporal sequence: A loud ringing in the left ear. Blinding light. The smell of an exotic herb. A toilet. A pair of used shoes. A disembodied voice screaming in Parsee. A kiss. A sea of shining clouds. Terror. Twilight in the branches of a tree outside the window of a strange room in an unknown city . . .

Are these the "primary experiences" experienced while her eyes move rapidly, furnishing material for the next dream? They could well be; but by following Aristotle's directions and making purely temporal connections between them, we can make of them a quite realistic narration of the day Edith woke up and turned off the alarm clock, got up and got dressed, had breakfast listening to the radio news, kissed Mr. Driemer goodbye, and took a plane to Cin-cinnati in order to attend a meeting of market analysts.

I submit that though this network of "secondary elaboration" may be more rationally controlled than that of the pretended dream, the primary material on which it must work can be considered inher-ently as bizarre, as absurd, as the crocodile on the roof, and that the factual account of Edith Driemer's day is no more and no less than the dream-story a "manoeuvre," "rendering sensible-seeming something that is not sensible in the least."

Dream narrative differs from conscious narrative in using sen-sory symbol more than language. In dream the sense of the direc-tionality of time is often replaced by spatial metaphor, or may be lowered, or reversed, or vanish. The connections dream makes between events are most often unsatisfactory to the rational intellect and the aesthetic mind. Dreams tend to flout Aristotle's rules of plausibility and muddle up his instructions concerning plot. Yet they are undeniably narrative: they connect events, fit things together in an order or a pattern that makes, to some portion of our mind, sense.

Looked at as a "primary visual (sensory) experience," in isolation, without connection to any context or event, each of our experiences is equally plausible or implausible, authentic or inauthentic, meaningful or absurd. But living creatures go to considerable pains to escape equality, to evade entropy, chaos, and old night. They arrange things. They make sense, literally. Molecule by molecule. In the cell. The cells arrange themselves. The body is an arrangement in spacetime, a patterning, a process; the mind is a process of the body, an organ, doing what organs do: organize. Order, pattern, connect. Do we have any better way to organize such wildly disparate experiences as a half-remembered crocodile, a dead great-aunt, the smell of coffee, a scream from Iran, a bumpy landing, and a hotel room in Cincinnati, than the narrative?—an immensely flexible technology, or life strategy, which if used with skill and resourcefulness presents each of us with that most fascinating of all serials, The Story of My Life.

I have read of a kind of dream that is symptomatic of one form of schizophrenia. The dream presents an object, a chair perhaps, or a coat, or a stump. Nothing happens, and there is nothing else in the dream.

Seen thus in spatial and temporal isolation, the primary experience or image can be the image of despair itself (like Sartre's tree root). Beckett's work yearns toward this condition. In the other direction, Rilke's celebration of "Things"—a chair, a coat, a stump—offers connection: a piece of furniture is part of the pattern of the room, of the life, a bed is a table in a swoon (in one of his French poems), forests are in the stump, the pitcher is also the river, and the hand, and the cup, and the thirst.

Whether the technique is narrative or not, the primary experience has to be connected with and fitted into the rest of experience to be useful, probably even to be available, to the mind. This may hold even for mystical perception. All mystics say that what they have experienced in vision cannot be fitted into ordinary time and space, but they try—they have to try. The vision is ineffable, but the story begins, "In the middle of the road of our life . . ."

It may be that an inability to fit events together in an order that at least seems to make sense, to make the narrative connection, is a radical incompetence at being human. So seen, stupidity could be defined as a failure to make enough connections, and insanity as severe repeated error in making connections—in telling The Story of My Life.

But nobody does it right all the time, or even most of the time. Even without identifying narration with falsification, one must admit that a vast amount of our life narration is fictional—how much, we cannot tell.

But if narration is a life stratagem, a survival skill, how can I get away, asleep and awake, with mistaking and distorting and omitting data, through wishful thinking, ignorance, laziness, and haste? If the ghostwriter in my head writing The Story of My Life is forgetful, careless, mendacious, a hack who doesn't care what happens so long as it makes some kind of story, why don't I get punished? Radical errors in interpreting and reacting to the environment aren't let off lightly, in either the species or the individual.

Is the truthfulness of the story, then, the all-important value; or is the quality of the fiction important too? Is it possible that we all keep going in very much the same way as Queen Dido or Don Quixote keeps going—by virtue of being almost entirely fictional characters?

Anyone who knows J. T. Fraser's work, such as his book *Of Time, Passion, and Knowledge,* and that of George Steiner, will have perceived my debt to them in trying to think about the uses of narrative. I am not always able to follow Mr. Steiner; but when he discusses the importance of the future tense, suggesting that statements about what does not exist and may never exist are central to the use of language, I follow him cheering and waving pompoms. When he makes his well-known statement "Language is the main instrument of man's refusal to accept the world as it is," I continue to follow, though with lowered pompoms. The proposition as stated worries me. Man's refusal to accept the world as it is? Do women also refuse? What about science, which tries so hard to see the world as it is? What about art, which not only accepts the dreadful world as it is but praises it for being so? "Isn't life a terrible thing, thank God!"

says the lady with the backyard full of washing and babies in *Under Milk Wood,* and the sweet song says, "Nobody knows the trouble I seen, Glory, Hallelujah!" I agree with them. All grand refusals, especially when made by Man, are deeply suspect.

So, caviling all the way, I follow Mr. Steiner. If the use of language were to describe accurately what exists, what, in fact, would we want it for?

Surely the primary, survival-effective uses of language involve stating alternatives and hypotheses. We don't, we never did, go about making statements of fact to other people, or in our internal discourse with ourselves. We talk about what may be, or what we'd like to do, or what you ought to do, or what might have happened: warnings, suppositions, propositions, invitations, ambiguities, analogies, hints, lists, anxieties, hearsay, old wives' tales, leaps and cross-links and spiderwebs between here and there, between then and now, between now and sometime, a continual weaving and restructuring of the remembered and the perceived and the imagined, including a great deal of wishful thinking and a variable quantity of deliberate or non-deliberate fictionalizing, to reassure ourselves or for the pleasure of it, and also some deliberate or semi-deliberate falsification in order to mislead a rival or persuade a friend or escape despair; and no sooner have we made one of these patterns of words than we may, like Shelley's cloud, laugh, and arise, and unbuild it again.

In recent centuries we speakers of this lovely language have reduced the English verb almost entirely to the indicative mood. But beneath that specious and arrogant assumption of certainty all the ancient, cloudy, moody powers and options of the subjunctive remain in force. The indicative points its bony finger at primary experiences, at the Things; but it is the subjunctive that joins them, with the bonds of analogy, possibility, probability, contingency, contiguity, memory, desire, fear, and hope: the narrative connection. As J. T. Fraser puts it, moral choice, which is to say human freedom, is made possible "by language, which permits us to give accounts of possible and impossible worlds in the past, in the future, or in a faraway land."

Fiction in particular, narration in general, may be seen not as a disguise or falsification of what is given but as an active encounter with the environment by means of posing options and alternatives, and an enlargement of present reality by connecting it to the unverifiable past and the unpredictable future. A totally factual narrative, were there such a thing, would be passive: a mirror reflecting all without distortion. Stendhal sentimentalized about the novel as such a mirror, but fiction does not reflect, nor is the narrator's eye that of a camera. The historian manipulates, arranges, and connects, and the storyteller does all that as well as intervening and inventing. Fiction connects possibilities, using the aesthetic sense of time's directionality defined by Aristotle as plot; and by doing so it is useful to us. If we cannot see our acts and being under the aspect of fiction, as "making sense," we cannot act as if we were free.

To describe narrative as "rationalization" of the given or of events is a blind alley. In the telling of a story, reason is only a support system. It can provide causal connections; it can extrapolate; it can judge what is likely, plausible, possible. All this is crucial to the invention of a good story, a sane fantasy, a sound piece of fiction. But reason by itself cannot get from the crocodile to Cincinnati. It cannot see that Elizabeth is, in fact, going to marry Darcy, and why. It may not even ever quite understand who it was, exactly, that Oedipus did marry. We cannot ask reason to take us across the gulfs of the absurd. Only the imagination can get us out of the bind of the eternal present, inventing or hypothesizing or pretending or discovering a way that reason can then follow into the infinity of options, a clue through the labyrinths of choice, a golden string, the story, leading us to the freedom that is properly human, the freedom open to those whose minds can accept unreality.

WORLD-MAKING

(1981)

I was invited to participate in a symposium called Lost Worlds and Future Worlds, at Stanford University in 1981. The text of my short contribution follows; a slightly garbled version of it was printed in Women Writers of the West Coast, *by Marilyn Yalom (Capra Press, 1983).*

We're supposed to be talking about world-making. The idea of making makes me think of making new. Making a new world: a different world: Middle Earth, say, or the planets of science fiction. That's the work of the fantastic imagination. Or there's making the world new: making the world different: a utopia or dystopia, the work of the political imagination.

But what about making the world, this world, the old one? That seems to be the province of the religious imagination, or of the will to survive (they may be the same thing). The old world is made new at the birth of every baby, and every New Year's Day, and every morning, and the Buddhist says at every instant.

That, in every practical sense, we make the world we inhabit is pretty well beyond question, but I leave it to the philosophers to decide whether we make it all from scratch—mmmm! tastes like a scratch world! but it's Bishop Berkeley's Cosmo-Mix!—or whether we patch it together by a more or less judicious selection of what strikes us as useful or entertaining in the inexhaustible chaos of the real.

In either case, what artists do is make a particularly skillful selection of fragments of cosmos, unusually useful and entertaining bits chosen and arranged to give an illusion of coherence and duration amidst the uncontrollable streaming of events. An artist makes the world her world. An artist makes her world the world. For a little while. For as long as it takes to look at or listen to or watch or read the work of art. Like a crystal, the work of art seems to contain the whole, and to imply eternity. And yet all it is is an explorer's sketch-map. A chart of shorelines on a foggy coast.

To make something is to invent it, to discover it, to uncover it, like Michelangelo cutting away the marble that hid the statue. Perhaps we think less often of the proposition reversed, thus: To discover something is to make it. As Julius Caesar said, "The existence of Britain was uncertain, until I went there." We can safely assume that the ancient Britons were perfectly certain of the existence of Britain, down to such details as where to go for the best woad. But, as Einstein said, it all depends on how you look at it, and as far as Rome, not Britain, is concerned, Caesar invented (*invenire*, "to come into, to come upon") Britain. He made it be, for the rest of the world.

Alexander the Great sat down and cried, somewhere in the middle of India, I think, because there were no more new worlds to conquer. What a silly man he was. There he sits sniveling, halfway to China! A conqueror. Conquistadores, always running into new worlds, and quickly running out of them. Conquest is not finding, and it is not making. Our culture, which conquered what is called the New World, and which sees the world of nature as an adversary to be conquered: look at us now. Running out of everything.

The name of our meeting is Lost Worlds and Future Worlds. Whether our ancestors came seeking gold, or freedom, or as slaves, we are the conquerors, we who live here now, in possession, in the New World. We are the inhabitants of a Lost World. It is utterly lost. Even the names are lost. The people who lived here, in this place, on these hills, for tens of thousands of years, are remembered (when they are remembered at all) in the language of the conquistadores: the "Costanos," the "Santa Claras," the "San Franciscos," names taken from foreign demigods. Sixty-three years ago, in the *Handbook of the Indians of California*, my father wrote:

> The Costanoan group is extinct so far as all practical purposes are concerned. A few scattered individuals survive. . . . The larger part of a century has passed since the missions were abolished, and nearly a century and a half since they commenced to be founded. These periods have sufficed to efface

even traditional recollections of the forefathers' habits, except
for occasional fragments.

Here is one such fragment, a song; they sang it here, under the
live oaks, but there weren't any wild oats here then, only the Californian bunch-grasses. The people sang:

> I dream of you,
> I dream of you jumping,
> Rabbit, jackrabbit, and quail.

And one line is left of a dancing song:

> Dancing on the brink of the world.

With such fragments I might have shored my ruin, but I didn't
know how. Only knowing that we must have a past to make a future
with, I took what I could from the European-based culture of my
own forefathers and mothers. I learned, like most of us, to use
whatever I could, to filch an idea from China and steal a god from
India, and so patch together a world as best I could. But still there is
a mystery. This place where I was born and grew up and love beyond
all other, my world, my California, still needs to be made. To make a
new world you start with an old one, certainly. To find a world,
maybe you have to have lost one. Maybe you have to be lost. The
dance of renewal, the dance that made the world, was always danced
here at the edge of things, on the brink, on the foggy coast.

HUNGER

(1981)

To publicize the Oxfam America Fast for the Hungry in 1981, the Portland Food Bank held a "food for thought" luncheon meeting, at which I was asked to speak briefly.

You probably didn't expect to hear anything about Macchu Picchu today—that lost city high in the Andes, built a thousand years ago—but the Chilean poet Pablo Neruda wrote a book about it, and I could find nothing to offer you that came closer to the heart of our subject here today. He describes the wonderful place in a long series of images—this is my own rather wild translation.

> Then up the ladder of the earth I climbed
> through the terrible mazes of lost jungles
> to reach you, Macchu Picchu.

> Tall city of stepped stone

> in you two lineages meet,
> the cradle of man, the cradle of light,
> rock together in the thorny wind.

> Mother of stone, foam of the condor,
> high reef of the human dawn . . .

And then the poet begins to ask who, in fact, built the city.

> Ancient America, bride of the depths,
> did you too, did your hands
> up from the forests to the high void of the gods,
> under the marriage-day banners of light and order,

49

mixed with the thunder of drums and lances,
did you too, did your hands
that wove the mind's rose and the snowline
and the blood-red grain of the furrows
into the web of shining matter, into the hollows of stone,
O buried America, did you too, did your hands hold down
in the under-depths, in the bitter pit, the eagle, hunger?

Hunger, coral of mankind,
hunger, did your steep reefs rise
as high as those high, ill-founded towers?

Macchu Picchu, did you build
stone upon stone, and the foundation, hunger?
diamond on diamond, and the foundation, tears?

That says to me what we have come here for. It says that so long as
the beautiful towers of stone, of concrete, of glass, are not well
founded, they are not habitable. No house worth living in has for its
cornerstone the hunger of those who built it. We in America now
raise our cities taller even than Macchu Picchu. But along with what
they call the "real" city, the "real estate," there is an invisible city. It is
to the stones of the city as the soul is to the body. And that's what
we're talking about. That is the city we're trying to build, to found,
not on hoarding and moneymaking and hunger, but on sharing and
on justice. A house that deserves its children.

We don't live in such a house. We never have, no doubt we never
will. But that doesn't matter. Whoever helps to build that house, to
lay a single stone of it, may feel that they've done more in their life
and with their life than all the Kings and Incas in all their power
ever did.

PLACES NAMES

(1981)

Specifications for this part of the journey: A middle-aged couple in a diesel VW starting east from Portland, Oregon, at six in the morning on the seventh of June, 1981, in the rain.

I
TO THE LITTLE BIGHORN

In the gorge of the Columbia
great grey shapes of mountain coming down
coming down
to the road
rain coming down
green forest and the rain coming down
and the river coming down.

Union Pacific going west
under the lava cliffs.
    Wasco County
Washington State now on a long, dry slant down
   to the river
and this side opening out,
getting lighter, getting dryer,
the rain a little sparser.

Suddenly the grass is yellow.
        We Can Handle It. The Dalles.
   Powerlines on the high bare hills.
   Blank wood walls.

The dam's open, Columbia roars out, white breakers
    in reverse,
a mist of water.
Washington lies in dim dun-gold levels in the rain.

It's sagebrush now and rabbitgrass,
the lava breaking through in buttresses,
pinnacles, organpipes, paws of iron-dark enormous
    lions.
Washington is sphinxes' feet.

    Sherman County
under rimrock by the big grey flood.
            Breakfast at Biggs Junction
            at the Riviera Cafe
            by the Nu-Vu Motel
            Greyhound and Trailways
            calling their passengers
            from the bacon-haunted restrooms.

    Morrow County
Cross the John Day River wide and flat
and the castles vanish:
    FLAT.
Sagebrush at its intervals.
Power poles at their intervals.
Raindrops at their intervals.
            Somewhere behind this
            Coyote is hiding.
    Umatilla County
    Fred's Melons.
    High Water.
Grey sage, grey black-stemmed willows in the reedy
    sloughs.
    Umatilla.
    Night Crawlers at the Western Auto,
    a gloomy wooden cowboy twenty feet tall at
        the Key Buy Store.
Gulls in the rain over irrigation arcs
in the desert of Irrigon, Oregon.

ENTERING WASHINGTON
   across the rainy river
   foaming from MacNary Dam.
Pale colors, pale browns of plowland, fading off
                                 and off
                                 and off.

Palouse.
Treeless.
No trees.
    Pasco: lines of morbid poplars
    blue in a vast swale.
    Snake meets Columbia, and we cross Columbia
    for the last time this time.
And the ash begins.
    Roadcuttings whitish.
    Top of every rock at the roadside white.
    The roadshoulder greyish-white.
The dry snow of the eighteenth of May, 1980,
   thirteen months ago.

As we turn from Washington 397 onto U.S. 90
   I remember the radio
that morning: Highway 90 is closed on account
   of DARKNESS.
Now the darkness
lies white on the roadsides.

    Spokane.
After the handsome city on its river the mountains
start to rise to the right hand,
westernmost Rockies,
forested, beclouded.
     And IDAHO WELCOMES YOU!

A wet white horse runs in the rain
over Lake Coeur d'Alene on steep cloudy pastures.
    Coeur d'Alene National Forest
    pine fir spruce pine fir spruce
Fourth of July Summit three thousand and eighty-one
   feet yoopee! over the top!

And we level down into parklands, lower, to a marsh
　　lonesome
　　hills and clouds on every side
and a great grey heron flops slowly south
over the lonesome marshes of the River Coeur
　　d'Alene.

　　　Shoshone County
　　　　　　Shoshone, Shoshone, Shoshone
　　　　　　　They didn't leave things
　　　　　　　only names, only words
　　　　　　　They owned very little
　　　　　　　other than breath
　　　　　　　a feather, a whisper
　　　　　　　Shoshone

　　　Smelterville.
A scruff of sheds and shacks and fences
under the steep hills;
high thin smokestacks of the mill, black,
and the black tip.
　　　Kellogg.
　　　　　　Kellogg Memorial Park No Bottles in Park
　　　　　　but a helluva lotta litter.
　　　　　　Vangs Shoe Repair
　　　　　　on the despairing wall of which is written
　　　　　　　　WALLACE SUX
The Shoshone Humane Society
　　　is a ten-by-twelve-foot building all alone on the
　　　　　river bank
　　　between the railroad and the highway
　　　in the Rocky Mountains.
　　　Heaven and Earth are not humane.

　　　Osburn, three mines, Silverton,
　　　and Welcome to Historic Wallace Silver Capital
　　　　of the World.
Somewhere in historic Wallace on a wall is written
　　KELLOGG SUX.
But the weary traveler benighted in the mountains
　　finds

a broasted chicken Sunday Dinner with slaw,
biscuits and honey, mashed potatoes, rain-
bow sherbet, beer and coffee, at Andersons
Hotel in the old, high dining room.
And all night in the motel in the silence of the
    mountains
the raingutters drummed on barrels in the alley
Rocky Mountain music.

                                    THE NEXT DAY
Six a.m. leave Wallace
in its high grey sodden solemn fir-dark cloud-encum-
    bered hills.
I-90 follows fast Gyro Creek past mines:
                Golconda District
                Compressor District
                Gold Creek
                tailings at Mullan
Lookout Pass, four thousand six hundred and eighty
    feet
            hello MONTANA!
        hello Rocky Mountain Time
        hello Lolo
We're doing 55 and so's the St. Regis River in the
    opposite direction,
jade green on granite
    Food Phone Gas Lodging
    No Services
            Breakfast in Superior
            at the Big Sky Cafe
        eggs up and square hashbrowns
    Alberton
across the wide Clark Fork, way down
at night in Alberton you must hear the river rivering
and see the car lights way up on the highway passing
    Missoula County
    Granite County
    Bearmouth
    Chalet Bearmouth

The rocks are pink, tawny, tawny red, orange, violet,
blond, gold, brown, purple, layered, lined, folded,
striped like Roman stripe.

>Drummond
>under the snowy mountains
>cottonwoods, church tower, wooden walls.
>What do you do in Drummond?

>>What you do in Drummond is climb up the
>>tall bare hill above I-90 and paint your high-
>>school class year on the granite cliffs near the
>>big white D for Drummond if you can find
>>any room left the highschool class years there
>>go back to 34 B.C.

Country Village Store 24 Miles. Gas Soup
   Moccasins.
That's what it said: Gas Soup Moccasins.

>Phosphate. NO SERVICES. Where do you pee
>   in Montana?
>Silver Bow County.
>Anaconda.

The huge dark rusty stack and flume under
   mountain shoulders,
rain coming fast from the west,
our rain, we're bringing it along,
traveling with our cloudy retinue from Oregon.

>Crackerville.

High sagebrush range, red caprock, pointed
   cedars scattered wide.

>Come to the IT Club in Rocker, Mont.
>Downtown Helena is FUN! NO SERVICES.

And after Butte under its terrific raped rich
   disemboweled mountain we go

UP.

Deerlodge Forest: sandstone pinnacles, I swear
   they are blanketed people
standing silent among the cedars
as the road goes winding fast and up
to the place where the rivers part.

Continental Divide
Homestake Pass, six thousand three
hundred and ninety-three feet.
Seabottom sandstone, ice-split, foliated, leaved by the
fingers of the cold,
dun and silver-grey, red and buff, big round worn
shapes, seabottom
here at the top of the continent
at the place my heart divides.
Farewell O rivers running to my sea.
Jefferson County.
Down we go and it begins to level down
rolling in hills and sweeps
and valleys and ranges and vast lovely reaches of land,
sagebrush and high grass, cedar and cottonwood,
the colors of cattle, the colors of horses.
Whitehall   stop stop stop we got to stop
it's a hundred miles
since breakfast—

In Whitehall at the gas station they won't let you
use the john unless you buy gas and they don't
have diesel O God but there's a semi-defunct self-
serve station and they don't give a damn they're in
there busy arguing toothlessly in low sullen voices
and the door of the john is propped open so it
won't lock so the builders working right outside
can use it if they need to and also they can see right
in and you can't shut the door but who cares, and
inside that door another traveler has written in
large letters:

THANK GOD FOR THIS TOILET

Amen, amen, amen.
Three Forks: the Jefferson, Madison, Gallatin
Rivers
the rivers with galloping names.
Horses, horses of Montana,
clump together in the great spaces of their
life,

have pony faces, clever faces, fat bellies,
are Indian colors, colors of Rockies rocks:
   buckskin, grey, roan, appaloosa, sorrel,
     paint.
Sweet Grass County.
The Yellowstone   goes shining off among
            cottonwoods and meadows
            towards lovely lines of rainy hills.
Big Timber.
        Frye's Charles M. Russell Motel.
I walked in the evening in Big Timber:

   a lot of trucks
   spits of rain
   far-off cobalt mountains streaked with white
   sweet grass of Sweet Grass County
   quaking aspen whispering in side yards of
     little wooden houses
   mountain ash in bloom in June
   birds whistling and whispering
   columbine: faint tawny pink and gold,
   color of the rocks, the Rockies' own
     wildflower.
I picked up a pink rock, granite, my piece of
   the action.

                 THE THIRD DAY ON THE ROAD
Under a bright and cloudy sky we go by
   Greycliff
   Stillwater
   Springtime
   Yellowstone
   Absarokee   That was what they called
            themselves,
         the ones we called the Crows.
Here by the Yellowstone lightly poised stood
   tall cities,
the city a circle, each house a circle,
twenty-eight lodgepoles, the door open to the
   east, the circle open.

Gone now. Empty.
White ranges in white clouds
above the river's green and empty valley:
    Absarokee.
A broom of light, amazing, sweeps through bluish
    mists
        over cliffs in a huge perspective
        beyond the pewter river, the cottonwoods,
        the pastures of the ghosts of the buffalo.
Big Horn County
    Bighorn River
        Little Bighorn River and Battlefield.
The battlefield. A middle-aged Crow Indian at the
Agency sent us to the detour, patient and polite. The Crow
were on Custer's side, a lot of good it did them. The stuff at
the building at the hilltop is all Custer, that vain and petty
man, and uniforms, and battle diagrams. One single postcard with the faces of the warchiefs of the Sioux and the
Cheyenne, heavy handsome fierce sad faces of old men,
but of Crazy Horse not even a postcard. He had no pictures taken. He didn't leave much behind. A name, a
breath, a feather on the wind.

    We walked down that long hill. Down from the
        building
    a small invisible voice led us,
    a voice in the grass of the battlefield
    beside the path, always just a couple of steps ahead
        chirk
            chirruk!
                leading us on
    invisible, a bird, a voice, a sweet, indifferent
        guide.
All around the battlefield
        (which stank of rotting bodies for weeks so
            that no sane man would go within a mile)
all around the battlefield between hilltop and river
larks trill and chirk in the long sweet grass and the
    sage,

the holy sage, that purifies.

Crickets. Cloudshadows.

Marble gravestones for the white men. Officers have
their names carved in the marble. Enlisted men do
not.

As for the others, they aren't there. The ones who
won the battle and lost the war. No stones to weigh
their feather spirits down.

> Wild roses
> prickly pear
> a lily like the mariposa
> bluebells
> tall milkweed stars
> and all the grass in bloom, long spiked or soft
>> or ruffled green
> and here and there a small, pale-scarlet Indian
>> paintbrush
> dipped in blood.

II
INDIANA AND POINTS EAST

We're doing 55 on Indiana 65.
    Jasper County.
    Flooded fields.
    Iroquois River spread way out, wide and
        brown as a Hershey bar.
    Distances in this glacier-flattened planed-down
        ground-level ground
    aren't blue, but whitish, and the sky is whitish-blue.
    It's in the eighties at 9:30 in the morning, the air
        is soft and humid,
    and the wind darkens the flooded fields
        between rows of oaks.
        Watch Your Speed—We Are.
Severely clean white farmhouses inside square
  white fences painted by
    Tom Sawyer yesterday produce
a smell of dung. A rich and heavy smell of dung on
  the southwest wind.
Can shit be heady?
La merde majestueuse.
    This is the "Old Northwest."
Not very old, not very north, not very west. And
  in Indiana
there are no Indians.

    Wabash River
right up to the road and the oaks are standing
ten feet out in the brown shadowmottled flood,
but the man at the diesel station just says:
You should of seen her yesterday.

The essence is motion being in motion moving on not
    resting at a point:
and so by catching at points and letting them go
    again without recurrence
or rhyme or rhythm I attempt to suggest or imitate
    that essence

the essence of which is that you cannot catch it.
Of course there are continuities:
the other aspect of the essence of moving on.
The county courthouses.
Kids on bikes.
White frame houses with high sashed windows.
Dipping telephone wires, telephone poles.
The names of the dispossessed.
The redwing blackbird singing to you from fencepost
    to fencepost.
Dave and Shelley singing "You're the Reason God
    Made Oklahoma" on the radio.
The yellow weedy clover by the road.
The flowering grasses.
And the crow, not the Indian, the bird, you seen one
    crow you seen 'em all,
kronk kronk.

CHEW MAIL POUCH TOBACCO
TREAT YOURSELF TO THE BEST

on an old plank barn, the letters half worn off, and that's a
continuity, not only in space but time: my California in the
thirties, & I at six years old would read the sign and
imagine a Pony Express rider at full gallop eating a candy
cigarette.

        Lafayette
        Greencastle
        And the roadsign points: Left to Indianapolis
                                Right to Brazil.
        Now there's some choice.

ANOTHER DAY

Ohio, south Ohio, Clermont County.
Cloudpuffs repeat roundtop treeshapes.
Under the grass you see the limestone layers, as if you
    drove on the ramparts
        of a fallen castle the size of Clermont County.
        Ohio 50, following Stonelick Creek.
        Daylilies dayglow orange in dark roadside woods

Brick farmhouses painted white, small, solid, far
between.
    Owensville founded 1839
    Monterey
    Milford
    Marathon   Little towns beads on a string
    Brown County
    Vera Cruz   A Spaniard in the works?
    Fayetteville   founded 1818 by Cornelion
        MacGroarty
    on the Little Miami River
    Nite Crawlers 65 cents a dozen

        There's a continuity, though the prices
            change:
        Nite Crawlers crawling clear across the
            continent.

    Highland County
    Dodsonville
    Allenburg   The road dips up and down
      in great swells like the sea
    Hoagland
    The Mad River, about one and one-half foot wide
    Hillsboro, home of Eliza Jane Thompson,
      Early Temperance Crusader
    Clearcreek
      Boston
        Rainsboro
    Ross County
      Bainbridge
      Paint Creek
    Seip—
        But Seip is older than Eliza Jane,
          and older than Ohio.
        Seip is a village twenty centuries old.

Posts mark the postholes of the houses within the encir-
cling wall; all walls are air, now; you rebuild them in your
mind. Beyond the little houses stands the long, steepsided

mound, silent in the sunlight, except for the bumblebee of
a power mower circling it, performing the clockwise spiral
rites of the god Technology, the god that cuts the grass;
the long, sweet grass on the enormous, ancient altar. A
church half the age of Stonehenge and twice the age of
Chartres. A country church.

> Onward past Bourneville, Slate Mill, North Fork
>   Farm, to Chillicothe.
>   At Chillicothe, the Hopewell Burial Mounds.

The people whom the White invaders dispossessed had
been living here for several hundred years; they called the
ones who built these mounds the Old Ones. Walk in the
silence of the vast sacred enclosure among the green
mounds built above the bones and ashes of the illustrious
dead

> laid between levels of mica, sheets of mica
> transparent and glittering as eyes, as souls.

> The pipes are stolen
> The sacred pipes are broken
> The beautiful carvings of Bobcat, Prairie-hen, Raven,
>   Turtle, Owl
> The sheets of pure thin copper cut in the shape of
>   the Bear,
>   of the Falcon, the soul-falcon,
>   of the falcon's foot
>   and the human hand.

> So, back to the New World, the thin, sick skin we laid
>   on this land,
>   the white skin. And onward past Londonderry,
>   Salt Creek, Ratcliffburg,
>   Allensville, Zaleski Freewill Baptist Church,
>   Lump Coal for Sale,
> and you can see the streaks of coal in the shaley
>   yellow soil. Prattsville.
> Dingers Motel in Prattsville. Athens County.
>   Greysville. Coolville.

Hey man I come from Coolville. And cross the brown
   Ohio
into WEST VIRGINIA.

AND ANOTHER DAY

Now here are Allegheny names as we went in the
   early morning
with the red sun rising over the misty heads and chill
   fog-filled
hollers of the hills:
> Buky Run
> Ellenboro
> Pennboro
> Burnells Run
> Spring Run

The sun is robed in a glory of mist enrayed by
   tree-branch shadows
shooting like arrows down.
> Snow Bird Road
> Smithburg
> Englands Run
> Morgans Run
> Buckeye Run
> Dark Hollow
> Fort New Salem
> Dog Run
> Cherry Camp
> Raccoon Run
> Salem Fork
> Flinderation.

After breakfast at Lums, the Entire Lums Family
   Thanks You,
comes the Child Evangelism Camp, and Harmony
   Grove,
and Pruntytown, 1798, Founded by John Prunty.
And we come over Laurel Mountain and from the top
   see all the misty ridges
and coming down we're into the Eastern Seabord
   smog, that yellow bile

that you see from airplanes, the yellow breath of our
    god.
Nite Crawlers 75 cents a dozen,
beside the Cheat River, a misty mirror for the hills.
Into Maryland at Backbone Mountain
and then right back into West Virginia, a state all
    backbone,
loyal to the union.

> Mineral County.
> Mount Storm.
> The Knobley Farm, 1766, on knobbly hills
> Ridgeville village on the hogback ridge
> Hampshire County, 1754, we keep going back
> The Stone House
> Little Cacapon River
> Paw Paw, on Short Mountain.
>> Where ye bin, honey?
>>> I bin to Paw Paw, maw.

WELCOME TO VIRGINIA!
> *Jesus is coming ready or not.*

And it's left one mile to Mecca, and right one mile
    to Gore.
We'd better go straight on.
So we went on to Georgia.

*Specifications for this part of the journey: Diesel VW, middle-
aged couple; daughter of 21; Englishwoman of 21 trying hard
not to melt; a lot of luggage, and a huge palmetto fan.*

III

THE DEEP AND SHALLOW SOUTHS

The names that run along the road that runs along the
coast in western Florida: Sea Breeze, Dolphin, Pine Tree,
Palm, Sun N Sand, Steak N Seafood, the Sand Flea, Lux-
ury Townhouses, Seafood, Luxury Highrise Condomin-
iums, The Hottest Place Under the Sun, The Outrigger,
Seafood, Vacation Forever on the Gulf, Solarcaine Stops
Sunburn Pain, Seafood, Riviera Cottages, Marina Towers,
Sandpiper Cove, Shrimp, Swimwear, T-Shirts, Seafood,
Shrimp,

    and dead trees and waterlilies in the swamps among
       the pines
    and the great melting clouds of faint cobalt blue ride
       easy inland off the azure Gulf
    and it's 83 degrees at nine a.m.
    Even So Come Lord Jesus, Are You Ready?

IT GOT TOO HOT TO WRITE
SO HERE'S ANOTHER DAY

It's 96 degrees at two p.m. as we leave the soggy bogs
    of Louisiana
for Mississippi green as green as green as grass
as green as Emerald.
       The Indian Mound at Emerald:
       a holy hill, handmade, where temples stood,
       a country cousin of the Great Pyramid in Mexico.
       Like a huge bed with a green bedspread
       emerald green
       in the infinite chanting of cicadas:
       in the cicadas are the souls of ancient priests.
  And now along the Natchez Trace, that dark and
    bloody trail,

in the sweet cool of shade,
from Natchez that looks down along the river of
    rivers
to Vicksburg where it's 91 degrees at seven p.m.

AND ANOTHER DAY

and at seven in the morning it's 83 degrees
and the soft wet air is bluish over the big bend of the
    big river.
Near Onward, Mississippi, the morning air is moist
    and easy.
Flat fields of the Delta, soy and cotton, run clean and
    even green
between bluish walls of trees.
A tractor goes slow down the rows.
Eight Black people in white shirts away off down the
    rows
hoeing cotton.
        Rolling Fork
        Nitta Yuma
        Estill
        Darlove
It's too damn hot to say hard names, they're soft as
    cottonballs.
It's 94 at noon as we come into Arkansas
across the mighty muddy milewide Mississippi.
And Arkansas is yellowish-brown under the even
    green.
Nobody moves
        in all of Arkansas
        except eight people in hats and kerchiefs going
            very slowly west in a beatup pickup truck
        and one old White man in a hat
            going very slowly south in his front yard on
            a tractor.
        Nobody else. Nobody else in all of Arkansas.

ANOTHER DAY

We started West from Russelville at five in the hot moist
dark just before daybreak. Rosyfingered dawn above the
Ozarks. Beside the road in the twilight of morning a little

yellow dog looked up at us: but no dog ever looked at
human eyes across so wide a gap.

>A little god in Arkansas.
>O Coyote, you made my country.

At Indian Nations Turnpike we have left the South.
There's a dry wind blowing over the scrub oaks on the
long, low ridges; and things aren't even green and humid
blue, but other colors, dry, distinct.

>Okfuskee County
>Weleetka
>Wetumka
>Okemah
>Shawnee
>Wevoka
>North Canadian River
>Seminole
>Pottawatomie
>Kickapoo
>Tecumseh
>Choctaw
>Anadarko
>Caddo   These are the names, the true names,
>   names of the world Coyote made.

At the Cherokee Trading Post there's lamps and cactus
jelly for sale, totem poles—Cherokee totem poles?—and
Perfumes of the Desert.

>O Coyote you always got things all wrong
>and then ran off with your tail between your legs
>laughing

There: all the little black elegance of foot and ear and
   jackrabbit brain
is gone to a bit of bloated bloody ragged mud by the
   tire-side.
A million times a night on our ten thousand roads.
The trouble with us is, you know what the trouble
   with us is?
>*we waste food.*
>   O Coyote get it right next time!

North Fork of the Red River
from this valley they say you are going, do not
   hasten to bid me adieu,
and there's sagebrush, yahoo sagebrush,
and we enter Texas at the Wheeler County Line.

ANOTHER DAY,

and here's a sunrise for you. In the Panhandle, dawn
among the thunderstorms. A gentle rain and lightning in
the dark, packing the car to leave Shamrock, Texas, and
the sky above I-40 mottled with black clouds and lighter
patches of sky holding one faint wet star. Thunder,
thunder near and far. From the dark, dark rain falls and
lightning flares in huge bright blurs northward, to the
right. And the earth is without form, and void. Slowly
light, slowly light slowly enlightens the soft fertile dark
world-cave, defines, separates Earth from Heaven.

   A fourlegged god with yellow eyes
   is making the world over.

And the roadside signs creep into being out of unbeing,
selling beds and goods and foods and Texas Souvenirs.

   At nine a.m. the road falls off the edge of things
      into the desert.
   Sagebrush ahead and mesas, far as the eye
      can see,
   under the sky of turquoise and white shell.
   NEW MEXICO. Names of New Mexico:
Tucumcari.
Santa Rosa.
      A heavy red river, the Gallina, like a red
        snake, crawls
      past Santa Rosa through rock-strewn,
        brush-dotted, red-green hills.
Colonias.
Pecos River, red, braiding red mud
San Miguel
      A sweet dry air.
      Dark green juniper

    dark red dirt
    dark blue sky
    bright white clouds
    Flowers: white stars, gold pads,
        purple spikes & yucca
Tecolote turnoff
These names are far between,
miles apart
Bernal
Behind the dark purple northern mesa is a great
Source of Clouds: from it clouds rise and float and
feather out and fade in silver shell-ripples above
the deserts.

Glorieta
Mesa Glorieta
Villanueva, San Juan, San José, and on to
Santa Fé.

                                                    ANOTHER DAY
Oh, one more sunrise, this is the next to last,
leaving Cortez, Colorado.
To the right a distant mesa is on fire.
Behind the San Miguels and Mesa Verde, a citron sky
    streaked orange-pink.
The lights of Cortez fade under the mountains,
    under grey-haired rainclouds;
and to the left, a full moon rides faint in veils of rose
    and blue,
over the long mountain called The Sleeping Ute.
The mesa on fire blazes up, and then a huge, soft
    raincloud
sits down on the sunrise and puts it out.
After a long time from the grey one shaft of pure
    light rises, white,
too white for the eye to bear, and Coyote wins again,
    and welcome
to Dove Creek, Colorado, pinto bean capital of the
    world!

IV

FAR WEST GOING WEST

WELCOME TO UTAH early in the morning.
The sunflowers are confused, haven't got turned
    sunwards yet, face every whichway.
Juniper. A good, strong, catspray smell of juniper in
    the high dry air.
Sagebrush, chamiso, the little yellow-flowered
    clover that's been along
our way from Oregon to Georgia and back. And
    crows.
Suddenly we descend from mountains into desert
where there are monsters.
A potbellied Mexican waterjug two hundred feet
    high
turns into a sphinx as you pass it.
A throne of red rock with no seat, a hundred feet
    high.
Red lumps and knobs and kneecaps and one-eyed
    skulls the size of a house.

The sunflowers now are all staring east like
    Parsees,
except a couple in the shadow of the roadcut, which
    haven't got the news
or received orders yet.
    There aren't a whole lot of names, in Utah,
      but here's one: Hole in the Rock:
        big white letters on a big red bluff with a
          hole in it, yessir,
        and also Paintings of Christ and
          Taxidermy.
A lone and conceivably insurgent but probably
    uninformed sunflower
stands in the shadow of a cliff, facing southwest, at
    7:41 a.m.
Well the last time *I* saw the sun it was over *there* and
    how do I know where the damn thing's got to?

Arches National Monument, near Moab: Red stone arches. Red stone lingams, copulating alligators, camels, triceratops, keyholes, elephants, pillows, towers, leaves, fins of the Ouroboros, lizard's heads. A woman of red stone and a man of red stone, very tall, stand facing the falconfaced god of the red stone. Many tall, strange stone people standing on the red sand under the red cliffs; and the sanddunes have turned to stone, and the Jurassic sea that lapped on these red beaches dried and dried and dried away and shrank to the Mormons' bitter lake. The sky is as blue as fire. Northward, stone dunes in white terraces and stairways pile up to the violet-red turrets and buttresses of a most terrible city inhabited by the Wind. A purple fortress stands before the gates, and in front of it, four tall, shapeless kings of stone stand guard.

NEXT MORNING

Heading out of green and gentle Delta to the Nevada line, early, to get across the desert in the cool.

> Jackrabbits flit
> on the moonlit salt pans
> to the left of the mountains of dawn.
>
> Jackrabbits dance
> in the moonlit sagebrush
> to the left of the mountains of dawn.
>
> Four pronghorn drift
> from the road into the sage
> in the twilight of morning
> to the left of the mountains of dawn.

Nevada
There are no names here.
> The rosepink shadowless mountains of dawn now
> are daylit,
> deepshadowed, and the moon has lost her
> dominion.
> In this long first sunlight the desert is greyish-
> gold.

By the road as straight as an imaginary canal on
　Mars are flowers:
　　　Michaelmas daisies, Matilija poppies white as the
　　　　moon up there,
　　　milkweed, blue chicory. The green lush South
　　　　was flowerless.
There are
five fenceposts
　　　in the middle of a vast sagebrush flat of which
　　　　the middle
　　　is everywhere and the circumference nowhere.
Five crows
one crow per post
soak up the morning sun.
　　　　　　Only Crow's been with us all the way,
　　　north, middle, south, and west. Even the
　　　　redwing blackbird
　　　gave out in Nevada, but Crow's here, Crow of the
　　　　Six Directions.
Jackrabbits go lolloping off like wallabies
　　　with magnificent blacktipped ears.
Gabbs Luning. There's a name for you!
　　　At Gabbs Luning there's a Schneelite Mine.
　　　I don't believe anything in Nevada. This is pure
　　　　Coyote country.
A vast lake that holds no water
is full to the brim of glittering light.
Far out, towards the center of the lake,
lie the bones of a wrecked ship
that struck on the reef of the mirage
and sank through heatwaves down and down
to lie now bleaching fathoms deep in blinding light,
all souls aboard her drowned in air.
Probably a potash mine. Who knows? We drive on
　　　west.

THE PRINCESS

(1982)

I was asked to give a keynote address to open a workshop conference of the Portland branch of the National Abortion Rights Action League, in January of 1982.

You are going to be working hard today on very serious and urgent work, matters literally of life and death, so I thought it might be a good idea to fool around a little first. I am going to tell you a fairy tale.

Once upon a time, long, long ago, in the Dark Ages, there was a princess. She was wealthy, well fed, well educated, and well beloved. She went to a college for training female royalty, and there, at the associated college for training male royalty, she met a prince. He, too, was wealthy, well fed, well educated, and well beloved. And they fell in love with each other and had a really royal time.

Although the princess was on the Honors List and the prince was a graduate student, they were remarkably ignorant about some things. The princess's parents, though modest and even inhibited, had been responsible and informative: she knew all about how babies are made. She had read books about it. But it had not occurred to her parents or the people who wrote the books that she might need to know how to *keep from making babies*. This was long ago, remember, in the Dark Ages, before sex was obligatory, before the Pill. All she knew was that there was something called a rubber, and boys always sniggered when the Trojan War was mentioned in high school. The prince, of course, knew everything. He'd been around. He'd had sex since he was fifteen, he said. He knew you had to wear a condom the first time each night. But the second or third time each night, you didn't. It was safe. He knew that.

Perhaps you can imagine what happens next in this story? Like all fairy tales, it follows a familiar path; there is a certain inevitable quality to the events.

"We have to get married!" the princess said to the prince.

"I'm going home to my mother," the prince said to the princess.

And he did. He went home to his family palace in Brooklyn Heights, and hid in the throne room.

The princess went to her family palace on Riverside Drive and cried a lot. She cried the Hudson River full of tears. But, though she had never been punished for anything in her life, she could not bring herself to tell her parents why she was crying. She made up a pretext to go to her mother's gynecologist and get a pregnancy test. They used rabbits; if the test was positive, the rabbit died; remember, this is the Dark Ages. The rabbit died. The princess didn't tell her parents, but went and dug the prince out and said, "We *really* have to get married."

"You're not a member of my religion, and anyhow, it's your baby," said the prince, and went back to Brooklyn Heights. And she went back home and cried so hard that her parents finally saw what had to be the matter. And they said, "O.K., it's O.K., honey, and if he won't marry you, you don't have to have the baby."

Now, you may recall that in the Dark Ages abortion was not legal. It was a crime, and not a minor one.

The princess's parents were not criminal types. They were the kind of people who obey the speed limit, and pay taxes and parking-ticket fines, and return borrowed books. I mean they were honest. They were neither square nor unsophisticated, they were not "religious," but they were intensely moral people, with a love of kindness and decency, and a strong respect for the law. And yet now, without hesitation, they resolved to break the law, to conspire to commit a felony. And they did so in the reasoned and deeply felt conviction that it was right, that indeed it was their *responsibility*, to do so.

The princess herself questioned the decision, not on legal grounds, of course, but ethically. She cried some more and said, "I'm being cowardly. I'm being dishonest. I'm evading the consequence of my own action."

Her father said, "That's right. You are. That cowardice, dishonesty, evasion, is a lesser sin than the crass irresponsibility of sacrificing your training, your talent, and the children you will want to have, in order to have one nobody wants to have."

He was a Victorian, you see, and a bit of a Puritan. He hated waste and wastefulness.

So the princess and her parents tried to find out how to get an abortion—and they got a little panicky, because they didn't know anybody who knew. The gynecologist got huffy when asked for a reference. "I don't handle A.B.'s," he said. After all, his license to a lucrative practice was at stake; he could have gone to jail; you can't blame him. It was an old family friend, a child psychologist, who finally found the right contact, the criminal connection. She made an appointment for "an examination."

They were really slick, that outfit. Dr. So-and-So. Nice office on the Lower East Side, polite smiling receptionist, *Esquire* and *National Geographic* on the waiting-room tables. Their reputation was "the highest-class abortionists in New York City," and it was probably deserved. They charged more for an abortion than most working families made in a year. This was no dirty backroom business. It was clean. It was class. They never said the word "abortion," not even that cute euphemism "A.B." The doctor offered to restore the hymen. "It's easy," he said. "No extra charge." The princess did not wish to be rebuilt like a Buick and said, "No. Get on with it." And they did. Did a fine job, I'm sure. As the princess left that office she passed a girl coming in, a college girl with red eyes and fear in her face, and she wanted to stop and say, "It's O.K., it's not so bad, don't be afraid," but she was afraid to. And she went back uptown in a taxi with her mother, both of them crying, partly out of grief, partly out of relief. "The endless sorrow . . ."

The princess went back to college to finish her degree. From time to time she would see the prince lurking and scuttling around behind the ivy on the buildings. I'm sure he has lived happily ever after. As for the princess, she got her B.A. a few months after she got her A.B., and then went on to graduate school, and then got married, and was a writer, and got pregnant by choice four times. One pregnancy ended in spontaneous abortion, miscarriage, in the third month; three pregnancies ended in live normal birth. She had three desired and beloved children, none of whom would have been born if her first pregnancy had gone to term.

If any birth is better than no birth, and more births are better than fewer births, as the "Right-to-Life" people insist, then they should approve of my abortion, which resulted in three babies instead of one. A curious but logical method of achieving their goal! But the preservation of life seems to be rather a slogan than a genuine goal of the anti-abortion forces; what they want is control.

Control over behavior: power over women. Women in the anti-
choice movement want to share in male power over women, and do
so by denying their own womanhood, their own rights and responsibilities.

If there is a moral to my tale, it's something like this. In spite of
everything the little princess had been taught by the male-suprema-
cist elements of her society, by high-school scandals about why Sallie
dropped out of school in March, by novels extolling motherhood as
woman's sole function, by the gynecologist's furtiveness, by the existence of a law declaring abortion to be a crime, by the sleek extor-
tionism of the abortionist—despite all those messages repeating
ABORTION IS WRONG!—when the terror was past, she pondered
it all, and she thought, "I have done the right thing."

What was wrong was not knowing how to prevent getting pregnant. What was wrong was my ignorance. To legislate that ignorance, that's the crime. I'm ashamed, she thought, for letting bigots
keep me ignorant, and for acting willfully in my ignorance, and for
falling in love with a weak, selfish man. I am deeply ashamed. But
I'm not guilty. Where does guilt come in? I did what I had to do so
that I could do the work I was put here to do. I will do that work.
That's what it's all about. It's about taking responsibility.

So I thought at the time, not very clearly. That I can think more
clearly about it now, and talk about it, to you and to others, is
entirely due to the moral courage and strength of women and men
who have been working these thirty years for the rights and dignity
and freedom of women, including the right to abortion. They set
me free, and I am here to thank them, and to promise solidarity.

Why did I tell you this tale, which is only too familiar? Well, I
called myself a princess in it, partly for the joke, and partly because
my parents were indeed royal, where it counts, in the soul; but also
to keep reminding myself and you that *I was privileged*. I had "the
best abortion in New York City." What was it like, in the Dark Ages
when abortion was a crime, for the girl whose dad couldn't borrow
the cash, as my dad could? What was it like for the girl who couldn't
even tell her dad, because he'd go crazy with shame and rage? Who
couldn't tell her *mother*? Who had to go alone to that filthy room
and put herself body and soul into the hands of a professional
criminal?—because that's what every doctor who did an abortion
was, whether he was an extortionist or an idealist. You know what it
was like for her. You know and I know; that's why we're here. We are
not going back to the Dark Ages. We are not going to let anybody in

this country have that kind of power over any girl or woman. There are great powers, outside the government and in it, trying to legislate the return of darkness. We are not great powers. But we are the light. Nobody can put us out. May all of you shine very bright and steady, today and always.

A NON-EUCLIDEAN VIEW
OF CALIFORNIA AS
A COLD PLACE TO BE

(1982)

Robert C. Elliott died in 1981 in the very noon of his scholarship, just after completing his book *The Literary Persona*. He was the truest of teachers, the kindest of friends. This paper was prepared to be read as the first in a series of lectures at his college of the University of California, San Diego, honoring his memory.

We use the French word *lecture*, "reading," to mean reading and speaking aloud, a performance; the French call such a performance not a *lecture* but a *conférence*. The distinction is interesting. Reading is a silent collaboration of reader and writer, apart; lecturing, a noisy collaboration of lecturer and audience, together. The peculiar patchwork form of this paper is my attempt to make it a "conference," a performable work, a piece for voices. The time and place, a warm April night in La Jolla in 1982, are past, and the warm and noisy audience must be replaced by the gentle reader; but the first voice is still that of Bob Elliott.

In *The Shape of Utopia*, speaking of our modern distrust of utopia, he said,

> If the word is to be redeemed, it will have to be by someone who has followed utopia into the abyss which yawns behind the Grand Inquisitor's vision, and who then has clambered out on the other side.[1]

That is my starting point, that startling image; and my motto is:

Usà puyew usu wapiw!

We shall be returning to both, never fear; what I am about here is returning.

In the first chapter of *The Shape of Utopia,* Bob points out that in the great participatory festivals such as Saturnalia, Mardi Gras, or Christmas, the age of peace and equality, the Golden Age, may be lived in an interval set apart for it, a time outside of daily time. But to bring perfect *communitas* into the structure of ordinary society would be a job only Zeus could handle; or, "if one does not believe in Zeus's good will, or even in his existence," says Bob, it becomes a job for the mind of man.

> Utopia is the application of man's reason and his will to the myth [of the Golden Age], man's effort to work out imaginatively what happens—or might happen—when the primal longings embodied in the myth confront the principle of reality. In this effort man no longer merely dreams of a divine state in some remote time: he assumes the role of creator.[2]

Now, the Golden Age, or Dream Time, is remote only from the rational mind. It is not accessible to euclidean reason; but on the evidence of all myth and mysticism, and the assurance of every participatory religion, it is, to those with the gift or discipline to perceive it, right here, right now. Whereas it is of the very essence of the rational or Jovian utopia that it is *not* here and *not* now. It is made by the reaction of will and reason against, away from, the here-and-now, and it is, as More said in naming it, nowhere. It is pure structure without content; pure model; goal. That is its virtue. Utopia is uninhabitable. As soon as we reach it, it ceases to be utopia. As evidence of this sad but ineluctable fact, may I point out that we in this room, here and now, are inhabiting utopia.

I was told as a child, and like to believe, that California was named "The Golden State" not just for the stuff Sutter found but for the wild poppies on its hills and the wild oats of summer. To the Spanish and Mexicans I gather it was the boondocks; but to the Anglos it has been a true utopia: the Golden Age made accessible by willpower, the wild paradise to be tamed by reason; the place where you go free of the old bonds and cramps, leaving behind your farm and your galoshes, casting aside your rheumatism and your inhibitions, taking up a new "life style" in a not-here-not-now where everybody gets rich quick in the movies or finds the meaning of life or anyhow gets a good tan hang-gliding. And the wild oats and the poppies still come up pure gold in cracks in the cement that we have poured over utopia.

In "assuming the role of creator," we seek what Lao Tzu calls "the profit of what is not," rather than participating in what is. To reconstruct the world, to rebuild or rationalize it, is to run the risk of losing or destroying what in fact is.

After all, California was not empty when the Anglos came. Despite the efforts of the missionaries, it was still the most heavily populated region in North America.

What the Whites perceived as a wilderness to be "tamed" was in fact better known to human beings than it has ever been since: known and named. Every hill, every valley, creek, canyon, gulch, gully, draw, point, cliff, bluff, beach, bend, good-sized boulder, and tree of any character had its name, its place in the order of things. An order was perceived, of which the invaders were entirely ignorant. Each of those names named, not a goal, not a place to get to, but a place where one is: a center of the world. There were centers of the world all over California. One of them is a bluff on the Klamath River. Its name was Katimin. The bluff is still there, but it has no name, and the center of the world is not there. The six directions can meet only in lived time, in the place people call home, the seventh direction, the center.

But we leave home, shouting Avanti! and Westward Ho!, driven by our godlike reason, which chafes at the limited, intractable, unreasonable present, and yearns to free itself from the fetters of the past.

"People are always shouting they want to create a better future," says Milan Kundera, in *The Book of Laughter and Forgetting*

> It's not true. The future is an apathetic void of no interest to anyone. The past is full of life, eager to irritate us, provoke and insult us, tempt us to destroy or repaint it. The only reason people want to be masters of the future is to change the past.[3]

And at the end of the book he talks to the interviewer about forgetting: forgetting is

> the great private problem of man: death as the loss of the self. But what is this self? It is the sum of everything we remember. Thus, what terrifies us about death is not the loss of the future but the loss of the past.[4]

And so, Kundera says, when a big power wants to deprive a smaller one of its national identity, of its self-consciousness, it uses what he calls the "method of organized forgetting."

And when a future-oriented culture impinges upon a present-centered one, the method becomes a compulsion. Things are forgotten wholesale. What are the names "Costanoan," "Wappo"? They are what the Spanish called the people around the Bay Area and in the Napa Valley, but what those people called themselves we do not know: the names were forgotten even before the people were wiped out. There was no past. Tabula rasa.

One of our finest methods of organized forgetting is called discovery. Julius Caesar exemplifies the technique with characteristic elegance in his *Gallic Wars*. "It was not certain that Britain existed," he says, "until I went there."

To whom was it not certain? But what the heathen know doesn't count. Only if godlike Caesar sees it can Britannia rule the waves.

Only if a European discovered or invented it could America exist. At least Columbus had the wit, in his madness, to mistake Venezuela for the outskirts of Paradise. But he remarked on the availability of cheap slave labor in Paradise.

The first chapter of *California: An Interpretive History*, by Professor Walton Bean, contains this paragraph:

> The survival of a Stone Age culture in California was not the result of any hereditary biological limitations on the potential of the Indians as a "race." They had been geographically and culturally isolated. The vast expanse of oceans, mountains, and deserts had sheltered California from foreign stimulation as well as from foreign conquest . . .

(being isolated from contact and protected from conquest are, you will have noticed, characteristics of utopia),

> . . . and even within California the Indian groups were so settled that they had little contact with each other. On the positive side, there was something to be said for their culture just as it was. . . . The California Indians had made a successful adaptation to their environment and they had learned to live without destroying each other.[5]

Professor Bean's excellent book is superior to many of its kind in the area of my particular interest: the first chapter. Chapter One of the American history—South or North America, national or regional—is usually short. Unusually short. In it, the "tribes" that "occupied" the area are mentioned and perhaps anecdotally described. In Chapter Two, a European "discovers" the area; and with a gasp of relief the historian plunges into a narration of the conquest, often referred to as settlement or colonization, and the acts of the conquerors. Since history has traditionally been defined by historians as the written record, this imbalance is inevitable. And in a larger sense it is legitimate; for the non-urban peoples of the Americas had no history, properly speaking, and therefore are visible only to the anthropologist, not to the historian, except as they entered into White history.

The imbalance is unavoidable, legitimate, and also, I believe, very dangerous. It expresses too conveniently the conquerors' wish to deny the value of the cultures they destroyed, and dehumanize the people they killed. It partakes too much of the method of organized forgetting. To call this "the New World"—there's a Caesarian birth!

The words "holocaust" and "genocide" are fashionable now; but not often are they applied to American history. We were not told in school in Berkeley that the history of California had the final solution for its first chapter. We were told that the Indians "gave way" before the "march of progress."

In the introduction to *The Wishing Bone Cycle*, Howard A. Norman says:

> The Swampy Cree have a conceptual term which I've heard used to describe the thinking of a porcupine as he backs into a rock crevice:
>
> *Usà puyew usu wapiw.*
>
> "He goes backward, looks forward." The porcupine consciously goes backward in order to speculate safely on the future, allowing him to look out at his enemy or the new day. To the Cree, it's an instructive act of self-preservation.[6]

The opening formula for a Cree story is "an invitation to listen, followed by the phrase, 'I go backward, look forward, as the porcupine does.' "[7]

In order to speculate safely on an inhabitable future, perhaps we would do well to find a rock crevice and go backward. In order to find our roots, perhaps we should look for them where roots are usually found. At least the Spirit of Place is a more benign one than the exclusive and aggressive Spirit of Race, the mysticism of blood that has cost so much blood. With all our self-consciousness, we have very little sense of where we live, where we are right here right now.

If we did, we wouldn't muck it up the way we do. If we did, our literature would celebrate it. If we did, our religion might be participatory. If we did—if we really lived here, now, in this present—we might have some sense of our future as a people. We might know where the center of the world is.

> ... Ideally, at its loftiest and most pure, the utopia aspires to (if it has never reached) the condition of the idyll as Schiller describes it—that mode of poetry which would lead man, not back to Arcadia, but forward to Elysium, to a state of society in which man would be at peace with himself and the external world.[8]

> The California Indians had made a successful adaptation to their environment and they had learned to live without destroying each other.[9]

It was Arcadia, of course; it was not Elysium. I heed Victor Turner's warning not to confuse archaic or primitive societies with the true *communitas,* "which is a dimension of all societies, past and present."[10] I am not proposing a return to the Stone Age. My intent is not reactionary, nor even conservative, but simply subversive. It seems that the utopian imagination is trapped, like capitalism and industrialism and the human population, in a one-way future consisting only of growth. All I'm trying to do is figure how to put a pig on the tracks.

Go backward. Turn and return.

> If the word [utopia] is to be redeemed, it will have to be by someone who has followed utopia into the abyss which yawns behind the Grand Inquisitor's vision.[11]

The utopia of the Grand Inquisitor

> is the product of "the euclidean mind" (a phrase Dostoyevsky often used), which is obsessed by the idea of regulating all life by reason and bringing happiness to man whatever the cost.[12]

The single vision of the Grand Inquisitor perceives the condition of man in a way stated with awful clarity by Yevgeny Zamyatin, in *We:*

> There were two in paradise, and the choice was offered to them: happiness without freedom, or freedom without happiness. No other choice.[13]

No other choice. Hear now the voice of Urizen!

> Hidden, set apart in my stern counsels
> Reserved for days of futurity,
> I have sought for a joy without pain,
> For a solid without fluctuation. . . .
>
> Lo, I unfold my darkness and on
> This rock place with strong hand the book
> Of eternal brass, written in my solitude.
>
> Laws of peace, of love, of unity,
> Of pity, compassion, forgiveness.
> Let each choose one habitation,
> His ancient infinite mansion,
> One command, one joy, one desire,
> One curse, one weight, one measure,
> One King, one God, one Law.[14]

In order to believe in utopia, Bob Elliott said, we must believe

> that through the exercise of their reason men can control and in
> major ways alter for the better their social environment. . . . One
> must have faith of a kind that our history has made nearly
> inaccessible.[15]

"When the Way is lost," Lao Tzu observed in a rather similar historical situation a few thousand years earlier,

> there is benevolence. When benevolence is lost there is justice.
> When justice is lost there are the rites. The rites are the end of
> loyalty and good faith, the beginning of disorder.[16]

"Prisons," said William Blake, "are built with stones of Law."[17] And coming back round to the Grand Inquisitor, we have Milan Kundera restating the dilemma of Happiness versus Freedom:

> Totalitarianism is not only hell, but also the dream of paradise—
> the age-old dream of a world where everybody would live in
> harmony, united by a single common will and faith, without
> secrets from one another. . . . If totalitarianism did not exploit
> these archetypes, which are deep inside us all and rooted deep
> in all religions, it could never attract so many people, especially
> during the early phases of its existence. Once the dream of

paradise starts to turn into reality, however, here and there people begin to crop up who stand in its way, and so the rulers of
paradise must build a little gulag on the side of Eden. In the
course of time this gulag grows ever bigger and more perfect,
while the adjoining paradise gets ever smaller and poorer.[18]

The purer, the more euclidean the reason that builds a utopia,
the greater is its self-destructive capacity. I submit that our lack of
faith in the benevolence of reason as the controlling power is well
founded. We must test and trust our reason, but to have *faith* in it is
to elevate it to godhead. Zeus the Creator takes over. Unruly Titans
are sent to the salt mines, and inconvenient Prometheus to the
reservation. Earth itself comes to be the wart on the walls of Eden.

The rationalist utopia is a power trip. It is a monotheocracy,
declared by executive decree, and maintained by willpower; as its
premise is progress, not process, it has no habitable present, and
speaks only in the future tense. And in the end reason itself must
reject it.

"O that I had never drank the wine nor eat the bread
Of dark mortality, nor cast my view into futurity, nor turned
My back darkening the present, clouding with a cloud,
And building arches high and cities, turrets and towers and domes
Whose smoke destroyed the pleasant garden, and whose running
    kennels
Choked the bright rivers. . . .

Then go, O dark futurity! I will cast thee forth from these
Heavens of my brain, nor will I look upon futurity more.
I cast futurity away, and turn my back upon that void
Which I have made, for lo! futurity is in this moment. . . ."

So Urizen spoke. . . .

    Then, glorious bright, exulting in his joy,
He sounding rose into the heavens, in naked majesty,
In radiant youth. . . .[19]

That is certainly the high point of this paper. I wish we could follow
Urizen in his splendid vertical jailbreak, but it is a route reserved to
the major poets and composers. The rest of us must stay down here
on the ground, walking in circles, proposing devious side trips, and
asking impertinent questions. My question now is: Where is the
place Coyote made?

In a paper about teaching utopia, Professor Kenneth Roemer says:

> The importance of this question was forced upon me several years ago in a freshman comp course at the University of Texas at Arlington. I asked the class to write a paper in response to a hypothetical situation: if you had unlimited financial resources and total local, state, and national support, how would you transform Arlington, Texas, into utopia? A few minutes after the class had begun to write, one of the students—a mature and intelligent woman in her late thirties—approached my desk. She seemed embarrassed, even upset. She asked, "What if I believe that Arlington, Texas, *is* utopia?"[20]

What do you do with *her* in Walden Two?

Utopia has been euclidean, it has been European, and it has been masculine. I am trying to suggest, in an evasive, distrustful, untrustworthy fashion, and as obscurely as I can, that our final loss of faith in that radiant sandcastle may enable our eyes to adjust to a dimmer light and in it perceive another kind of utopia. As this utopia would not be euclidean, European, or masculinist, my terms and images in speaking of it must be tentative and seem peculiar. Victor Turner's antitheses of structure and *communitas* are useful to my attempt to think about it: structure in society, in his terms, is cognitive, *communitas* existential; structure provides a model, *communitas* a potential; structure classifies, *communitas* reclassifies; structure is expressed in legal and political institutions, *communitas* in art and religion.

> Communitas breaks in through the interstices of structure, in liminality; at the edges of structure, in marginality; and from beneath structure, in inferiority. It is almost everywhere held to be sacred or "holy," possibly because it transgresses or dissolves the norms that govern structured or institutionalized relationships and is accompanied by experiences of unprecedented potency.[21]

Utopian thought has often sought to institutionalize or legislate the experience of *communitas*, and each time it has done so it has run up against the Grand Inquisitor.

> The activities of a machine are determined by its structure, but the relation is reversed in organisms—organic structure is determined by its processes.[22]

That is Fritjof Capra, providing another useful analogy. If the attempt to provide a structure that will ensure *communitas* is impaled on the horns of its own dilemma, might one not abandon the machine model and have a go at the organic—permitting process to determine structure? But to do so is to go even further than the Anarchists, and to risk not only being called but being in fact regressive, politically naive, Luddite, and anti-rational. Those are real dangers (though I admit that the risk of being accused of not being in the Main Current of Western Thought is one I welcome the opportunity to run). What kind of utopia can come out of these margins, negations, and obscurities?* Who will even recognize it as a utopia? It won't look the way it ought to. It may look very like some kind of place Coyote made after having a conversation with his own dung.

The symbol which Trickster embodies is not a static one.

Paul Radin speaking. You will recall that the quality of static perfection is an essential element of the non-inhabitability of the euclidean utopia (a point that Bob Elliott discusses with much cogency).

> The symbol which Trickster embodies is not a static one. It contains within itself the promise of differentiation, the promise of god and man. For this reason every generation occupies itself with interpreting Trickster anew. No generation understands him fully but no generation can do without him . . . for he represents not only the undifferentiated and distant past, but likewise the undifferentiated present within every individual. . . . If we laugh at him, he grins at us. What happens to him happens to us.[23]

---

* When I was struggling with the writing of this piece, I had not read the four volumes of Robert Nichols' *Daily Lives in Nghsi-Altai* (New York: New Directions, 1977–79). I am glad that I had not, because my thoughts could not then have so freely and fecklessly coincided, collided, and intersected with his. My paper would have been written in the consciousness of the existence of Nghsi-Altai, as Pierre Menard's *Quixote* was written in the consciousness of the existence of Cervantes' *Quixote*, and might have been even more different from what it is than Menard's *Quixote* from Cervantes'. But it can be and I hope will be *read* in the consciousness of the existence of Nghsi-Altai; and the fact that Nghsi-Altai is in some respects the very place I was laboriously trying to get to, and yet lies in quite the opposite direction, can only enlarge the use and meaning of my work. Indeed, if this note leads some readers to go find Nghsi-Altai for themselves, the whole thing will have been worthwhile.

And he never was in Eden, because coyotes live in the New World. Driven forth by the angel with the flaming sword, Eve and Adam lifted their sad heads and saw Coyote, grinning.

Non-European, non-euclidean, non-masculinist: they are all negative definitions, which is all right, but tiresome; and the last is unsatisfactory, as it might be taken to mean that the utopia I'm trying to approach could only be imagined by women—which is possible—or only inhabited by women—which is intolerable. Perhaps the word I need is yin.

Utopia has been yang. In one way or another, from Plato on, utopia has been the big yang motorcycle trip. Bright, dry, clear, strong, firm, active, aggressive, lineal, progressive, creative, expanding, advancing, and hot.

Our civilization is now so intensely yang that any imagination of bettering its injustices or eluding its self-destructiveness must involve a reversal.

> The ten thousand things arise together
> and I watch their return.
> They return each to its root.
> Returning to one's roots is known as stillness.
> Returning to one's destiny is known as the constant.
> Knowledge of the constant is known as discernment.
> To ignore the constant
> is to go wrong, and end in disorder.[24]

To attain the constant, to end in order, we must return, go round, go inward, go yinward. What would a yin utopia be? It would be dark, wet, obscure, weak, yielding, passive, participatory, circular, cyclical, peaceful, nurturant, retreating, contracting, and cold.

Now on the subject of heat and cold: a reference in *The Shape of Utopia* sent me to a 1960 lecture by M. Lévi-Strauss, "The Scope of Anthropology," which so influenced my efforts to think out this paper that I wish to quote from it at some length, with apologies to those of you to whom the passage[25] is familiar. He is speaking of "primitive" societies.

> Although they exist in history, these societies seem to have worked out or retained a certain wisdom which makes them desperately resist any structural modification which might afford history a point of entry into their lives. The societies which have best protected their distinctive character appear to be those concerned above all with persevering in their existence.

Persevering in one's existence is the particular quality of the organism; it is not a progress towards achievement, followed by stasis, which is the machine's mode, but an interactive, rhythmic, and unstable process, which constitutes an end in itself.

> The way in which they exploit the environment guarantees them a modest standard of living as well as the conservation of natural resources. Though various, their rules of marriage reveal to the demographer's eye a common function; to set the fertility rate very low, and to keep it constant. Finally, a political life based upon consent, and admitting of no decisions but those arrived at unanimously, would seem designed to preclude the possibility of calling on that driving force of collective life which takes advantage of the contrast between power and opposition, majority and minority, exploiter and exploited.

Lévi-Strauss is about to make his distinction between the "hot" societies, which have appeared since the Neolithic Revolution, and in which "differentiations between castes and between classes are urged without cease, in order that social change and energy may be extracted from them," and the "cold" societies, self-limited, whose historical temperature is pretty near zero.

The relevance of this beautiful piece of anthropological thinking to my subject is immediately proven by Lévi-Strauss himself, who in the next paragraph thanks Heaven that anthropologists are not expected to predict man's future, but says that if they were, instead of merely extrapolating from our own "hot" society, they might propose a progressive integration of the best of the "hot" with the best of the "cold."

If I understand him, this unification would involve carrying the Industrial Revolution, already the principal source of social energy, to its logical extreme: the completed Electronic Revolution. After this, change and progress would be strictly cultural and, as it were, machine-made.

> With culture having integrally taken over the burden of manufacturing progress, society . . . , placed outside and above history, could once more assume that regular and as it were crystalline structure, which the surviving primitive societies teach us is not antagonistic to the human condition.

The last phrase, from that austere and somber mind, is poignant.
  As I understand it, Lévi-Strauss suggests that to combine the hot

and the cold is to transfer mechanical operational modes to machines while retaining organic modes for humanity. Mechanical progress; biological rhythm. A kind of superspeed electronic yang train, in whose yin pullmans and dining cars life is serene and the rose on the table does not even tremble. What worries me in this model is the dependence upon cybernetics as the integrating function. Who's up there in the engineer's seat? Is it on auto? Who wrote the program—old Nobodaddy Reason again? Is it another of those trains with no brakes?

It may simply be the bad habits of my mind that see in this brief utopian glimpse a brilliant update of an old science-fiction theme: the world where robots do the work while the human beings sit back and play. These were always satirical works. The rule was that either an impulsive young man wrecked the machinery and saved humanity from stagnation, or else the machines, behaving with impeccable logic, did away with the squashy and superfluous people. The first and finest of the lot, E. M. Forster's "The Machine Stops," ends on a characteristic double chord of terror and promise: the machinery collapses, the crystalline society is shattered with it, but outside there are free people—how civilized, we don't know, but outside and free.

We're back to Kundera's wart on the walls of Eden—the exiles from paradise in whom the hope of paradise lies, the inhabitants of the gulag who are the only free souls. The information systems of the train are marvelous, but the tracks run through Coyote country.

> In ancient times the Yellow Emperor first used benevolence and righteousness and meddled with the minds of men. Yao and Shun followed him and worked till there was no more hair on their shins . . . in the practice of benevolence and righteousness, taxed their blood and breath in the establishment of laws and standards. But still some would not submit to their rule, and had to be exiled, driven away. . . . The world coveted knowledge, . . . there were axes and saws to shape things, ink and plumblines to trim them, mallets and gouges to poke holes in them, and the world, muddled and deranged, was in great confusion.[26]

That is Chuang Tzu, the first great Trickster of philosophy, sending a raspberry to the Yellow Emperor, the legendary model of rational control. Things were hot in Chuang Tzu's day, too, and he proposed a radical cooling-off. The best understanding, he said, "rests in what it cannot understand. If you do not understand this, then Heaven the Equalizer will destroy you."27*

Having copied out this sentence, I obeyed, letting my understanding rest in what it could not understand, and went to the *I Ching*. I asked that book please to describe a yin utopia for me. It replied with Hexagram 30, the doubled trigram Fire, with a single changing line in the first place taking me to Hexagram 56, the Wanderer. The writing of the rest of this paper and the revisions of it were considerably influenced by a continuing rumination of those texts.

If utopia is a place that does not exist, then surely (as Lao Tzu would say) the way to get there is by the way that is not a way. And in the same vein, the nature of the utopia I am trying to describe is such that if it is to come, it must exist already.

I believe that it does:† most clearly as an element in such deeply unsatisfactory utopian works as Hudson's *A Crystal World* or Aldous Huxley's *Island*. Indeed Bob Elliott ended his book on utopia with a discussion of *Island*. Huxley's "extraordinary achievement," he says, "is to have made the old utopian goal—the central human goal—thinkable once more."28 Those are the last words of the book. It is very like Bob that they should be not the closing but the opening of a door.

The major utopic element in my novel *The Dispossessed* is a variety of pacifist anarchism, which is about as yin as a political ideology can get. Anarchism rejects the identification of civilization with the state, and the identification of power with coercion; against the inherent violence of the "hot" society it asserts the value of such antisocial behavior as the general refusal of women to bear arms in war, and other coyote devices. In these areas anarchism and Taoism converge both in matter and manner, and so I came there to play my fictional games. The structure of the book may suggest the balance-in-motion and rhythmic recurrence of the Tai Chi, but its excess yang shows: though the utopia was (both in fact and in fiction) founded by a woman, the protagonist is a man; and he dominates it in, I must say, a very masculine fashion. Fond as I am of him, I'm not

---

* "Heaven the Equalizer" was translated by James Legge as "the Lathe of Heaven," a fine phrase, from which I have got considerable mileage; but Joseph Needham has gently pointed out to me that when Chuang Tzu was writing the Chinese had not yet invented the lathe. Fortunately we now have Burton Watson's wonderfully satisfying translation to turn to.

† In Nghsi-Altai—partly.

going to let him talk here. I want to hear a different voice. This is Lord Dorn, addressing the Council of his country, on June 16, 1906. He is talking not to, but about, us.

> With them the son and the father are of different civilizations and are strangers to each other. They move too fast to see more than the surface glitter of a life too swift to be real. They are assailed by too many new things ever to find the depths in the old before it has gone by. The rush of life past them they call progress, though it is too rapid for them to move with it. Man remains the same, baffled and astonished, with a heap of new things around him but gone before he knows them. Men may live many sorts of lives, and this they call "opportunity," and believe opportunity good without ever examining any one of those lives to know if it is good. We have fewer ways of life and most of us never know but one. It is a rich way, and its richness we have not yet exhausted. . . . They cannot be blamed for seeing nothing good in us that will be destroyed by them. The good we have they do not understand, or even see.[29]

Now, this speech might have been made in the council of any non-Western nation or people at the time of its encounter with Europeans in numbers. This could be a Kikuyu talking, or a Japanese—and certainly Japan's decision to Westernize was in the author's mind—and it is almost painfully close to the observations of Black Elk, Standing Bear, Plenty-Coups, and other native North American spokesmen.

Islandia is not a hot but a warm society: it has a definite though flexible class hierarchy, and has adopted some elements of industrial technology; it certainly has and is conscious of its history, though it has not yet entered into world history, mainly because, like California, it is geographically marginal and remote. In this central debate at the Council of Islandia, the hinge of the book's plot and structure, a deliberate choice is made to get no hotter: to reject the concept of progress as a wrong direction, and to accept persevering in one's existence as a completely worthy social goal.

In how many other utopias is this choice rationally propounded, argued, and made?

It is easy to dismiss Islandia as a mere fantasy of the Golden Age, naively escapist or regressive. I believe it is a mistake to do so, and that the options it offers are perhaps more realistic and more urgent than those of most utopias.

Here is M. Lévi-Strauss once more, this time on the subject of viruses:

> The reality of a virus is almost of an intellectual order. In effect, its organism is reduced practically to the genetic formula that it injects into simple or complex beings, thus forcing their cells to betray their characteristic formula in order to obey its own and to manufacture beings like itself.
>
> In order for our civilization to appear, the previous and simultaneous existence of other civilizations was necessary. And we know, since Descartes, that its originality consists essentially of a method which, because of its intellectual nature, is not suited to generating other civilizations of flesh and blood, but one which can impose its formula on them and force them to become like it. In comparison with these civilizations—whose living art expresses their corporeal quality because it relates to very intense beliefs and, in its conception as much as in its execution, to a certain state of equilibrium between man and nature—does our own civilization correspond to an animal or a viral type?[30]

This is the virus that Lord Dorn saw carried by the most innocent tourist from Europe or the United States: a plague against which his people had no immunity. Was he wrong?

Any small society that tried to make Lord Dorn's choice has, in fact, been forcibly infected; and the big, numerous civilizations—Japan, India, and now China—have either chosen to infect themselves with the viral fever or have failed to make any choice, all too often mixing the most exploitive features of the hot world with the most passive of the cold in a way that almost guarantees the impossibility of their persevering in their own existence or allowing local nature to continue in health. I wanted to speak of *Islandia* because I know no other utopian work that takes for its central intellectual concern this matter of "Westernization" or "progress," which is perhaps the central fact of our times. Of course the book provides no answer or solution; it simply indicates the way that cannot be gone. It is an enantiodroma, a *reculer pour mieux sauter*, a porcupine backing into a crevice. It goes sideways. That's very likely why it gets left out of the survey courses in Utopian Lit. But side trips and reversals are precisely what minds stuck in forward gear most need, and in its very quality of forswearing "futurity," of standing aside—and of having been left aside—*Islandia* is, I suggest, a valuable as well as an endearing book.

It is to some degree a Luddite book as well; and I am forced now to ask: Is it our high technology that gives our civilization its invasive, self-replicating, mechanical forward drive? In itself, any technology is "infectious" only as other useful or impressive elements of culture are; ideas, institutions, fashions too, may be self-replicating and irresistibly imitable. Obviously, technology is an essential element of all cultures and very often, in the form of potsherds or bits of styrofoam, all they leave behind in time. It is far too basic to all civilization to be characterized in itself as either yin or yang, I think. But at this point, here and now, the continuously progressing character of our technology, and the continuous change that depends upon it—"the manufacture of progress," as Lévi-Strauss called it— is the principal vehicle of the yang, or "hotness," of our society.

One need not smash one's typewriter and go bomb the laundromat, after all, because one has lost faith in the continuous advance of technology as the way towards utopia. Technology remains, in itself, an endless creative source. I only wish that I could follow Lévi-Strauss in seeing it as leading from the civilization that turns men into machines to "the civilization that will turn machines into men."[31] But I cannot. I do not see how even the almost ethereal technologies promised by electronics and information theory can offer more than the promise of the simplest tool: to make life materially easier, to enrich us. That is a great promise and gain! But if this enrichment of one type of civilization occurs only at the cost of the destruction of all other species and their inorganic matrix of earth, water, and air, and at increasingly urgent risk to the existence of all life on the planet, then it seems fairly clear to me that to count upon technological advance for *anything but* technological advance is a mistake. I have not been convincingly shown, and seem to be totally incapable of imagining for myself, how any further technological advance of any kind will bring us any closer to being a society predominantly concerned with preserving its existence; a society with a modest standard of living, conservative of natural resources, with a low constant fertility rate and a political life based upon consent; a society that has made a successful adaptation to its environment and has learned to live without destroying itself or the people next door. But that is the society I want to be able to imagine—I must be able to imagine, for one does not get on without hope.

What are we offered by way of hope? Models, plans, blueprints, wiring diagrams. Prospects of ever more inclusive communications systems linking virus to virus all over the globe—no secrets, as Kundera says. Little closed orbiting test-tubes full of viruses, put up by the L-5 Society, in perfect obedience to our compulsion to, as they say, "build the future"—to be Zeus, to have power over what happens, to control. Knowledge is power, and we want to know what comes next, we want it all mapped out.

Coyote country has not been mapped. The way that cannot be gone is not in the road atlas, or is every road in the atlas.

In the *Handbook of the Indians of California,* A. L. Kroeber wrote, "The California Indians . . . usually refuse pointblank to make even an attempt [to draw a map], alleging utter inability."[32]

The euclidean utopia is mapped; it is geometrically organized, with the parts labeled *a, a', b:* a diagram or model, which social engineers can follow and reproduce. Reproduction, the viral watchword.

In the *Handbook,* discussing the so-called Kuksu Cult or Kuksu Society—a clustering of rites and observances found among the Yuki, Pomo, Maidu, Wintu, Miwok, Costanoan, and Esselen peoples of Central California—Kroeber observed that our use of the terms "the cult" or "a society," our perception of a general or abstract entity, Kuksu, falsifies the native perception:

> The only societies were those of the town unit. They were not branches, because there was no parent stem. Our method, in any such situation, religious or otherwise, is to constitute a central and superior body. Since the day of the Roman empire and the Christian church, we hardly think of a social activity except as it is coherently organized into a definite unit definitely subdivided.
>
> But it must be recognized that such a tendency is not an inherent and inescapable one of all civilization. If we are able to think socially only in terms of an organized machine, the California native was just as unable to think in those terms.
>
> When we recall with how slender a machinery and how rudimentary an organization the whole business of Greek civilization was carried out, it becomes easily intelligible that the . . . Californian could dispense with almost all endeavors in this direction, which to us seem vital.[33]

Copernicus told us that the earth was not the center. Darwin told us that man is not the center. If we listened to the anthropologists we might hear them telling us, with appropriate indirectness, that the

White West is not the center. The center of the world is a bluff on the Klamath River, a rock in Mecca, a hole in the ground in Greece, nowhere, its circumference everywhere.

Perhaps the utopist should heed this unsettling news at last. Perhaps the utopist would do well to lose the plan, throw away the map, get off the motorcycle, put on a very strange-looking hat, bark sharply three times, and trot off looking thin, yellow, and dingy across the desert and up into the digger pines.

I don't think we're ever going to get to utopia again by going forward, but only roundabout or sideways; because we're in a rational dilemma, an either/or situation as perceived by the binary computer mentality, and neither the either nor the or is a place where people can live. Increasingly often in these increasingly hard times I am asked by people I respect and admire, "Are you going to write books about the terrible injustice and misery of our world, or are you going to write escapist and consolatory fantasies?" I am urged by some to do one—by some to do the other. I am offered the Grand Inquisitor's choice. Will you choose freedom without happiness, or happiness without freedom? The only answer one can make, I think, is: No.

Back round once more. *Usà puyew usu wapiw!*

> If the word [utopia] is to be redeemed, it will have to be by someone who has followed utopia into the abyss which yawns behind the Grand Inquisitor's vision, and who then has clambered out on the other side.[34]

Sounds like Coyote to me. Falls into things, traps, abysses, and then clambers out somehow, grinning stupidly. Is it possible that we are in fact no longer confronting the Grand Inquisitor? Could he be the Father Figure whom we have set up before us? Could it be that by turning around we can put him behind us, and leave him staring like Ozymandias King of Kings out across the death camps, the gulags, the Waste Land, the uninhabitable kingdom of Zeus, the binary-option, single-vision country where one must choose between happiness and freedom?

If so, then we are in the abyss behind him. Not out. A typical Coyote predicament. We have got ourselves into a really bad mess and have got to get out; and we have to be sure that it's the other side we get out to; and when we do get out, we shall be changed.

I have no idea who we will be or what it may be like on the other side, though I believe there are people there. They have always lived there. It's home. There are songs they sing there; one of the songs is called "Dancing at the edge of the world." If we, clambering up out of the abyss, ask questions of them, they won't draw maps, alleging utter inability; but they may point. One of them might point in the direction of Arlington, Texas. I live there, she says. See how beautiful it is!

This is the New World! we will cry, bewildered but delighted. We have discovered the New World!

Oh, no, Coyote will say. No, this is the old world. The one I made.

You made it for us! we will cry, amazed and grateful.

I wouldn't go so far as to say that, says Coyote.

Notes

1. Robert C. Elliott, *The Shape of Utopia* (Chicago: University of Chicago Press, 1970), p. 100.

2. Ibid., pp. 8, 9.

3. Milan Kundera, *The Book of Laughter and Forgetting*, trans. Michael Henry Heim (New York: Penguin Books, 1981), p. 22.

4. Ibid., pp. 234–35.

5. Walton Bean, *California: An Interpretive History* (New York: McGraw-Hill, 1968), p. 4.

6. Howard A. Norman, introduction to *The Wishing Bone Cycle* (New York: Stonehill Publishing Co., 1979).

7. Ibid.

8. Elliott, p. 107.

9. Bean, p. 4.

10. Victor W. Turner, *The Ritual Process: Structure and Anti-Structure* (Chicago: Aldine Publishing Co., 1969), p. 129.

11. Elliott, p. 100.

12. Ibid.

13. Quoted in Elliott, p. 94.

14. William Blake, *The Book of Urizen*, lines 52–55, 75–84.

15. Elliott, p. 87.

16. Lao Tzu, *Tao Teh Ching*, Book II, Chapter 38.

17. William Blake, *The Marriage of Heaven and Hell*, Book III, *Proverbs of Heaven and Hell*, line 21.

18. Kundera, p. 233.

19. William Blake, *Vala, or the Four Zoas*, Book IX, lines 162–167, 178–181, 186, 189–191.

20. Kenneth Roemer, "Using Utopia to Teach the Eighties," *World Future Society Bulletin* (July–August 1980).

21. Turner, p. 128.

22. Fritjof Capra, *The Turning Point* (New York: Simon & Schuster, 1982). Excerpted in *Science Digest* (April 1982), p. 30.

23. Paul Radin, *The Trickster* (New York: Philosophical Library, 1956), p. 168.

24. Lao Tzu, Book I, Chapter 16.

25. Claude Lévi-Strauss, *The Scope of Anthropology* (London: Jonathan Cape, 1968), pp. 46–47. Also included in *Structural Anthropology II* (New York: Basic Books, 1976), pp. 28–30. The version here is my own amalgam of the two translations.

26. *The Complete Works of Chuang Tzu,* trans. Burton Watson (New York: Columbia University Press, 1968), p. 116.

27. Ibid., p. 254.

28. Elliott, p. 153.

29. Austin Tappan Wright, *Islandia* (New York: Alfred A. Knopf, 1942), p. 490.

30. Lévi-Strauss, "Art in 1985," in *Structural Anthropology II*, p. 283.

31. Lévi-Strauss, *Scope of Anthropology*, p. 49.

32. Alfred L. Kroeber, *Handbook of the Indians of California*, Smithsonian Institution, Bureau of American Ethnology Bulletin no. 78 (Washington, D.C., 1925), p. 344.

33. Ibid., p. 374.

34. Elliott, p. 100.

FACING IT

(1982)

In December of 1982, the Portland Fellowship of Reconciliation held a symposium called Facing It. I was invited to join one of the panels and give a short talk about science fiction and how it faces the issue of nuclear war.

Modern science fiction begins with H. G. Wells, and as far as I know, it is also with Wells that the apocalypse, the end of the world, becomes a subject of fiction. The stories he called his "scientific romances" run the apocalyptic gamut, from a cometary Judgment Day followed by a very boring earthly paradise, to one of the most terribly beautiful nightmares of all fiction, the beach at the end of the world at the end of *The Time Machine*.

That great vision is the end as seen by science: entropy, the cold, dark chaos that is the target of Time's arrow. Usually, since Wells, the speculative storyteller has chosen a livelier finale. The sun goes nova, or aliens invade, or we perish from overpopulation or pollution or plague, or we mutate into higher forms, or whatever. Round about 1945 a specific kind of apocalypse, not surprisingly, became common in science fiction: the After-the-Bomb, or Post-Holocaust, story.

In the typical After-the-Bomb story, the characters are survivors of what is typically referred to as the Five-Minute War. Some of the options offered these survivors are:

1. Not to survive at all. The characters all kill each other off in the shelters and the ruins. Or, more tidily, as in *On the Beach,* they commit suicide.

2. To survive by killing and dominating other survivors who happen not to be Social Darwinists.

3. To survive by digging in and hanging on and battling mutant monsters with strange powers in the ruins of Chicago.

4. To survive by *being* mutants—often living a pleasant, rural life, far from the ruins of Chicago; kind of like Grandma Moses with telepathy.

5. To survive by leaving the Earth and getting away just in time in a space ship. These characters may sit by a canal on Mars and watch the rest of us go incandescent, or dwell for generations in their space ship, or colonize other planets; they certainly have the best options.

Many, many stories using these or similar scenarios were written and published between the late forties and the present. I wrote some myself, in the early sixties. Most of them were trivial, inadequate to their terrible subject. Some, like Walter Miller's *A Canticle for Leibowitz*, remain rich and durable works of imagination. The radioactive wasteland of glowing slagheaps populated by feral mutants is now a commonplace, perhaps a genuine archetype, available to beginners, hacks, film-makers, and the Collective Unconscious. Recently the Post-Holocaust story seems to be enjoying a revival, I should like to say thanks to President Reagan, but more honestly perhaps as a symptom of the world mood of which the Reagan presidency, and our presence here tonight, are also symptoms.

The Post-Holocaust story must be in part rehearsal, or acting out, variously motivated. One motivation is unmistakably desire. Rage, frustration, and infantile egoism play out the death wish: *Let's press that button and see what happens!* Another motivation is fear, the obsessive anxiety that keeps the mind upon the worst that could happen, dwelling on it, in the not entirely superstitious hope that *if I talk enough about it maybe it won't happen.* Rationally controlled, this fear motivates the cautionary tale: *Look what would happen if— ! so don't!* And the stories where people flee the Earth altogether would seem to be pure wish fulfillment, escapism.

Very few After-the-Bomb tales seem to have come out of South America, I wish I had time to speculate why; but a great many have come from America and England. (One might propose Samuel Beckett as the prophet of the post-apocalypse; his writings are drawn towards, yearn towards, the condition of utter silence.) European science-fiction writers have done their share, but across the Iron Curtain writers seem not to write about World War III. It may be the government demanding optimism, censoring speculation.

Or perhaps those Russian and Polish science-fiction writers who are
not timid yes-men, and often use use their art to say quite subversive
and unacceptable things, feel it ethically wrong to write about
nuclear holocaust, because by doing so they would trivialize and
familiarize the ultimate act of evil.

And this is a real issue, I think: the question of "the unspeakable."
If one believes that words are acts, as I do, then one must hold
writers responsible for what their words do.

The pornography of violence of course far exceeds, in volume
and general acceptance, sexual pornography, in this Puritan land of
ours. Exploiting the apocalypse, selling the holocaust, is a pornography; the power fantasies of the survivalists, which seem to origi-
nate in certain works of science fiction such as Robert Heinlein's
Farnham's Freehold, are pornographic. But for the ultimate selling
job on ultimate violence one must read those works of fiction issued
by our government as manuals of civil defense, in which, as a friend
of mine puts it, you learn that there's nothing to be afraid of if
you've stockpiled lots of dried fruit.

The question is that of false reassurance. Is the writer "facing it"
or, by pretending to face it, evading, lying? In many cases it's not
easy to decide. Those stories in which Life Goes On, even though
two-headed and glowing faintly in the dark, may be seen as
false reassurance or may find justification in the necessity of hope.
However ill-founded, however misguided, hope is the basic stratagem of mortality. We need it, and an art that fails to offer it
fails us.

Still, I see much current fantasy and science fiction in full retreat
from real human needs. Where a Tolkien prophetically faced the
central fact of our time, our capacity to destroy ourselves, the present spate of so-called heroic fantasy, in which Good defeats Evil by
killing it with a sword or staff or something phallic, seems to have
nothing in mind beyond instant gratification, the avoidance of discomfort, in a fake-medieval past where technology is replaced by
magic and wishful thinking works. But the science-fiction books
about endless wars in space, where technology *is* magic and the
killing proceeds without moral or psychological justification of any
kind, probably are written from the same unadmitted despair. The
future has become uninhabitable. Such hopelessness can arise, I
think, only from an inability to face the present, to live in the
present, to live as a responsible being among other beings in this
sacred world here and now, which is all we have, and all we need, to
found our hope upon.

RECIPROCITY OF
PROSE AND POETRY

(1983)

This talk was written for and given as part of the 1983 Poetry Series at the Folger Shakespeare Library. Jean Nordhaus, who was running the series, needed a title to put in her flyer long before the talk was written, so I said off the top of my head, "Oh, call it 'Reciprocity of Prose and Poetry,'" figuring that "reciprocity" was one of those Humpty Dumpty words that can mean anything you like while sounding deeply meaningful. Unfortunately it is not only a meaningful word but a strong-minded one, and every time I turned a corner in the writing of my talk, there was Reciprocity waiting for me with a stern expression, saying, "What, exactly, do you mean?"

People who read use the words "prose" and "poetry" with perfect confidence, and generally without trying to define them either in themselves or in contrast to each other. In this they are probably wise. The borderline between prose and poetry is one of those fog-shrouded literary minefields where the wary explorer gets blown to bits before ever seeing anything clearly. It is full of barbed wire and the stumps of dead opinions. It has been no-man's-land ever since the Bourgeois Gentleman blundered into it in Molière's play, three hundred years ago.

> M. JOURDAIN: I want you to help me write a little billydoo.
> THE PHILOSOPHY TEACHER: Certainly. Would you like it to be poetry?
> M. JOURDAIN: No. No poetry.

THE PHILOSOPHY TEACHER: Prose, then.

M. JOURDAIN: No. Not poetry, and not prose.

THE PHILOSOPHY TEACHER: It has to be one or the other.

M. JOURDAIN: Why?

THE PHILOSOPHY TEACHER: Well, sir, the only means of expression we possess are prose and poetry.

M. JOURDAIN: There isn't anything besides prose and poetry?

THE PHILOSOPHY TEACHER: Correct. Whatever is not prose is poetry; and whatever is not poetry is prose.

M. JOURDAIN: But, talking—what's talking?

THE PHILOSOPHY TEACHER: Prose.

M. JOURDAIN: What? You mean, when I say, "Hey, Nick, bring my slippers and get me a hot toddy"—that's prose?

THE PHILOSOPHY TEACHER: Yes, sir.

M. JOURDAIN: By God! I've been talking prose for forty years and never knew it![1]

Now, here is a remarkably similar conversation from the much admired *Random House Dictionary of the English Language* (1967):

POETRY: 1. The art of rhythmical composition, written or spoken, for exciting pleasure by beautiful, imaginative, or elevated thoughts.   2. Literary work in metrical form; verse.   3. Prose with poetic qualities. . . .

PROSE: 1. The ordinary form of written or spoken language, without metrical structure, as distinguished from poetry or verse.   2. Matter-of-fact, commonplace, dull expression. . . .

The vigorous ignorance of the Bourgeois Gentleman may be a better guide through the minefield than the certainties of the Philosophy Teacher and the dictionary. Indeed the dictionary seems to create its own fog. Definition 1 of poetry is rather fine, but is badly undercut by Definition 1 of prose, which limits rhythm to "metrical structure" and limits prose to being ordinary (although things get worse in Definition 2, which asserts it is dull). These definitions when applied to cases would unequivocally put *Jane Eyre* and *Our Mutual Friend* into the category of poetry, while excluding from it the *Cantos* and *The Waste Land*. Evidently we need some devices to probe for mines with, such as a clear and practicable conception of what rhythm in language is and where it coincides with metrics; after which we could begin to explore the vast area in which a rhythmic structure or pattern exists in language but does not coincide with metrics.

In 1917 William Patterson of Columbia University wrote a book called *The Rhythm of Prose,* an interesting attempt to use experiment to supplement opinion and authority, and an excellent summary of the theories and research on the subject in his day. It remains so far as I know the only book on the subject of prose rhythms. There is need for a book on the rhythms of literature or artfully used language—rhythms in the largest sense, as organizing or patterning principles—and their relation to the rhythms of ordinary speech, prose in the Bourgeois Gentleman's sense. Fascinating studies in this latter area exist, mostly in the specialized journals of linguistics. The research of such scholars as the Drs. Scollon in Alaska on spoken rhythms is related to the work done by such scholar-poets as Dell Hymes and Dennis Tedlock in bringing the oral literatures of other cultures into the English ken, and, in so doing, examining the whole nature of the artful use of language. If this work could be brought together into a "state of the art," as Patterson did sixty-five years ago, it would be a very exciting book.

Without it, all I can do is blunder on through the minefield. At once I step straight onto Gertrude Stein, and leap into the air.

> Poetry is I say essentially a vocabulary just as prose is essentially not.
>
> And what is the vocabulary of which poetry absolutely is. It is a vocabulary based on the noun as prose is essentially and determinately and vigorously not based on the noun.
>
> Poetry is concerned with using with abusing, with losing with wanting with denying with avoiding with adoring with replacing the noun. It is doing that always doing that, doing that and doing nothing but that. Poetry is doing nothing but using losing refusing and pleasing and betraying and caressing nouns. . . .
>
> So that is poetry really loving the name of anything and that is not prose.[2]

That is a charming hand grenade, but the pin's missing, I think. To define poetry as naming not telling—to exclude narrative—was useful fifty years ago, seventy years ago, when poetry was ridding itself of regular meter, rhyme, and a fixed poetic diction and matter. Poetry had to be redefined as independent of verse (an independence still ignored by Definition 2 of poetry and Definition 1 of prose in the *Random House Dictionary*). Like all revolutions, this one broke down barriers indiscriminately; like all revolutions, its acts of freedom tended to harden into dogmas. Poetry was defined not

only as independent of metrical verse but as exclusive of and superior to it—which is historically nonsense; poetry was further defined as exclusive of narration, exposition, discussion, and drama—
which is demented. The lava had hardened to basalt by the time I
came to Gertrude Stein's college; she was off in Paris happily digging holes in English prose, but in English-A we were solemnly
informed that "a poem must not mean, but be." Some of us wanted
to ask, Why? Why can't it do both, if it likes, or perhaps something
else entirely? But freshmen, especially freshwomen, did not ask
questions like that where the Lowells spoke only to the Cabots and
you know who the Cabots spoke to; so we swallowed the dogma in
class, and spat it out at the door. The children of the revolution are
always ungrateful, and the revolution must be grateful that it is so.

Pursuing the Snark of definition through the fog, one comes
upon a statement by Huntington Brown that is far more cautious,
specious, and dangerous than Gertrude Stein's.

> If it be asked wherein a poet's attitude toward his matter differs
> from that of a prose writer, my answer would be that in prose the
> characteristic assumption of both writer and reader is that the
> subject has an identity and an interest apart from the words,
> whereas in poetry it is assumed that word and idea are insepa-
> rable.[3]

This one ticks.

As a distinction of fantasy from realistic fiction, it would be of
considerable interest, but as a distinction of poetry from prose it is
very odd. I do not think Mr. Brown meant to imply that the subject
or matter of poetry is unidentifiable and of no inherent interest,
though he comes very near saying so; but there is in his definition an
implication that cannot be avoided and should be made clear: *It is
the language that counts in poetry and the ideas that count in prose.*
Corollary: Poetry is untouchable, but prose may be freely para-
phrased.

This is indeed a very common assumption, shared by readers and
writers alike: Mr. Brown is absolutely correct in that. But I question
the assumption, which he does not.

The integrity of a piece of language, poetry or prose, is a function of its quality; and an essential element of its quality is the
inseparability of idea and language. When a thing is said right it is
said right, whether in prose or poetry, formal discourse or cursing

the cat. If it is said wrong, if it lacks quality, if it is stupid poetry or careless prose, you may paraphrase it all you like; chances are you will improve it. But how are word and idea to be separated in this?

> "What child is it?" cried several ladies at once, and, among the rest, Nancy Lammeter, addressing Godfrey.
>
> "I don't know—some poor woman's who has been found in the snow, I believe," was the answer Godfrey wrung from himself with a terrible effort. ("After all, *am* I certain?" he hastened to add, silently, in anticipation of his own conscience.)
>
> "Why, you'd better leave the child here, then, Master Marner," said good-natured Mrs. Kimble, hesitating, however, to take those dingy clothes into contact with her own ornamented satin bodice. "I'll tell one o' the girls to fetch it."
>
> "No—no—I can't part with it, I can't let it go," said Silas, abruptly. "It's come to me—I've a right to keep it."
>
> The proposition to take the child from him had come to Silas quite unexpectedly, and his speech, uttered under a strong sudden impulse, was almost like a revelation to himself: a minute before, he had no distinct intention about the child.[4]

That the subject of that passage has an identity and interest apart from the words is true, but to what degree is it genuinely separable from them? If they are separable, it should be easy to make a satisfactory paraphrase of Godfrey's curious aside, which though set in parentheses and qualified as silent, is written as if spoken out loud, almost as if the others could hear him thinking, or as if he thought they could hear him thinking. . . . It should be easy to write another sentence characterizing the good-natured Mrs. Kimble who sees the clothes, not the child, touch her breast; and to rewrite Silas's speech, all broken monosyllables; and to find equally appropriate words in which to express the ideas of the final paragraph.

I do not believe that any of this is easy, or possible; in fact, I believe that any tampering with that passage would be as offensive as tampering with a bit of Shakespeare or Keats. And not only was the passage taken truly at random—the first novel my hand touched in the bookcase, opened to the page it chose to open at—but it is a fragment out of context from a large-scale work that gains its power and the real "identity and interest of its subject" less from the sense and sound of any sentence or paragraph than from the pacing and rhythm of paragraphs and chapters and the shape and pace of the actions described: large, slow movements, taking real

time to read, and occupying considerable psychological and intellectual space. Eliot was certainly not a great stylist, like Dickens, but
she wrote *prose:* and no paraphrase or rewrite or update or *Cliffs
Notes* can do anything to it but weaken and destroy it.

This "characteristic assumption" that poetry is the beautiful
dumb blonde, all words, and prose is the smart brunette with
glasses, all ideas, is certainly a common one; it lurks at the heart of
the poem that must not mean but be, as well as in the tiny mind of
the average best-seller writer. But here is somebody who I think
does not share it. This is Gary Snyder, being asked by an interviewer
what is the difference between his poetry and his prose.

> My own prose . . . does not have the musical phrase or the
> rhythm behind it. Nor does it have the constant density or the
> complexity [of my poetry]. . . . I don't really think of them as
> different so much—I adopt whatever structure seems to be
> necessary to the communication in mind. And I try to keep a
> clear line between, say . . . journal jottings and poems—and
> again, the real line is in the music and the density—although
> again, to be fair, not all my poems are that dense in terms of
> content analysis, but have maybe a musical density sometimes.[5]

The modesty and candor of that reply is an essential element of
its meaning, I think. Snyder brings out what he thinks character-
izes poetry—rhythm and density—so that one can make a kind
of definition from his statement: Poetry tends to be more rhythmic and denser in texture than prose. But clearly they aren't,
in his mind, "all that different"—the difference is of degree
not kind.

For that kind of easy, laid-back attitude, and for moving easily
between poetry and prose, Snyder gets put down. He lacks rigor. To
which I would reply, at least he isn't rigid. My concern here is
personal. I also write both prose and poetry and move freely
between them, and so am curious to know why and how I know that
I write both, and how I know that they are not the same thing. And I
am interested because, although I wrote and published poetry first,
my reputation was made as a prose writer, and I find my poetry
quite often dismissed on the sole ground that it was written by "a
novelist" and so cannot be taken seriously.

Are prose and poetry activities so far from being reciprocal that
they are incompatible, then? Poets have to defend poetry with fierce

intelligence against the dead weight and corruption of non-poetry
and anti-poetry, as Sidney and Shelley did, and renew that defense
in every generation. But poetry is not anti-prose; and intelligent
defense is not mere territorialism. Sometimes a Westerner like
myself even gets the impression that the territory of poetry lies east
of the Mississippi . . . but generally it seems more like a big fish tank,
and its inhabitants come rushing out of their nests of weed like
sticklebacks in mating season, shouting, Out! Out! Go write novels,
go tell stories, go write plays and libretti and screenplays and television scripts and radio dramas and descriptions of the universe and
histories and speculations on the nature of mankind and the cosmos
and all that prose, but keep out of our territory where nothing is
allowed to happen except poetry which is none of the above! In here
we are poets: and we write for one another.

Goethe wrote both prose and poetry, in large quantities and of
indisputable quality; and he said, "Occasional poetry is the highest
form." I am sure he didn't mean the kind of stuff that poet laureates
emit to please the ruling classes, but a poetry that escapes the
private, the confessional, and the merely esoteric, by observing—in
lament or celebration, in drama or description or narration or lyric,
in any mode or tone—a shared occasion. Such poetry may be
mysterious but is not idiosyncratic. Its movement is outward from
the individual center to the center of a larger whole, a community.
That movement is the energy of all theater, and of all oral literatures, performance of which, whether ritual or casual, is their own
occasion. It is surely the native movement or gesture of poetry.

Occasional poetry as the highest poetry is an idea worth keeping
in mind, though it is a daunting ideal in this time of supercom-
munication and superweapons, when, whether we like it or not, and
whether or not we like one another, all occasions include us all. At
any rate it is an idea that serves as an antidote to the defensive
definition of poetry as anti-prose—a hermetic art. I'd like to see
that definition neutralized, because when people take it seriously it
not only mandarinizes poetry but narrows and lowers the expectations and standards for the writing of novels, screenplays, descriptions of baseball games and remote galaxies, and so on, all of which
should surely be in free communication and having intercourse in
every sense of the word all the time with poetry.

All the same, all the same, there is a difference . . . isn't there? In
the work, not the worker, says Shelley. "The distinction between
poets and prose writers," he says in the *Defense of Poetry*, "is a vul-

gar error."[6] Now, there's a man who swatted Philosophy Teachers like flies.

The distinction Shelley makes is between

> measured and unmeasured language; for the popular division into prose and verse is inadmissible in accurate philosophy.
>
> Sounds as well as thoughts have relation both between each other and towards that which they represent, and a perception of the order of those relations has always been found connected with a perception of the order of the relations of thoughts. Hence the language of poets has ever affected a certain uniform and harmonious recurrence of sound, without which it were not poetry, and which is scarcely less indispensable to the communication of its influence, than the words themselves, without reference to that peculiar order.[7]

It is a difficult passage. I understand it to say that the measure—not the meter, which he specifically dismisses as accidental—the measure, what Gary Snyder calls rhythm, is the expression of the relations of sounds and of thoughts among themselves and to one another: the perception of a larger order in which sounds and ideas move together: word-music. This certainly does not (and he says that it does not) define poetry and prose as different things, for prose could have its own proper, looser rhythms and measures. But Shelley goes on to talk about translation:

> Hence the vanity of translation; it were as wise to cast a violet into a crucible that you might discover the formal principle of its colour and odour, as seek to transfuse from one language into another the creations of a poet. The plant must spring again from its seed, or it will bear no flower—and this is the burthen of the curse of Babel.[8]

Scientists do cast violets into crucibles and discover the principles of their color and odor. Shelley did not say it was impossible; he said it was unwise. We also translate poetry. And here, with the metaphor of translation, I think I can finally get at what has been worrying me all along.

A poem is its words. It may be recreated in a different language, but then it is a new poem, a new plant, as Shelley says, sprung from the idea-seed of the old one. You cannot change the words and still have the poem. This is inarguable. But it is also an inarguable fact that many poets delight in translating poetry and many readers delight in translations: I call John Keats to witness, Chapman's Homer in hand.

This is a bit of a paradox, but worse, it leads back to the blonde-brunette fallacy. Nobody even tries to argue that prose can't be translated. Everybody knows it can. Everybody who can read the original and compare the translation knows what gets lost in translation, and writhes and groans and shouts, How could the stupid ass miss *that*! . . . But still, most of us here read *War and Peace* in one of the variously inadequate and (we are told) inept translations, and we talk about it quite as if in fact we had read *War and Peace*, and I think we are right to do so. But is a novel not its words, then?

If not, what is it?

There is not, nor ever was, a Real Natasha; nor is the Napoleon of *War and Peace* the Real Napoleon; far from it. He is Tolstoy's invention, and a good thing too. But then, what is a novel, if not a web of words? Ideas? Is a novel all ideas? Far from it, and a good thing too. But let us call the emotions and perceptions and complex apprehensions aroused by a novel "ideas," since nobody seems to know what else to call them. Well, then, are words and ideas so easily separable in prose? Does an ineffable yet durable idea-ness exist, a Shelleyan idea-seed, a soul, immaterial yet capable of being *trans-lated*, of being *brought across* the gap between two languages/cultures/ages, and fitted into a new and totally different word-body, without itself undergoing any substantial change or loss? This is metempsychosis—reincarnation. I believe it because I see it happen, but I don't understand it, because I also believe that a novel, just as much as a poem, is its words.

Translation is entirely mysterious. Increasingly I have felt that the act of writing is itself translating, or more like translating than it is like anything else. What is the other text, the original? I have no answer. I suppose it is the source, the deep sea where ideas swim, and one catches them in nets of words and swings them shining into the boat . . . where in this metaphor they die and get canned and eaten in sandwiches. To bring something across, one needs a boat; or a bridge; what bridge? The metaphors all self-destruct. I am left with the stubborn feeling that composition, whether of poetry or prose, is not all that different from translation. In translating you have a text of words to work from; in composing or creating you don't; you have a text that is not words, and you find the words. That's a difference, of course, but the job, getting the right words in the right order, getting the measure right, is the same. Feels the same.

Perhaps this is why sometimes a lot of writers writing in different languages, in different countries, all seem to be going the same direction without communicating about it, like a flock of birds or fish, suddenly all doing the same new thing and understanding what the others are trying to do. They are all translating into their own idiom or idiolect from the same nonverbal text.

It is also because of this that I feel that the area where Hymes, Tedlock, and others[9] have been working—not abstract theories of translation but actual translations across the widest possible gaps, from an oral, performed text in the totally alien language of a radically different culture, into written English—that this is where something exciting is going on; this is one of the places where our literature is alive, unfixed, on the move, defying definition. What is this stuff? Is it spoken or written? Both. Is it narrative or ritual? Both. Is it poetry or prose? Both. That's the sort of stuff I want to be able to compose myself. I want to learn how to make translations from the languages nobody knows, nobody speaks. The translations will not be as good as the originals, but then, they never are.

Notes

1. Molière, *Le Bourgeois Gentilhomme*, Act II, Scene 4 (my translation).

2. Gertrude Stein, *Lectures in America* (New York: Random House, 1935), pp. 231–32.

3. Huntington Brown, *Prose Styles* (Minneapolis: University of Minnesota Press, 1966), p. 55.

4. George Eliot, *Silas Marner* (New York: Harcourt, Brace, and World, 1962), p. 140.

5. Gary Snyder, *The Real Work: Interviews and Talks, 1964–1979* (New York: New Directions, 1980), p. 36.

6. Percy Bysshe Shelley, *A Defense of Poetry;* Thomas Love Peacock, *The Four Ages of Poetry,* ed. John E. Jordan (Indianapolis and New York: Bobbs-Merrill Co., Library of Liberal Arts, 1965), p. 34.

7. Ibid., p. 33.

8. Ibid.

9. To anyone interested in pursuing this indication, I would recommend the following books and their rich bibliographies: Karl Kroeber, ed., *Traditional Literatures of the American Indian: Texts and Interpretations* (Lincoln: University of Nebraska Press, 1981); Dell Hymes, *"In Vain I Tried to Tell You": Essays in Native*

American Ethnopoetics (Philadelphia: University of Pennsylvania Press, 1981); Dennis Tedlock, *The Spoken Word and the Work of Interpretation* (Philadelphia: University of Pennsylvania Press, 1983); Jarold Ramsay, *Reading the Fire: Essays in Traditional Indian Literatures of the Far West* (Lincoln: University of Nebraska Press, 1983); and Brian Swann, ed., *Smoothing the Ground: Essays on Native American Oral Literature* (Berkeley: University of California Press, 1983). See also "Text, Silence, Performance," p. 182n, in this volume.

A LEFT-HANDED
COMMENCEMENT ADDRESS

(1983)

I want to thank the Mills College Class of '83 for offering me a rare chance: to speak aloud in public in the language of women.

I know there are men graduating, and I don't mean to exclude them, far from it. There is a Greek tragedy where the Greek says to the foreigner, "If you don't understand Greek, please signify by nodding." Anyhow, commencements are usually operated under the unspoken agreement that everybody graduating is either male or ought to be. That's why we are all wearing these twelfth-century dresses that look so great on men and make women look either like a mushroom or a pregnant stork. Intellectual tradition is male. Public speaking is done in the public tongue, the national or tribal language; and the language of our tribe is the men's language. Of course women learn it. We're not dumb. If you can tell Margaret Thatcher from Ronald Reagan, or Indira Gandhi from General Somoza, by anything they say, tell me how. This is a man's world, so it talks a man's language. The words are all words of power. You've come a long way, baby, but no way is long enough. You can't even get there by selling yourself out: because there is theirs, not yours.

Maybe we've had enough words of power and talk about the battle of life. Maybe we need some words of weakness. Instead of saying now that I hope you will all go forth from this ivory tower of college into the Real World and forge a triumphant career or at least help your husband to and keep our country strong and be a success in everything—instead of talking power, what if I talked like a woman right here in public? It won't sound right. It's going to sound terrible. What if I said what I hope for you is first, if—only if—you want kids, I hope you have them. Not hordes of them. A couple, enough. I hope they're beautiful. I hope you and they have enough to eat, and a place to be warm and clean in, and friends, and work you like doing. Well, is that what you went to college for? Is that all? What about success?

Success is somebody else's failure. Success is the American Dream we can keep dreaming because most people in most places, including thirty million of ourselves, live wide awake in the terrible reality of poverty. No, I do not wish you success. I don't even want to talk about it. I want to talk about failure.

Because you are human beings, you are going to meet failure. You are going to meet disappointment, injustice, betrayal, and irreparable loss. You will find you're weak where you thought yourself strong. You'll work for possessions and then find they possess you. You will find yourself—as I know you already have—in dark places, alone, and afraid.

What I hope for you, for all my sisters and daughters, brothers and sons, is that you will be able to live there, in the dark place. To live in the place that our rationalizing culture of success denies, calling it a place of exile, uninhabitable, foreign.

Well, we're already foreigners. Women as women are largely excluded from, alien to, the self-declared male norms of this society, where human beings are called Man, the only respectable god is male, and the only direction is up. So, that's their country; let's explore our own. I'm not talking about sex; that's a whole other universe, where every man and woman is on their own. I'm talking about society, the so-called man's world of institutionalized competition, aggression, violence, authority, and power. If we want to live as women, some separatism is forced upon us: Mills College is a wise embodiment of that separatism. The war-games world wasn't made by us or for us; we can't even breathe the air there without masks. And if you put the mask on you'll have a hard time getting it off. So how about going on doing things our own way, as to some extent you did here at Mills? Not *for* men and the male power hierarchy—that's their game. Not *against* men, either—that's still playing by their rules. But *with* any men who are with us: that's our game. Why should a free woman with a college education either fight Machoman or serve him? Why should she live her life on his terms?

Machoman is afraid of our terms, which are not all rational, positive, competitive, etc. And so he has taught us to despise and deny them. In our society, women have lived, and have been despised for living, the whole side of life that includes and takes responsibility for helplessness, weakness, and illness, for the irrational and the irreparable, for all that is obscure, passive, uncontrolled, animal, unclean—the valley of the shadow, the deep, the depths of life. All that the Warrior denies and refuses is left to us and the men who share it with us and therefore, like us, can't play doctor, only nurse, can't be warriors, only civilians, can't be chiefs, only indians. Well, so that is our country. The night side of our country. If there is a day side to it, high sierras, prairies of bright grass, we only know pioneers' tales about it, we haven't got there yet. We're never going to get there by imitating Machoman. We are only going to get there by going our own way, by living there, by living through the night in our own country.

So what I hope for you is that you live there not as prisoners, ashamed of being women, consenting captives of a psychopathic social system, but as natives. That you will be at home there, keep house there, be your own mistress, with a room of your own. That you will do your work there, whatever you're good at, art or science or tech or running a company or sweeping under the beds, and when they tell you that it's second-class work because a woman is doing it, I hope you tell them to go to hell and while they're going to give you equal pay for equal time. I hope you live without the need to dominate, and without the need to be dominated. I hope you are never victims, but I hope you have no power over other people. And when you fail, and are defeated, and in pain, and in the dark, then I hope you will remember that darkness is your country, where you live, where no wars are fought and no wars are won, but where the future is. Our roots are in the dark; the earth is our country. Why did we look up for blessing—instead of around, and down? What hope we have lies there. Not in the sky full of orbiting spy-eyes and weaponry, but in the earth we have looked down upon. Not from above, but from below. Not in the light that blinds, but in the dark that nourishes, where human beings grow human souls.

ALONG THE PLATTE

(1983)

Some people fly to Tierra del Fuego and Katmandu; some people drive across Nebraska in a VW bus.

Living in Oregon, with family in Georgia, we drive the United States corner to corner every now and then. It takes a while. On the fifth day out of Macon, just crossing the Missouri, we look up to see a jet trail in the big sky. That plane going west will do two thousand miles while we do two hundred. A strange thought. But the strangeness works both ways. We'll drive about four hundred miles today. On foot with an ox-drawn wagon, that distance would take up to a month.

These are some notes from a day and a half on the Oregon Trail.

About ten in the morning we cross the wide Missouri into the West. Nebraska City looks comfortable and self-reliant, with its railyards and grain elevators over the big brown river. From it we drive out into rolling, spacious farmlands, dark green corn, pale yellow hay stubble, darkening gold wheat. The farmhouses, with big barns and a lot of outbuildings, come pretty close together: prosperous land. The signs say: Polled Shorthorns . . . Hampshire Swine . . . Charolais . . . Yorkshire and Spotted Swine.

We cross the North Fork of the Little Nemaha. The rivers of America have beautiful names. What was the language this river was named in? Nemaha—Omaha—Nebraska . . . Eastern Siouan, I guess. But it's a guess. We don't speak the language of this country.

Down in the deep shade of trees in high thick grass stand three horses, heads together, tails swishing, two black and one white with black tail and mane. Summertime . . .

Around eleven we're freewaying through Lincoln, a handsome city, the gold dome on its skyscraper capitol shining way up in the pale blue sky, and on our left the biggest grain elevator I ever saw, blocks long, a cathedral of high and mighty cylinders of white. On KECK, Shelley and Dave are singing, "Santa Monica freeway, sometimes makes a country girl blue . . ." After a while the DJ does the announcements. There will be a State Guernsey Picnic on Saturday, if I heard right.

Now we're humming along beside the Platte—there's a language I know. Platte means Flat. It's pretty flat along the Platte, all right, but there are long swells in this prairie, like on the quietest sea, and the horizon isn't forever: it's a blue line of trees way off there, under the farthest line of puffball fair-weather clouds.

We cross some channels of the braided Platte at Grand Island and stop for lunch at a State Wayside Park called Mormon Island, where it costs two bucks to eat your picnic. A bit steep. But it's a pretty place, sloughs or channels of the river on all sides, and huge black dragonflies with silver wingtips darting over the shallows, and blue darning-needles in the grass. The biggest mosquito I ever saw came to eat my husband's shoulder. I got it with my bare hand, but a wrecking ball would have been more appropriate. There used to be buffalo here. They were replaced by the mosquitoes.

On along the Platte, which we're going to cross and recross eleven times in Nebraska and one last time in Wyoming. The river is in flood, running hard between its grey willows and green willows, aspens and big cottonwoods. Some places the trees are up to their necks in water, and west of Cozad the hayfields are flooded, hayrolls rotting in the water, grey-white water pouring through fields where it doesn't belong.

The cattle are in pure herds of Black Angus, Aberdeen, Santa Gertrudis, and some beautiful mixed herds, all shades of cream, dun, brown, roan. There's a Hereford bull in with his harem and descendants, big, frowning, curly-headed, like an angry Irishman.

In 1976 Nebraska commissioned ten sculptures for the roadside rest areas along Interstate 80, and going west you see five of them; we stop at each one to see and photograph it, as does the grey-haired man with two daughters who pose with the sculpture for his photograph. The pieces are all big, imaginative, bold. The one we like best resides in a pond a couple miles west of Kearny. It's aluminum in planes and curves and discs; parts of it are balanced to move softly, without sound; all of it floats on the flickering, reflecting water. It's called *The Nebraska Wind Sculpture*. "What is it?" says a grinning man. I say, "Well, the AAA tourbook says it looks like H. G. Wells's Time Machine." He says, "O.K., but what *is* it?"—and I realize he thinks it may be "something," not "just" a work of art; and so he's looking at it and grinning, enjoying the damfool thing. If he knew it was Art, especially Modern Art, would he be afraid of it and refuse to see it at all? A fearless little boy, meanwhile, haunts the pool and shouts, "Look! A lobster!" pointing at a crayfish, and nearly falls into the scummy shallows reflecting the silver Nebraska Wind.

Down the road a town called Lexington advertises itself:

ALL-AMERICAN CITY
ALL-NEBRASKA COMMUNITY

Those are some kind of national and state awards for something, I suppose, but how disagreeable, how unfriendly and exclusive they sound. But then, what other state of the union thought of celebrating the Bicentennial with big crazy sculptures right out for every stranger driving I-80 to see? Right on, Nebraska!

We pull in for the night at a motel in North Platte, a town that has a rodeo every night of every summer every year, and we sure aren't going to miss that. After dinner we drive out Rodeo Road to Buffalo Bill Avenue to the Cody Arena (by now we have the idea that that old fraud came from around here), and the nice cowgirl selling tickets says, trying to give us a senior citizen savings, "Would you be over sixty at all?" No, we can't manage that yet, so she gives us full-price tickets and a beautiful smile. All the seats are good. It's a warm dry prairie evening, the light getting dusty and long. Young riders on young horses mill around the arena enjoying the attention till the announcer starts the show the way all rodeos start, asking us to salute "the most beautiful flag in the world," a pleasure, while the horses fidget and the flag bearer sits stern, but the announcer goes on about how this flag has been "spat and trampled and mocked and burned on campuses," boy, does he have it in for campuses, what decade is he living in? The poison in his voice is pure Agent Orange. More of this "patriotism" that really means hating somebody. Shut up, please, and let's get on with what all us Americans are here to see—and here to do, for ten bucks prize money.

The first cowboy out of the chute, bareback bronc-riding, gets thrown against the fence, and another gets his leg broken right under the stands. Rodeos are hard on horses, hard on cattle, hard on men. A lousy way to earn ten bucks. Ladies, don't let your sons grow up to be cowboys, as the song says. But the calf-roping is done for the joy of skill, of teamwork, horse and man, and the barrel-

riding girls are terrific, whipping around those barrels like the
spinning cars on a fairground octopus, and then the quirt flicks and
the snorting pony lays out blurry-legged and belly to the ground on
the home stretch with the audience yipping and yahooing all the
way. By now the lady from Longview, Washington, with the six-pack
on the next bench is feeling no pain. A bull is trying to destroy the
chutes before the rider even gets onto him. The rodeo is one of the
few places where people and animals still fully interact. How vain
and gallant horses are, not intelligent, but in their own way wise;
how fine the scared, wily vigor of the calves and the power of the big
Brahma bulls—the terrific vitality of cattle, which we raise to kill.
People who want matadors mincing around can have them, there's
enough moments of truth for me in a two-bit rodeo.

Driving back after the show over the viaduct across Bayley Yard, a
huge Union Pacific switching center, we see high floodlights far
down the line make gold rivers of a hundred intertwining tracks
curving off into the glare and dazzling dark. Trains are one of the
really good things the Industrial Revolution did—totally practical
and totally romantic. But on all those tracks, one train.

Next morning we stop at Ogallala for breakfast at the Pioneer
Trails Mall. I like that name. Two eggs up, hashbrowns, and biscuits.
The restaurant radio loudspeaker plays full blast over the South
Platte River roaring past full of logs and junk and way over the
speed limit for rivers.

We leave that river at last near where the Denver road splits off,
and come into the low, bare hills across it. As the water dries out of
the ground and air, going west, the blur of humidity is gone; colors
become clear and pale, distance vivid. Long, light-gold curves of
wheat and brown plowed land stripe the hills. At a field's edge the
stiff wheat sticks up like a horse's mane cropped short. The wind
blows in the tall yellow clover on the roadsides. Sweet air, bright
wind. Radio Ogallala says that now is the time to be concerned about
the European corn borer.

Between the wheat and corn fields scarped table-lands begin to
rise, and dry washes score the pastures. The bones of the land show
through, yellowish-white rocks. There's a big stockyard away off the
road, the cattle, dark red-brown, crowded together, looking like
stacked wood in a lumberyard. Yucca grows wild on the hills here;
this is range land. Horses roam and graze far off in the soft-colored
distances. We're coming to the Wyoming border, leaving this big,
long, wide, bright Nebraska; a day and a half, or forty minutes, or a

month in the crossing. From a plane I would remember nothing of Nebraska. From driving I will remember the willows by the river, the sweet wind. Maybe that's what they remembered when they came across afoot and horseback, and camped each night a few miles farther west, by the willows and the cottonwoods down by the Platte.

WHOSE LATHE?

(1984)

This piece was written for the "Forum" section of my regional major newspaper, The Oregonian, *in May of 1984. The arguments made are local and specific; the problem addressed is national and general. Any author who boasts about freedom of the press in the United States should, perhaps, make certain that none of his or her books has been banned, dropped from a reading list as immoral or anti-religious or "secular humanist" (that bogey includes almost all science fiction), or weeded out or locked away by a public librarian or school librarian under pressure. The trouble is, it's not a matter the author is likely to hear about. I would not have known that one of my books was to have a censorship hearing in Washougal, Washington, a town twenty minutes' drive from my city, if a librarian in that school district had not alerted me the night before the hearing. Little as I wish to, I have to assume that censorship has been and is being imposed on my books, and on all literature, in school districts, schools, and libraries all over the country, and that there is nothing I can do about it except protest against it whenever and wherever I can; a protest I know other writers, and readers, will share.*

In a small town near Portland late this spring, a novel, *The Lathe of Heaven,* was the subject of a hearing concerning its suitability for use in a senior-high-school literature class. I took a lively interest in the outcome, because I wrote the novel.

The case against the book was presented first. The man who was asking that it be withdrawn stated his objections to the following elements in the book: fuzzy thinking and poor sentence structure; a mention of homosexuality; a character who keeps a flask of brandy in her purse, and who remarks that her mother did not love her. (It seemed curious to me that he did not mention the fact that this same character is a Black woman whose lover/husband is a White man. I had the feeling that this was really what he hated in the book, and that he was afraid to say so; but that was only my feeling.)

He also took exception to what he described as the author's advocacy of non-Christian religions and/or of non-separation of Church and State (his arguments on this point, or these points, were not clear to me).

Finally, during discussion, he compared the book to junk food, apparently because it was science fiction.

The English Department of the school then presented a carefully prepared, spirited defense of the book, including statements by students who had read it. Some liked it, some didn't like it, most objected to having it, or any other book, banned.

In discussion, teachers pointed out that since it is the policy of the Washougal School District to assign an alternative book to any student who objects on any grounds to reading an assigned one, the attempt to prevent a whole class from reading a book was an attempt to change policy, replacing free choice by censorship.

When the Instructional Materials Committee of the district voted on the motion to ban the book, the motion was defeated twenty votes to five. The hearing was public and was conducted in the most open and democratic fashion. I did not speak, as I felt the teachers and students had spoken eloquently for me.

Crankish attacks on the freedom to read are common at present. When backed and coordinated by organized groups, they become sinister. In this case, I saw something going on that worried me a good deal because it did not seem to be coming from an outside pressure group, but from elements of the educational establishment itself: this was the movement to change policy radically by instituting, or "clarifying," guidelines or criteria for the selection/elimination of books used in the schools. The motion on which this committee of the school district voted was actually that the book be withdrawn *"while guidelines and policies for the district are worked out."* Those guidelines and policies were the real goal, I think, of the motion.

Guidelines? That sounds dull. Innocent. Useful. Of course we have to be sure about the kinds of books we want our kids to read in school. Don't we?

Well, do we? The dangerous vagueness of the term "guidelines and policies for the district" slides right past such questions as: Who are "we"? Who decides what the children read? Does "we" include you? Me? Teachers? Librarians? Students? Are fifteen-to-eighteen-year-olds ever "we," or are they always "they"?

And what are the guidelines to be? On what criteria or doctrines are they to be based?

The people concerned with schools in Oregon try, with ever decreasing budgets, to provide good, sound food in the school cafeterias, knowing that for some students that's the only real meal they get. They try, with ever decreasing budgets, to provide beautiful, intelligent books in classes and school libraries, knowing that for many students those are the only books they read. To provide the best: everyone agrees on that (even the people who vote against school levies). But we don't and we can't agree on what books are the best. And therefore what is vital is that we provide variety, abundance, plenty—not books that reflect one body of opinion or doctrine, not books that one group or sect thinks good, but the broadest, richest range of intellectual and artistic material possible.

Nobody is forced to read any of it. There is that very important right to refuse and choose an alternative.

When a bad apple turns up, it can be taken out of the barrel on a case-by-case, book-by-book basis—investigated, defended, prosecuted, and judged, as in the hearing on my *Lathe of Heaven*.* But this can't be done wholesale by using "guidelines," instructions for censorship. There is no such thing as a moral filter that lets good books through and keeps bad books out. Such criteria of "goodness" and "badness" are a moralist's dream but a democrat's nightmare.

Censorship, here or in Russia or wherever, is absolutely antidemocratic and elitist. The censor says: You don't know enough to choose, but we do, so you will read what we choose for you and nothing else. The democrat says: The process of learning is that of learning how to choose. Freedom isn't given, it's earned. Read, learn, and earn it.

I fear censorship in this Uriah Heepish guise of "protecting our

---

* Currently (1987) a textbook written for Oregon schools called *Let's Oregonize* is going through this process on the state level. The arguments against it were brought by environmentalists and others who found it tendentious and biased towards certain industries and interests. From my point of view it certainly sounds like a rather bad apple. But it is getting a scrupulously fair hearing.

children," "stricter criteria," "moral guidance," "a more definite policy," and so on. I hope administrators, teachers, librarians, parents, and students will resist it. Its advocates are people willing to treat others not only as if they were not free but were not even worthy of freedom.

THE WOMAN
WITHOUT ANSWERS

(1984)

Invited to come to the Cooper Union for a New School conference, The Presence of Myth in Contemporary Life, I asked if instead of preparing a paper I could participate on a panel as a respondent. As the date of the conference (in October of 1984) drew near, impressive lists of speakers were issued; but I had received only one of the several papers to which I was supposed to respond, and that one was a short story, a kind of statement not ordinarily considered to need a response. I began to panic, and did what I generally do in a panic: I tried to make my situation make sense, to make it into a story—in the circumstances, inevitably, a myth. Among all the various presentations given during the three days of the conference, it is distinguished by being the only one not meant to be taken seriously. Nor will it be found in the handsome volume of the proceedings of the conference issued the following year, in which the subject of myth is approached from practically every direction except, perhaps, the direction Coyote comes from.

There was a woman from the town upriver from where the Willamette comes into the Columbia. She wasn't so young any more, and she said to her husband, "I'd like to go east a while and see our son who's staying there." So she started out and went east for a long way but a short time, till she got to that island where her son was. He was doing fine there. After she saw him she saw a big, old, strange house there among all the other houses, and she said, "I've heard of this place." So she went in and found a lot of people there having a meeting, talking together. Some of them knew her and said, "Come on in, Little Bear Woman! We're playing a game here. We tell stories and then you have to answer what we said." She said, "All right." She was afraid of them; it was their territory, and some of them were really big people. So she said, "All right, I'll try." Then they began talking again, telling stories and telling stories about the stories, and Little Bear Woman got to feeling smaller and smaller. The ones that talked were almost all men, and they mostly talked about men, so that she wondered if there was a shortage of women in the eastern part of the country; but then she saw lots of women listening to the men talking. By then she was feeling a good deal like running away back west, but she was too old to run well, so she stayed. And besides, these people weren't malevolent, they were generous people. So she sent her mind in the six directions and back to the center and invoked her Ancestors, especially those of the Boas Totem: "Please help me, Ancestors! I am a respondent and I don't know what to respond."

Over there in Illo Tempore her Ancestors said, "Listen, that one's in trouble again," and they decided to send some people across to help her.

The first one came—it was Claude Lévi-Strauss riding on a jaguar. And Claude Lévi-Strauss said, "Myths get thought, myth thinks itself, in humankind, unbeknownst to humankind. . . . And my own work gets thought in me, it thinks itself in me, without my knowing." The woman agreed with that. Then the Ancestors sent Mircea Eliade riding on the east wind, and he said, "In myth the Cosmos is articulate: the world reveals itself as language." She agreed with that, too. Then Lao Tzu came by riding on a dragon and laughed and said nothing at all, and the woman agreed with that, too. Then finally Coyote came along, Coyote who made everything, even if maybe she didn't make it quite the way she meant to or the way we'd like it, and she said, "What's wrong?"

Little Bear Woman said, "I said I'd respond, and I have no responses."

"So, what else is new?" says Coyote.

Little Bear Woman thought, "She's right. It happens all the time. The dream where I stand up to play the viola concerto, only as I stand up it occurs to me that I have never learned to play the viola. The voice in the silence of three in the morning that says inside my head, *Why* did you say *that* to the dean's wife at dinner? The supermarket checkout where you open your bag to pay and your wallet isn't in it. The child that asks you, But do the soldiers want to kill *me*? The jailed poet in a foreign country whose silence asks you continually, How long will you, who are able to speak, be silent? The Sphinx that asks you what goes on four and two and three legs in Greek and you don't speak Greek so the Sphinx eats you. The labyrinth you can't get out of because you aren't the one with the sword and the thread, you aren't the hero but only the monster, the animalhead, the dumb one who doesn't have the answers."

"Happens all the time," says Coyote. "That's what myths do. They happen all the time. Presence of myth in contemporary life, and vice versa. You are a Myth who married a History, and you both have to make the best of it. Think yourself: articulate: be still. Each at the appropriate time and in the appropriate place. Have you seen any mice around this house?"

"No," the woman said, "I haven't seen any mice."

So Coyote went on along, and the Woman Without Answers and the others went on playing the game according to Coyote's rules, by which you always get yourself into trouble.

THE SECOND REPORT OF THE SHIPWRECKED FOREIGNER TO THE KADANH OF DERB

(1984)

In November of 1984, the Seattle branch of Antioch University invited Vonda N. McIntyre and myself to chair a daylong conference on Women, Power, and Leadership. Expecting fifteen or twenty participants, and faced with ninety-five women and three men, Vonda and I were pretty well floored. We floundered about all morning trying to pull the thing together: object lessons in the inexperience of Women given the Power of Leadership, certainly. We asked the group for help, and a quiet woman at the back proposed a format that satisfied both those who wanted to hear us speak as "successful" women and writers, and those who, like Vonda and me, preferred a general discussion in which as many voices as possible might be heard. The lot-drawn panel format she suggested worked splendidly, and people talked that afternoon about living and working in a society that conceives of power and leadership almost totally in male terms—talked with a cogency and often a poignancy that have stayed with me and enriched my understanding ever since.

I read this piece as my opening statement. At the time I was thinking about a series of these "Reports" (the "First Report" was published in Antaeus *and then in my story collection* The Compass Rose), *but so far there are only two. Communications from Derb seem to have been interrupted.*

Your Highness:

I have been trying to figure out how to tell you a story about a Representative Person of Earth, so that you might be amused by the tale while learning from it, or from the spaces between the words, something about my world, or yours. The trouble is, I have not been able to think of a Representative Person.

I met a member of the House of Representatives once. He was an odd person, not representative at all. He entered the room when the party had been going on for an hour or so, and from the way the host and hostess and others went to him like bits of iron to a magnet, and from the way he spoke in rich tones, it was evident that he was important. Unfortunately I lived in the wrong district and had never heard his name, and so when we were introduced I was puzzled by the curiously professional way he shook my hand, as if handshaking were a profession, and by the way he used his eyes. He used them as a means of looking straight into my eyes with an expression of intense sincerity. I had the impression that he did not see me. I don't know who, or what, he did see. He talked well and loudly, told two fairly dirty jokes at dinner, and laughed. He impinged upon all of us, while none of us seemed to affect him in any way. He exuded himself, while absorbing nothing. From what inexhaustible source, since he never replenished it by drawing upon the rest of the universe, did he draw so much self to exude? When I found out (on the way home) that he was a Representative, I thought that that explained it: his inexhaustible source was power—power itself. He was, as it were, plugged into the main. But this disqualified him as a Representative *Person*. Most people have to generate their own power.

Once upon a time a baby was born and named Soru. When she was little her mother carried her into the fields and laid her in the shade at the field's edge while the work went on. When Soru got bigger she ran about in the village with the other little children, and played down by the stream. The children made toy boats out of big leaves; Soru liked to make little mud figures of people and set them in the boats. The boats always sank, and the mud figures dissolved quickly in the muddy water, becoming swirls of tiny particles drifting downstream. Soru learned how to prepare food with her mother and aunt and elder sister. With other girls she learned other necessary skills such as sewing, mat-making, roof repair, dancing, fire-tending, milking, storytelling, genealogy, and all the labors of the fields. She was healthy, merry, and industrious, and not long after she attained puberty Anfe's family came to ask about her dowry; presently she became Anfe's wife and went to live in that household. There she worked very hard, but Anfe's three younger sisters were jolly and affectionate, and the four of them were always laughing and playing and joking. Soru's first baby was born on the day it rained after the long drought; the rain beat like great drums, and the child was a beautiful and healthy girl. The next year she had a boy, and the year after that a girl. Anfe's father died then, and the man from Monoy came and insisted that the debt be paid. The family could not pay it all, and he would not accept part payment, so they lost the land. Soru and Anfe and the three babies and Anfe's youngest sister had to move in with Anfe's mother's sister, who was a mean, lazy old woman. That house was so dirty it could not be cleaned, and far too small for them all, but Soru managed. She worked for Tima in the fields. When the chance for a good marriage for Anfe's youngest sister came up, Soru saw to it that a dowry was provided, though she missed her sister-in-law's company, and now while she was in the fields she had to leave the children in the care of the old woman. Anfe was a good-natured man and a hard worker, but he hated being tied down to one job for long; he quit work so often that he couldn't always find it, and went without work some-times for weeks and months. At such times he would hang around with other men and drink, and come home drunk and treacherous and full of rage; then he and the old woman would quarrel, and the children would hide from them until Soru came home from the fields. One day in the long rains Anfe and the old woman began quarreling again. He began swearing and hitting her. The eldest girl knew that after her father left, the old woman would beat the children, so she took the two little ones and ran to hide down by the river where they often played. The river was swollen with rain and the banks were caving in. The bank fell away under the eldest girl's feet and she was swept away by the river. The little ones came crying to the house. When people came to the field where Soru was work-ing and told her, she sat down on the wet ground and rocked her body, crying out, "Oh, oh, my child of the rain, my child of the rain!" She was five months pregnant then. After that happened, Anfe drove the old woman out of her own house, and she went to live with her granddaughter in Monoy. Anfe got a job he liked, working on the dam they were building upriver; he could only come home twice a month, but he got very good pay. Soru was not well and had to stop working in the fields. She got the house as clean as it could be got, and was content looking after the two children, but she still did not feel well. More than a month before her time she began to bleed, and they could not stop the bleeding; and so she died, and the baby was stillborn. Anfe's elder sister took the two children. Soru lived twenty years, eight months, and four days.

What I don't know how to do, you see, is put Soru and the member of the House of Representatives together so that they make any sense. Soru seems to say, "Work, laugh, grieve, die," and the Representative says, "I, I, I, I," and neither can hear the other. If you put the two together, it does make sentences: I work, I laugh, I grieve, I die. But these sentences mean such different things to Soru and to the Representative! He might even deny that the last two sentences—I grieve, I die—were true. Soru would deny none of them, but she probably would have seen little sense in talking about such things; she went ahead and did them. And maybe sang about them. The Representative also indubitably has worked and laughed and will die, but he does not want these matters mentioned, preferring such terms as "profit incentive," "recreation," "life expectancy." I can't think how he would refer to grief at all—perhaps as "mental health problems." But since Soru simply did not exist, was a total blank, in respect to profit incentive, recreation, life expectancy, and mental health problems, the Representative would be unable to comprehend the fact that she existed, or indeed that anyone else exists; so we are back to his "I, I, I, I." And to the subject of power.

Power is said to be the most important thing on earth. It is said that if Soru had had power—various sorts of power, but all deriving from the sort of power the Representative has—if Soru had been plugged into the main, her life would have been three or four times longer and happier.

The life expectancy of the Representative is certainly more than three times longer than Soru's life and ten times longer than Soru's eldest daughter's life. Is a life expectancy, however, a life? At eleven years old, Soru was a very good dancer. Can people who are plugged into the main dance? Or can they only twitch as the electricity courses through their veins? They say the victims of electrocution and the subjects of electroshock therapy, when the power is switched on, do a sort of dance.

I have a notion that the word "power" has become a form empty of content, which has meaning only as the individual fills it, pours the molten bronze of a life and self into that empty mold. Other such words are "God," "Country," "justice," "rights." They are words frequently used by the Representative. But has he ever filled them with anything? Is "I, I, I, I" what should fill those great empty forms?

The architect gives me the blueprint. "There," he says, "there's your house!"

"Very nice! When will you start work on it?"

"Start work? I'm an architect, not a carpenter. It's finished—I've done my work! Why don't you move in?"

So I move into the blueprint. I become very clever at cooking nutritious paper stew, which my family eats all grouped cheerily together in the Dining Area of the blueprint. We furnish the living room with cutouts from an advertisement for a Colonial American Living Room Suite in the daily paper. We find a color TV in the Sunday supplement. Sometimes the Representative appears on our TV, in one dimension, since it is only a two-dimensional set; and he talks about power. Other men appear, talking about Power to the People, the Power Struggle in South Erewhon, the Orderly Transfer of Power, the Power Shortage, and so on. It was a tricky job cutting out the little tiny paper cord and plug for the TV set, but it works fine.

Your Highness:

I am still looking for a Representative Person of Earth, but there seems to have been a power failure somewhere. Please give me some time.

ROOM 9, CAR 1430

(1985)

The view, where I sit writing this, is of frozen Klamath Lake, a sweep of bluish white, and the dawn-bright mountains above it—a picture postcard of Oregon winter. Ten minutes from now my view will be of fences zigzagging past farms among the snowy hills, a whole new postcard. And soon after that it will be great, solemn, snow-hung firs and the peaks and chasms of the Cascades. Because I'm sitting in Room 9, Car 1430, of the Coast Starlight, coming north to Portland. And the whole trip is beautiful.

President Reagan has decided he can do without Amtrak and has left it out of his budget. I suppose the last time Mr. Reagan rode a train was before I was born, and by now he probably doesn't know anybody who ever travels by train. He only knows Important People, people whose time is money. Only unimportant people take trains. People to whom time isn't money, but life, their life lived and to be lived.

Quite a few young families are on this train. The kids patter up and down the aisles and corridors, merry; it's all a thrill to them. Quite a few elderly women and men are traveling together or alone, maybe grandparents like me coming back from a visit to the daughter's new daughter. There are some single men—businessmen? Are there still businessmen who take the train for a break? They sit there (like me) with their briefcases, reading and writing, looking out the window to follow an idea or see a snowy mountain swinging by. There are quite a few people on this train, and not many empty seats or compartments. Nearly twenty million people rode the trains of America last year. Unimportant people.

The administration's dislike of Amtrak may be rooted in a perception of the system as vaguely socialistic. It is supported by the government, to be sure. So are the auto and plane industries, of course, but they can't be called public transportation, and therefore they escape suspicion.

The usual justification, however, for killing the passenger trains is that train travel is "outmoded." The private car for short trips, the airplane for long trips—that's Progress, the Future.

(Hold on for just a moment, please, while I watch the big engine up there kicking out a spray of shining snow like a skier on a graceful turn . . .)

It can be seen just the other way round. Commuting by car is increasingly difficult; in the big Eastern cities it is simply impossible—a thing of the past. As for the airplane, it's beautiful, useful, and wasteful. It has one and only one advantage as a passenger carrier: speed. If speed really matters, if you have to be at a funeral in Kansas tomorrow or if you only get two weeks off a year and want to spend them in Hawaii or Mexico, then it is good to be able to fly there. If speed is not essential, then it is good to have the option of *not* flying. Why should we be forced to undergo the incredible and increasing discomfort, danger, and indignity that the airlines inflict on their passengers?

Trains are not deliberately overbooked.

Train stations are downtown—not in some dreary boondock twenty-five dollars away from where you want to be.

Train seats in coaches are deep, wide, and comfortable.

Train rooms in the sleepers are genuinely luxurious.

Train food isn't much good any more, since Amtrak's budget has been cut and cut and cut, but at least you can eat when and how you choose. Instead of being strapped into a seat with a plastic platter of stuff slapped down in front of you, like a kid in a highchair, you can get up and walk to the diner (they still use linen tablecloths) or the snack bar or the lounge, and eat and drink like a grownup. Or you can bring a sack and have a moveable feast. A croissant and a tangerine just out of Klamath Falls (the car porter brought me coffee), a cheese-and-tomato sandwich as we cross the Cascades . . .

The airplane does not represent the future of passenger transportation. This country's days of blind wastefulness are past and gone; any attempt to continue them is not progressive but deeply reactionary. The plane, with its tremendous inefficiency as a passenger vehicle, is the anachronism. It is out of date. An administration seeking a sound economy would (like Japan and most European countries) be refunding its passenger train system, enlarging and improving it. Not wrecking it through underfunding and then, like a spoiled kid with a toy he doesn't understand, trashing it.

Let's save our trains for human beings, unimportant as they may be—people who know that how you go matters just as much as where you get. Roll on, Coast Starlight! Take us to those far places your lonesome whistle tells about, and bring us on back home!

THEODORA

(1985)

Written as the introduction to the Yolla Bolly Press edition of The Inland Whale, *Theodora Kroeber's retellings of Native American stories.*

Some people lead several lives all at once; my mother lived several lives one at a time. Her names reflect this serial complexity: Theodora Covel Kracaw Brown Kroeber Quinn. The last four are the names of men: Kracaw her father's name (and the source of her lifelong nickname Krakie), Brown, Kroeber, and Quinn her three husbands. Covel is a family name on her mother's side, used as a girl's middle name for several generations. Her first name came from a novel her mother liked, *Theodora Goes Wild*. She was Theo to some, Dora to none.

The (auto)biographical note about the author on the jacket of the first edition of *The Inland Whale* reads in part:

> Theodora Kroeber was born in Denver and spent her early years in the mining camp of Telluride, Colorado. She earned a B.A. in psychology and economics and an M.A. in clinical (then called "abnormal") psychology at the University of California. Offered a position in a boys' reformatory, she got married instead and had three sons and a daughter. When the children were grown and raising their own families, she began to write. Part of the background for her writing comes from Indians, rivers, and deserts encountered while accompanying her husband, A. L. Kroeber, the noted anthropologist, on professional journeys and field trips.

The bit about the boys' reformatory is a characteristically graceful piece of legerdemain: Theodora took her master's degree in 1920 and married Clifton Brown that same year; three years later, with two baby sons, she was widowed; in 1925 she met Alfred Kroeber; they married, and in 1926 and 1929 her other two children were born. Where the boys' reformatory comes in this crowded decade I can't quite figure out. Although she wrote two biographies notable for their exhaustive research and scrupulous selection of fact, Theodora's native gift was for the brilliant shortcut that reveals an emotional or dramatic truth, the event turned legend—not raw fact, but cooked fact, fact made savory and digestible. She was a great cook both of foods and of words.

The Inland Whale was written in the late 1950s, when, as she says, her children were off having children, and she and Alfred were enjoying the freedom of his long emeritus career, during which he taught at Harvard and Columbia and was a resident of various think tanks—well-traveled, unhurried, productive years. Work, writing, was pretty much like breathing to Alfred Kroeber; he just quietly did it all the time. With time and energy now to spare, Theodora soon found her own breath. First she wrote a couple of essays with Alfred (interesting pre-computer attempts at counting word frequency in poetry), then some children's stories (often a woman's way into literature—threatening to no one, including herself). Then a first novel. And then this book.

I don't know the genesis of the book, but would guess that separate stories, which she had tried retelling for their own sake and the work's sake, began to make a whole, a shape in her mind. Perhaps she set out to write a book of stories about women, but I think it more likely that the pattern became apparent and the connections imperative as she worked and reworked and re-reworked the material—for she was a hard writer, a merciless reviser. The coherence of the book and the clarity of her prose are the result of the kind of distillation that makes fine liquors, the kind of pressure that makes diamonds. She strove for a vivid simplicity, but she was never artless.

People ask if she told stories like these to her children. She read to us, but it is her aunt Betsy and my father whose storytelling I remember. Only a few times do I recall her making the "breakthrough into performance," as Dell Hymes calls it. Once when she was eighty or so, six or eight kids and grandkids at table, John Quinn presiding, one of us asked her about her experiences as a child of nine on a visit to San Francisco when the great earthquake of 1906 struck. All the storytelling power of her books got unleashed, and none of us will forget that hour. But usually it was conversational give-and-take that she wanted and created among family and friends. And one sees her valuation of written narrative as "higher" or more "finished" than oral—the conventional and almost universal judgment of her time both in literature and anthropology—in her notes to *The Inland Whale*.

Still, it is very like her to have chosen from all the stories of the peoples of California nine stories about women, at a time when even in anthropology the acts of women were easy to dismiss as secondary, women being subsumed (oddly enough) in Man. From her mother Phebe and other strong women of her late-frontier Western childhood, Theodora had a firm heritage of female independence and self-respect. Her sense of female solidarity was delicate and strong. She made her daughter feel a lifelong welcome, giving me the conviction that I had done the right thing in being born a woman—a gift many woman-children are denied. But also she would say that she "liked men better than women"; her temperament inclined her to the conventional supporting roles of wife and mother; and she detested the direct opposition of a woman's will to a man's. She must have thought her loving empire was endangered by feminism, for her intolerance of what she called "women's lib" went beyond her general distrust of ideologies. But all the same, in her life as a writer, I think she was a true feminist.

Look for Native American women in White literature before 1960: if you find any at all, you generally find something called a "squaw." There are no squaws in *The Inland Whale*—only human beings. This is not freedom from racist stereotyping only, but also freedom from masculinist prejudice, and a deliberate search for the feminine. Theodora kept telling me to write about women, not men, years before I (the "women's libber") was able to do so. She did so herself from the start, not only because the feminists of her mother's generation had freed us both, but also because she was true to her being, her perceptions, her female humanity. In all her different lives she was entirely woman.

The book was written and published, and *Ishi* was begun, while Alfred was alive. After his death came her life as widow, soon famous in her own right for her great book *Ishi;* and then a new life, and new directions in writing, as Mrs. John Quinn. She never wrote till she was over fifty and she never stopped writing till she died at eighty-three. I wish she had started earlier: we might have had more books from her; her novels might have found a publisher; and she wouldn't have had to wait for validation and self-confidence till a time in life when most artists are at ease with their craft and are getting the recognition they deserve. I know she regretted having started writing so late. But not bitterly. She wasn't a regretter, or a blamer. She kept going on, out of an old life, into a new one. So I imagine she goes now.

SCIENCE FICTION AND
THE FUTURE

(1985)

In February of 1985 the Oregon Museum of Science and Industry
invited me to participate on a panel, Science Fiction and the Future, and
the following was my prepared statement for that discussion.

We know where the future is. It's in front of us. Right? It lies before
us—a great future lies before us—we stride forward confidently
into it, every commencement, every election year. And we know
where the past is. Behind us, right? So that we have to turn around
to see it, and that interrupts our progress ever forward into the
future, so we don't really much like to do it.

It seems that the Quechua-speaking peoples of the Andes see all
this rather differently. They figure that because the past is what you
know, you can see it—it's in front of you, under your nose. This is a
mode of perception rather than action, of awareness rather than
progress. Since they're quite as logical as we are, they say that the
future lies behind—behind your back, over your shoulder. The
future is what you *can't* see, unless you turn around and kind of
snatch a glimpse. And then sometimes you wish you hadn't, because
you've glimpsed what's sneaking up on you from behind. . . . So, as
we drag the Andean peoples into our world of progress, pollution,
soap operas, and satellites, they are coming backwards—looking
over their shoulders to find out where they're going.

I find this an intelligent and appropriate attitude. At least it
reminds us that our talk about "going forward into the future" is a

142

metaphor, a piece of mythic thinking taken literally, perhaps even a bluff, based on our macho fear of ever being inactive, receptive, open, quiet, still. Our unquiet clocks make us think that we make time, that we control it. We plug in the timer and make time happen. But in fact the future comes, or is there, whether we rush forward to meet it in supersonic jets with nuclear warheads, or sit on a peak and watch the llamas graze. Morning comes whether you set the alarm or not.

The future is not mere space. This is where I part company with a whole variety of science fiction, the imperialistic kind, as seen in all the Space Wars and Star Wars novels and films and the whole branch of sf that reduces technology to hi-tech. In such fictions, space and the future are synonymous: they are a place we are going to get to, invade, colonize, exploit, and suburbanize.

If we do "get to" space, it's not unlikely that that's how we'll behave there. It is possible that we will "conquer" space. But it is not possible that we will "conquer" the future, because there is no way we can get there. The future is the part of the spacetime continuum from which—in the body and in ordinary states of consciousness—we are excluded. We can't even see it. Except for little glimpses over the shoulder.

When we look at what we can't see, what we do see is the stuff inside our heads. Our thoughts and our dreams, the good ones and the bad ones. And it seems to me that when science fiction is really doing its job that's exactly what it's dealing with. Not "the future." It's when we confuse our dreams and ideas with the non-dream world that we're in trouble, when we think the future is a place we own. Then we succumb to wishful thinking and escapism, and our science fiction gets megalomania and thinks that instead of being fiction it's prediction, and the Pentagon and the White House begin to *believe* it, and we get True Believers conquering the future by means of SDI.

As a science-fiction writer I personally prefer to stand still for long periods, like the Quechua, and look at what is, in fact, in front of me: the earth; my fellow beings on it; and the stars.

THE ONLY GOOD AUTHOR?

(1985)

When writing about the work of a living author, some critics send their article, chapter, or book to that author, either in draft, for comment, or when printed, as a courtesy. Other critics do not. It is my impression that the ones who do not are getting more numerous. Trying to imagine their reason for ignoring the existence of the person probably most interested in their work, I have come up with several possible lines of argument.

1. *Live authors have an unfair advantage over dead authors, which can be removed by treating live authors as if they were dead.*

This is a nice idea, but I don't think it motivates a great many critics.

2. *Critics know better than most authors what the work means to the reader, as a thing in itself, as a part of literature, as an event in the history of literature or ideas.*

This is, or ought to be, true. The author's responses, however, might still be of interest; and if critics know better than the author, then they will know when to discount the author's responses as arising from wishful thinking, defensiveness, or ignorance.

3. *Critics are objective about the work; the author cannot be.*

This I suspect to be the usual rationale. I want to question it radically, as follows:

Is it true? In all cases? In which cases?

What is meant by "objectivity" in literary criticism? If it means something other than the vigilant effort to think clearly and eschew fad, partiality, bigotry, and judgmentalism, what does it mean?

If by "objectivity" is meant an imitation or application of the scientific method, is this method clearly understood by the critic? Does the critic firmly believe it to be appropriate to the study of literature, and, if appropriate, adequate?

144

4. *If the critic were in correspondence with the author or intended from the start to ask the author for a response, the critic's thinking and writing might be affected, influenced, changed.*

This I believe to be true, even though most critics are pretty sure of their ideas and not easily shaken by a mere author. It is also true that such a correspondence, an undertaking of mutual *responsibility,* can be hard going, hard work for both parties, often unsettling or distressing, and sometimes unrewarding. Yet I do think it humanly and intellectually altogether preferable to the lack of communication, the stupid, embarrassed, perhaps resentful silence that seems to be increasingly taken for granted. Critics whose principal goal or interest is power will of course not share this preference; I am talking only to those whose principal interest as critics is their work.

My judgment in the matter is based mostly on "anecdotal" or "soft" data, to use the currently fashionable unexamined pejoratives; that is to say, on my own experience, which has ranged from the satisfaction of giving useful answers to intelligent questions concerning both fact and theory or intention, to the frustration of reading errors of fact, date, order, and sense, and erroneous assertions of influence or intention, all of which could have been set straight very easily, and then reading the same errors repeated by other critics who choose to get their data anywhere but from the horse's mouth; sometimes indeed it would seem from the other end. Even a direct quote from the author can mislead when taken from something written a decade or two ago and used without historical context, as if the author's mind were incapable of change.

But perhaps some critics are simply reluctant to pester; their rationale would be:

5. *Critics should allow authors to get on with new work.*

I wish grade-school teachers would ponder this one instead of giving out the pestering of authors as an assignment (the result being such letters as one I got recently: "We all have to write some author, I have not read your book actually but the cover is very interesting . . ."). Some authors welcome spontaneous letters, from kids or from critics. Others don't; they refuse to be bothered, and let the questioner know it either by not responding or by a few rude words. We must all expect a few rude words from time to time; if we are either authors or critics, more than a few.

But even when both critic and author desire cooperation, intellectual or temperamental disagreement may be so strong, or the theoretical approach so different, that useful interchange is impossible.

In this case the author can really do nothing but sulk and fume while the critic gallops on. It is worth remembering that the critic is always in control in this situation—choosing what to show the author, when to show it, and whether to give the author's responses any weight at all. There is absolutely no risk unless the critic chooses to take it.

What there might be to gain, that risk taken, is well expressed in the paragraph that enabled me to write this statement, and to whose author I am very grateful. Explaining that she sent a draft of the relevant section of her critical work *For the Record* (Women's Press, 1984) to each of the feminist theorists whose ideas she discussed, Dale Spender writes:

> Initially, it was a theoretical consideration which led me to adopt this method and, in practice, I have learnt that it makes an enormous difference to what one writes. It has astonished me just how much more care I have taken to be accurate, how much more thoughtfully I have perused the texts (and how often I have completely revised my opinion and evaluation) simply because my portrayal of a particular woman's ideas was going to her for comment. I have learnt a great deal from the exercise. . . . We need to devise more means of dialogue and validation in a society where these are not readily sought.

BRYN MAWR
COMMENCEMENT ADDRESS

(1986)

Thinking about what I should say to you made me think about what
we learn in college; and what we unlearn in college; and then how
we learn to unlearn what we learned in college and relearn what we
unlearned in college, and so on. And I thought how I have learned,
more or less well, three languages, all of them English; and how one
of these languages is the one I went to college to learn. I thought I
was going to study French and Italian, and I did, but what I learned
was the language of power—of social power; I shall call it the father
tongue.

This is the public discourse, and one dialect of it is speech-
making—by politicians, commencement speakers, or the old man
who used to get up early in a village in Central California a couple of
hundred years ago and say things very loudly on the order of
"People need to be getting up now, there are things we might be
doing, the repairs on the sweathouse aren't finished and the tarweed is in seed over on Bald Hill; this is a good time of day for doing
things, and there'll be plenty of time for lying around when it gets
hot this afternoon." So everybody would get up grumbling slightly,
and some of them would go pick tarweed—probably the women.
This is the effect, ideally, of the public discourse. It makes something happen, makes somebody—usually somebody else—do
something, or at least it gratifies the ego of the speaker. The difference between our politics and that of a native Californian people is
clear in the style of the public discourse. The difference wasn't clear
to the White invaders, who insisted on calling any Indian who made
a speech a "chief," because they couldn't comprehend, they

wouldn't admit, an authority without supremacy—a non-dominating authority. But it is such an authority that I possess for the brief—we all hope it is decently brief—time I speak to you. I have no right to speak to you. What I have is the responsibility you have given me to speak to you.

The political tongue speaks aloud—and look how radio and television have brought the language of politics right back where it belongs—but the dialect of the father tongue that you and I learned best in college is a written one. It doesn't speak itself. It only lectures. It began to develop when printing made written language common rather than rare, five hundred years ago or so, and with electronic processing and copying it continues to develop and proliferate so powerfully, so dominatingly, that many believe this dialect—the expository and particularly the scientific discourse—is the *highest* form of language, the true language, of which all other uses of words are primitive vestiges.

And it is indeed an excellent dialect. Newton's *Principia* was written in it in Latin, and Descartes wrote Latin and French in it, establishing some of its basic vocabulary, and Kant wrote German in it, and Marx, Darwin, Freud, Boas, Foucault—all the great scientists and social thinkers wrote it. It is the language of thought that seeks objectivity.

I do not say it is the language of rational thought. Reason is a faculty far larger than mere objective thought. When either the political or the scientific discourse announces itself as the voice of reason, it is playing God, and should be spanked and stood in the corner. The essential gesture of the father tongue is not reasoning but distancing—making a gap, a space, between the subject or self and the object or other. Enormous energy is generated by that rending, that forcing of a gap between Man and World. So the continuous growth of technology and science fuels itself; the Industrial Revolution began with splitting the world-atom, and still by breaking the continuum into unequal parts we keep the imbalance from which our society draws the power that enables it to dominate every other culture, so that everywhere now everybody speaks the same language in laboratories and government buildings and headquarters and offices of business, and those who don't know it or won't speak it are silent, or silenced, or unheard.

You came here to college to learn the language of power—to be empowered. If you want to succeed in business, government, law, engineering, science, education, the media, if you want to succeed, you have to be fluent in the language in which "success" is a meaningful word.

White man speak with forked tongue; White man speak dichotomy. His language expresses the values of the split world, valuing the positive and devaluing the negative in each redivision: subject/object, self/other, mind/body, dominant/submissive, active/passive, Man/Nature, man/woman, and so on. The father tongue is spoken from above. It goes one way. No answer is expected, or heard.

In our Constitution and the works of law, philosophy, social thought, and science, in its everyday uses in the service of justice and clarity, what I call the father tongue is immensely noble and indispensably useful. When it claims a privileged relationship to reality, it becomes dangerous and potentially destructive. It describes with exquisite accuracy the continuing destruction of the planet's ecosystem by its speakers. This word from its vocabulary, "ecosystem," is a word unnecessary except in a discourse that excludes its speakers from the ecosystem in a subject/object dichotomy of terminal irresponsibility.

The language of the fathers, of Man Ascending, Man the Conqueror, Civilized Man, is not your native tongue. It isn't anybody's native tongue. You didn't even hear the father tongue your first few years, except on the radio or TV, and then you didn't listen, and neither did your little brother, because it was some old politician with hairs in his nose yammering. And you and your brother had better things to do. You had another kind of power to learn. You were learning your mother tongue.

Using the father tongue, I can speak of the mother tongue only, inevitably, to distance it—to exclude it. It is the other, inferior. It is primitive: inaccurate, unclear, coarse, limited, trivial, banal. It's repetitive, the same over and over, like the work called women's work; earthbound, housebound. It's vulgar, the vulgar tongue, common, common speech, colloquial, low, ordinary, plebeian, like the work ordinary people do, the lives common people live. The mother tongue, spoken or written, expects an answer. It is conversation, a word the root of which means "turning together." The mother tongue is language not as mere communication but as relation, relationship. It connects. It goes two ways, many ways, an exchange, a network. Its power is not in dividing but in binding, not in distancing but in uniting. It is written, but not by scribes and secretaries for posterity; it flies from the mouth on the breath that is our life and is gone, like the outbreath, utterly gone and yet returning, repeated,

the breath the same again always, everywhere, and we all know it by
heart. John have you got your umbrella I think it's going to rain.
Can you come play with me? If I told you once I told you a hundred
times. Things here just aren't the same without Mother, I will now
sign your affectionate brother James. Oh what am I going to do? So
I said to her I said if he thinks she's going to stand for that but then
there's his arthritis poor thing and no work. I love you. I hate you. I
hate liver. Joan dear did you feed the sheep, don't just stand around
mooning. Tell me what they said, tell me what you did. Oh how my
feet do hurt. My heart is breaking. Touch me here, touch me again.
Once bit twice shy. You look like what the cat dragged in. What a
beautiful night. Good morning, hello, goodbye, have a nice day,
thanks. God damn you to hell you lying cheat. Pass the soy sauce
please. Oh shit. Is it grandma's own sweet pretty dear? What am I
going to tell her? There there don't cry. Go to sleep now, go to
sleep. . . . Don't go to sleep!

It is a language always on the verge of silence and often on the
verge of song. It is the language stories are told in. It is the language
spoken by all children and most women, and so I call it the mother
tongue, for we learn it from our mothers and speak it to our kids. I'm
trying to use it here in public where it isn't appropriate, not suited to
the occasion, but I want to speak it to you because we are women and
I can't say what I want to say about women in the language of capital
M Man. If I try to be objective I will say, "This is higher and that is
lower," I'll make a commencement speech about being successful in
the battle of life, I'll lie to you; and I don't want to.

Early this spring I met a musician, the composer Pauline
Oliveros, a beautiful woman like a grey rock in a streambed; and to
a group of us, women, who were beginning to quarrel over theories
in abstract, objective language—and I with my splendid Eastern-
women's-college training in the father tongue was in the thick of the
fight and going for the kill—to us, Pauline, who is sparing with
words, said after clearing her throat, "Offer your experience as your
truth." There was a short silence. When we started talking again, we
didn't talk objectively, and we didn't fight. We went back to feeling
our way into ideas, using the whole intellect not half of it, talking
with one another, which involves listening. We tried to offer our
experience to one another. Not claiming something: offering something.

How, after all, can one experience deny, negate, disprove, another
experience? Even if I've had a lot more of it, *your* experience is your
truth. How can one being prove another being wrong? Even if

you're a lot younger and smarter than me, *my* being is my truth. I can offer it; you don't have to take it. People can't contradict each other, only words can: words separated from experience for use as weapons, words that make the wound, the split between subject and object, exposing and exploiting the object but disguising and defending the subject.

People crave objectivity because to be subjective is to be embodied, to be a body, vulnerable, violable. Men especially aren't used to that; they're trained not to offer but to attack. It's often easier for women to trust one another, to try to speak our experience in our own language, the language we talk to each other in, the mother tongue; so we empower one another.

But you and I have learned to use the mother tongue only at home or safe among friends, and many men learn not to speak it at all. They're taught that there's no safe place for them. From adolescence on, they talk a kind of degraded version of the father tongue with each other—sports scores, job technicalities, sex technicalities, and TV politics. At home, to women and children talking mother tongue, they respond with a grunt and turn on the ball game. They have let themselves be silenced, and dimly they know it, and so resent speakers of the mother tongue; women babble, gabble all the time. . . . Can't listen to that stuff.

Our schools and colleges, institutions of the patriarchy, generally teach us to listen to people in power, men or women speaking the father tongue; and so they teach us not to listen to the mother tongue, to what the powerless say, poor men, women, children: not to hear that as valid discourse.

I am trying to unlearn these lessons, along with other lessons I was taught by my society, particularly lessons concerning the minds, work, works, and being of women. I am a slow unlearner. But I love my unteachers—the feminist thinkers and writers and talkers and poets and artists and singers and critics and friends, from Wollstonecraft and Woolf through the furies and glories of the seventies and eighties—I celebrate here and now the women who for two centuries have worked for our freedom, the unteachers, the unmasters, the unconquerors, the unwarriors, women who have at risk and at high cost offered their experience as truth. "Let us NOT praise famous women!" Virginia Woolf scribbled in a margin when she was writing *Three Guineas,* and she's right, but still I have to praise these women and thank them for setting me free in my old age to learn my own language.

The third language, my native tongue, which I will never know though I've spent my life learning it: I'll say some words now in this language. First a name, just a person's name, you've heard it before. Sojourner Truth. That name is a language in itself. But Sojourner Truth spoke the unlearned language; about a hundred years ago, talking it in a public place, she said, "I have been forty years a slave and forty years free and would be here forty years more to have equal rights for all." Along at the end of her talk she said, "I wanted to tell you a mite about Woman's Rights, and so I came out and said so. I am sittin' among you to watch; and every once and awhile I will come out and tell you what time of night it is." She said, "Now I will do a little singing. I have not heard any singing since I came here."[1]

Singing is one of the names of the language we never learn, and here for Sojourner Truth is a little singing. It was written by Joy Harjo of the Creek people and is called "The Blanket Around Her."[2]

> maybe it is her birth
> which she holds close to herself
> or her death
> which is just as inseparable
> and the white wind
> that encircles her is a part
> just as
> 　　　　the blue sky
> hanging in turquoise from her neck
>
> oh woman
> remember who you are
> woman
> it is the whole earth

So what am I talking about with this "unlearned language"— poetry, literature? Yes, but it can be speeches and science, any use of language when it is spoken, written, read, heard as art, the way dancing is the body moving as art. In Sojourner Truth's words you hear the coming together, the marriage of the public discourse and the private experience, making a power, a beautiful thing, the true discourse of reason. This is a wedding and welding back together of the alienated consciousness that I've been calling the father tongue and the undifferentiated engagement that I've been calling the mother tongue. This is their baby, this baby talk, the language you can spend your life trying to learn.

We learn this tongue first, like the mother tongue, just by hearing it or reading it; and even in our overcrowded, underfunded public high schools they still teach *A Tale of Two Cities* and *Uncle Tom's Cabin;* and in college you can take four solid years of literature, and even creative writing courses. But. It is all taught as if it were a dialect of the father tongue.

Literature takes shape and life in the body, in the womb of the mother tongue: always: and the Fathers of Culture get anxious about paternity. They start talking about legitimacy. They steal the baby. They ensure by every means that the artist, the writer, is male. This involves intellectual abortion by centuries of women artists, infanticide of works by women writers, and a whole medical corps of sterilizing critics working to purify the Canon, to reduce the subject matter and style of literature to something Ernest Hemingway could have understood.

But this is our native tongue, this is our language they're stealing: we can read it and we can write it, and what we bring to it is what it needs, the woman's tongue, that earth and savor, that relatedness, which speaks dark in the mother tongue but clear as sunlight in women's poetry, and in our novels and stories, our letters, our journals, our speeches. If Sojourner Truth, forty years a slave, knew she had the right to speak that speech, how about you? Will you let yourself be silenced? Will you listen to what men tell you, or will you listen to what women are saying? I say the Canon has been spiked, and while the Eliots speak only to the Lowells and the Lowells speak only to God, Denise Levertov comes stepping westward quietly, speaking to us.[3]

> There is no savor
> more sweet, more salt
>
> than to be glad to be
> what, woman,
>
> and who, myself,
> I am, a shadow
>
> that grows longer as the sun
> moves, drawn out
>
> on a thread of wonder.
> If I bear burdens
>
> they begin to be remembered
> as gifts, goods, a basket

of bread that hurts
my shoulders but closes me

in fragrance. I can
eat as I go.

As I've been using the word "truth" in the sense of "trying hard
not to lie," so I use the words "literature," "art," in the sense of
"living well, living with skill, grace, energy"—like carrying a basket
of bread and smelling it and eating as you go. I don't mean only
certain special products made by specially gifted people living in
specially privileged garrets, studios, and ivory towers—"High" Art;
I mean also all the low arts, the ones men don't want. For instance,
the art of making order where people live. In our culture this
activity is not considered an art, it is not even considered work. "Do
you work?"—and she, having stopped mopping the kitchen and
picked up the baby to come answer the door, says, "No, I don't
work." People who make order where people live are by doing so
stigmatized as unfit for "higher" pursuits; so women mostly do it,
and among women, poor, uneducated, or old women more often
than rich, educated, and young ones. Even so, many people want
very much to keep house but can't, because they're poor and haven't
got a house to keep, or the time and money it takes, or even the
experience of ever having seen a decent house, a clean room, except
on TV. Most men are prevented from housework by intense cultural
bias; many women actually hire another woman to do it for them
because they're scared of getting trapped in it, ending up like the
woman they hire, or like that woman we all know who's been pushed
so far over by cultural bias that she can't stand up, and crawls
around the house scrubbing and waxing and spraying germ killer
on the kids. But even on her kneebones, where you and I will never
join her, even she has been practicing as best she knows how a great,
ancient, complex, and necessary art. That our society devalues it is
evidence of the barbarity, the aesthetic and ethical bankruptcy, of
our society.

As housekeeping is an art, so is cooking and all it involves—it
involves, after all, agriculture, hunting, herding. . . . So is the making of clothing and all it involves. . . . And so on; you see how I want
to revalue the word "art" so that when I come back as I do now to
talking about words it is in the context of the great arts of living, of
the woman carrying the basket of bread, bearing gifts, goods. Art
not as some ejaculative act of ego but as a way, a skillful and

powerful way of being in the world. I come back to words because words are my way of being in the world, but meaning by language as art a matter infinitely larger than the so-called High forms. Here is a poem that tries to translate six words by Hélène Cixous, who wrote *The Laugh of the Medusa;* she said, "Je suis là où ça parle," and I squeezed those six words like a lovely lemon and got out all the juice I could, plus a drop of Oregon vodka.

> I'm there where
> it's talking
> Where that speaks I
> am in that talking place
> > Where
> that says
> my being is
> > Where
> my being there
> is speaking
> I am
> > And so
> laughing
> in a stone ear

The stone ear that won't listen, won't hear us, and blames us for its being stone. . . . Women can babble and chatter like monkeys in the wilderness, but the farms and orchards and gardens of language, the wheatfields of art—men have claimed these, fenced them off: No Trespassing, it's a man's world, they say. And I say,

> oh woman
> remember who you are
> woman
> it is the whole earth

We are told, in words and not in words, we are told by their deafness, by their stone ears, that our experience, the life experience of women, is not valuable to men—therefore not valuable to society, to humanity. We are valued by men only as an element of their experience, as things experienced; anything we may say, anything we may do, is recognized only if said or done in their service.

One thing we incontestably do is have babies. So we have babies as the male priests, lawmakers, and doctors tell us to have them, when and where to have them, how often, and how to have them; so that is all under control. But we are *not to talk about* having babies, because that is not part of the experience of men and so nothing to do with reality, with civilization, and no concern of art. —A rending scream in another room. And Prince Andrey comes in and sees his poor little wife dead bearing his son— Or Levin goes out into his fields and thanks his God for the birth of his son— And we know how Prince Andrey feels and how Levin feels and even how God feels, but we don't know what happened. Something happened, something was done, which we know nothing about. But what was it? Even in novels by women we are only just beginning to find out what it is that happens in the other room—what women do.

Freud famously said, "What we shall never know is what a woman wants." Having paused thoughtfully over the syntax of that sentence, in which WE are plural but "a woman" apparently has no plural, no individuality—as we might read that a cow must be milked twice a day or a gerbil is a nice pet—WE might go on then to consider whether WE know anything about, whether WE have ever noticed, whether WE have ever asked a woman what she *does*—what women do.

Many anthropologists, some historians, and others have indeed been asking one another this question for some years now, with pale and affrighted faces—and they are beginning also to answer it. More power to them. The social sciences show us that speakers of the father tongue are capable of understanding and discussing the doings of the mothers, if they will admit the validity of the mother tongue and listen to what women say.

But in society as a whole the patriarchal mythology of what "a woman" does persists almost unexamined, and shapes the lives of women. "What are you going to do when you get out of school?" "Oh, well, just like any other woman, I guess I want a home and family"—and that's fine, but what is this home and family just like other women's? Dad at work, mom home, two kids eating apple pie? This family, which our media and now our government declare to be normal and impose as normative, this nuclear family now accounts for seven percent of the arrangements women live in in America. Ninety-three percent of women don't live that way. They don't do that. Many wouldn't if you gave it to them with bells on. Those who want that, who believe it's their one true destiny—what's their chance of achieving it? They're on the road to Heartbreak House.

But the only alternative offered by the patriarchal mythology is that of the Failed Woman—the old maid, the barren woman, the castrating bitch, the frigid wife, the lezzie, the libber, the Unfeminine, so beloved of misogynists both male and female.

Now indeed there are women who want to be female men; their role model is Margaret Thatcher, and they're ready to dress for success, carry designer briefcases, kill for promotion, and drink the Right Scotch. They want to buy into the man's world, whatever the cost. And if that's true desire, not just compulsion born of fear, O.K.; if you can't lick 'em join 'em. My problem with that is that I can't see it as a good life even for men, who invented it and make all the rules. There's power in it, but not the kind of power I respect, not the kind of power that sets anybody free. I hate to see an intelligent woman voluntarily double herself up to get under the bottom line. Talk about crawling! And when she talks, what can she talk but father tongue? If she's the mouthpiece for the man's world, what has she got to say for herself?

Some women manage it—they may collude, but they don't sell out as women; and we know that when they speak for those who, in the man's world, are the others: women, children, the poor. . . .

But it is dangerous to put on Daddy's clothes, though not, perhaps, as dangerous as it is to sit on Daddy's knees.

There's no way you can offer your experience as your truth if you deny your experience, if you try to be a mythical creature, the dummy woman who sits there on Big Daddy's lap. Whose voice will come out of her prettily hinged jaw? Who is it says yes all the time? Oh yes, yes, I will. Oh I don't know, you decide. Oh I can't do that. Yes hit me, yes rape me, yes save me, oh yes. That is how A Woman talks, the one in What-we-shall-never-know-is-what-A-Woman-wants.

A Woman's place, need I say, is in the home, plus at her volunteer work or the job where she's glad to get sixty cents for doing what men get paid a dollar for but that's because she's always on pregnancy leave but childcare? No! A Woman is home caring for her children! even if she can't. Trapped in this well-built trap, A Woman blames her mother for luring her into it, while ensuring that her own daughter never gets out; she recoils from the idea of sisterhood and doesn't believe women have friends, because it probably means something unnatural, and anyhow, A Woman is afraid of women. She's a male construct, and she's afraid women will deconstruct her. She's afraid of everything, because she can't change. Thighs forever thin and shining hair and shining teeth and she's my Mom, too, all seven percent of her. And she never grows old.

There are old women—little old ladies, as people always say; little bits, fragments of the great dummy statue goddess A Woman. Nobody hears if old women say yes or no, nobody pays them sixty cents for anything. Old men run things. Old men run the show, press the buttons, make the wars, make the money. In the man's world, the old man's world, the young men run and run and run until they drop, and some of the young women run with them. But old women live in the cracks, between the walls, like roaches, like mice, a rustling sound, a squeaking. Better lock up the cheese, boys. It's terrible, you turn up a corner of civilization and there are all these old women running around on the wrong side—

I say to you, you know, you're going to get old. And you can't hear me. I squeak between the walls. I've walked through the mirror and am on the other side, where things are all backwards. You may look with a good will and a generous heart, but you can't see anything in the mirror but your own face; and I, looking from the dark side and seeing your beautiful young faces, see that that's how it should be.

But when you look at yourself in the mirror, I hope you see yourself. Not one of the myths. Not a failed man—a person who can never succeed because success is basically defined as being male— and not a failed goddess, a person desperately trying to hide herself in the dummy Woman, the image of men's desires and fears. I hope you look away from those myths and into your own eyes, and see your own strength. You're going to need it. I hope you don't try to take your strength from men, or from a man. Secondhand experience breaks down a block from the car lot. I hope you'll take and make your own soul; that you'll feel your life for yourself pain by pain and joy by joy; that you'll feed your life, eat, "eat as you go"— you who nourish, be nourished!

If being a cog in the machine or a puppet manipulated by others isn't what you want, you can find out what you want, your needs, desires, truths, powers, by accepting your own experience as a woman, as this woman, this body, this person, your hungry self. On the maps drawn by men there is an immense white area, terra incognita, where most women live. That country is all yours to explore, to inhabit, to describe.

But none of us lives there alone. Being human isn't something people can bring off alone; we need other people in order to be people. We need one another.

If a woman sees other women as Medusa, fears them, turns a stone ear to them, these days, all her hair may begin to stand up on end hissing, *Listen, listen, listen!* Listen to other women, your sisters,

your mothers, your grandmothers—if you don't hear them how will
you ever understand what your daughter says to you?

And the men who can talk, converse with you, not trying to talk
through the dummy Yes-Woman, the men who can accept your
experience as valid—when you find such a man love him, honor
him! But don't obey him. I don't think we have any right to obedience. I think we have a responsibility to freedom.

And especially to freedom of speech. Obedience is silent. It does
not answer. It is contained. Here is a disobedient woman speaking,
Wendy Rose of the Hopi and Miwok people, saying in a poem called
"The Parts of a Poet,"[4]

> parts of me are pinned
> to earth, parts of me
> undermine song, parts
> of me spread on the water,
> parts of me form a rainbow
> bridge, parts of me follow
> the sandfish, parts of me
> are a woman who judges.

Now this is what I want: I want to hear your judgments. I am sick
of the silence of women. I want to hear you speaking all the languages, offering your experience as your truth, as human truth,
talking about working, about making, about unmaking, about eating, about cooking, about feeding, about taking in seed and giving
out life, about killing, about feeling, about thinking; about what
women do; about what men do; about war, about peace; about who
presses the buttons and what buttons get pressed and whether
pressing buttons is in the long run a fit occupation for human
beings. There's a lot of things I want to hear you talk about.

This is what I don't want: I don't want what men have. I'm glad to
let them do their work and talk their talk. But I do not want and will
not have them saying or thinking or telling us that theirs is the only
fit work or speech for human beings. Let them not take our work,
our words, from us. If they can, if they will, let them work with us
and talk with us. We can all talk mother tongue, we can all talk
father tongue, and together we can try to hear and speak that
language which may be our truest way of being in the world, we who
speak for a world that has no words but ours.

I know that many men and even women are afraid and angry
when women do speak, because in this barbaric society, when

women speak truly they speak subversively—they can't help it: if
you're underneath, if you're kept down, you break out, you subvert.
We are volcanoes. When we women offer our experience as our
truth, as human truth, all the maps change. There are new mountains.

That's what I want—to hear you erupting. You young Mount St.
Helenses who don't know the power in you—I want to hear you. I
want to listen to you talking to each other and to us all: whether
you're writing an article or a poem or a letter or teaching a class or
talking with friends or reading a novel or making a speech or
proposing a law or giving a judgment or singing the baby to sleep or
discussing the fate of nations, I want to hear you. Speak with a
woman's tongue. Come out and tell us what time of night it is! Don't
let us sink back into silence. If we don't tell our truth, who will?
Who'll speak for my children, and yours?

So I end with the end of a poem by Linda Hogan of the Chickasaw people, called "The Women Speaking."[5]

> Daughters, the women are speaking.
> They arrive
> over the wise distances
> on perfect feet.
> Daughters, I love you.

Notes

1. Sojourner Truth, in *The Norton Anthology of Literature by Women,* ed. Sandra M.
Gilbert and Susan Gubar (New York: W. W. Norton & Co., 1985), pp. 255–56.

2. Joy Harjo, "The Blanket Around Her," in *That's What She Said: Contemporary
Poetry and Fiction by Native American Women,* ed. Rayna Green (Bloomington: Indiana University Press, 1984), p. 127.

3. Denise Levertov, "Stepping Westward," in *Norton Anthology,* p. 1951.

4. Wendy Rose, "The Parts of a Poet," in *That's What She Said,* p. 204.

5. Linda Hogan, "The Women Speaking," in ibid., p. 172.

WOMAN/WILDERNESS

(1986)

*In June of 1986, Gary Snyder invited me to come talk to his class in
Wilderness at the University of California at Davis. I told him I would
say a little about woman and wilderness and read some poetry, mostly
from my book* Always Coming Home. *What follows is what I said before
getting into the reading. Highly tendentious, it was meant to, and did,
provoke lively discussion.*

Civilized Man says: I am Self, I am Master, all the rest is Other—
outside, below, underneath, subservient. I own, I use, I explore, I
exploit, I control. What I do is what matters. What I want is what
matter is for. I am that I am, and the rest is women and the wilderness, to be used as I see fit.

To this, Civilized Woman, in the voice of Susan Griffin, replies as
follows:

> We say there is no way to see his dying as separate from her
> living, or what he had done to her, or what part of her he had
> used. We say if you change the course of this river you change
> the shape of the whole place. And we say that what she did then
> could not be separated from what she held sacred in herself,
> what she had felt when he did that to her, what we hold sacred to
> ourselves, what we feel we could not go on without, and we say if
> this river leaves this place, nothing will grow and the mountain
> will crumble away, and we say what he did to her could not be
> separated from the way that he looked at her, and what he felt
> was right to do to her, and what they do to us, we say, shapes how
> they see us. That once the trees are cut down, the water will wash
> the mountain away and the river be heavy with mud, and there

will be a flood. And we say that what he did to her he did to all of
us. And that one fact cannot be separated from another. And
had he seen more clearly, we say, he might have predicted his
own death. How if the trees grew on that hillside there would be
no flood. And you cannot divert this river. We say look how the
water flows from this place and returns as rainfall, everything
returns, we say, and one thing follows another, there are limits,
we say, on what can be done and everything moves. We are all a
part of this motion, we say, and the way of the river is sacred, and
this grove of trees is sacred, and we ourselves, we tell you, are
sacred.[1]

What is happening here is that the wilderness is answering. This
has never happened before. We who live at this time are hearing
news that has never been heard before. A new thing is happening.

> Daughters, the women are speaking.
> They arrive
> over the wise distances
> on perfect feet.

The women are speaking: so says Linda Hogan of the Chickasaw
people.[2] The women are speaking. Those who were identified as
having nothing to say, as sweet silence or monkey-chatterers, those
who were identified with Nature, which listens, as against Man, who
speaks—those people are speaking. They speak for themselves and
for the other people, the animals, the trees, the rivers, the rocks.
And what they say is: We are sacred.

Listen: they do not say, "Nature is sacred." Because they distrust
that word, Nature. Nature as not including humanity, Nature as
what is not human, that Nature is a construct made by Man, not a
real thing; just as most of what Man says and knows about women is
mere myth and construct. Where I live as woman is to men a
wilderness. But to me it is home.

The anthropologists Shirley and Edwin Ardener, talking about
an African village culture, made a useful and interesting mental
shape. They laid down two circles largely but not completely over-
lapping, so that the center of the figure is the tall oval of interlap,
and on each side of it are facing crescents of non-overlap. One of the
two circles is the Dominant element of the culture, that is, Men. The
other is the Muted element of the culture, that is, Women. As Elaine
Showalter explains the figure, "All of male consciousness is within
the circle of the Dominant structure and thus accessible to or struc-

tured by language." Both the crescent that belongs to men only and the crescent that belongs to women only, outside the shared, central, civilized area of overlap, may be called "the wilderness." The men's wilderness is real; it is where men can go hunting and exploring and having all-male adventures, away from the village, the shared center, and it is accessible to and structured by language. "In terms of cultural anthropology, women know what the male crescent is like, even if they have never seen it, because it becomes the subject of legend. . . . But men do not know what is in the wild,"[3] that is, the no-man's-land, the crescent that belongs to the Muted group, the silent group, the group within the culture that *is not spoken,* whose experience is not considered to be part of human experience, that is, the women.

Men live their whole lives within the Dominant area. When they go off hunting bears, they come back with bear stories, and these are listened to by all, they become the history or the mythology of that culture. So the men's "wilderness" becomes Nature, considered as the property of Man.

But the experience of women as women, their experience unshared with men, that experience is the wilderness or the wildness that is utterly other—that is in fact, to Man, unnatural. That is what civilization has left out, what culture excludes, what the Dominants call animal, bestial, primitive, undeveloped, unauthentic—what has not been spoken, and when spoken, has not been heard—what we are just beginning to find words for, our words not their words: the experience of women. For dominance-identified men and women both, that is true wildness. Their fear of it is ancient, profound, and violent. The misogyny that shapes every aspect of our civilization is the institutionalized form of male fear and hatred of what they have denied and therefore cannot know, cannot share: that wild country, the being of women.

All we can do is try to speak it, try to say it, try to save it. Look, we say, this land is where your mother lived and where your daughter will live. This is your sister's country. You lived there as a child, boy or girl, you lived there—have you forgotten? All children are wild. You lived in the wild country. Why are you afraid of it?

Notes

1. Susan Griffin, *Woman and Nature* (New York: Harper & Row, Colophon Books, 1978), p. 186.

2. Linda Hogan, "The Women Speaking," in *That's What She Said: Contemporary Poetry and Fiction by Native American Women,* ed. Rayna Green (Bloomington: Indiana University Press, 1984), p. 172.

3. Elaine Showalter, "Feminist Criticism in the Wilderness," in *The New Feminist Criticism,* ed. Elaine Showalter (New York: Pantheon Books, 1985), p. 262. See also Shirley Ardener, ed., *Perceiving Women* (New York: Halsted Press, 1978).

THE CARRIER BAG THEORY
OF FICTION

(1986)

In the temperate and tropical regions where it appears that hominids evolved into human beings, the principal food of the species was vegetable. Sixty-five to eighty percent of what human beings ate in those regions in Paleolithic, Neolithic, and prehistoric times was gathered; only in the extreme Arctic was meat the staple food. The mammoth hunters spectacularly occupy the cave wall and the mind, but what we actually did to stay alive and fat was gather seeds, roots, sprouts, shoots, leaves, nuts, berries, fruits, and grains, adding bugs and mollusks and netting or snaring birds, fish, rats, rabbits, and other tuskless small fry to up the protein. And we didn't even work hard at it—much less hard than peasants slaving in somebody else's field after agriculture was invented, much less hard than paid workers since civilization was invented. The average prehistoric person could make a nice living in about a fifteen-hour work week.

Fifteen hours a week for subsistence leaves a lot of time for other things. So much time that maybe the restless ones who didn't have a baby around to enliven their life, or skill in making or cooking or singing, or very interesting thoughts to think, decided to slope off and hunt mammoths. The skillful hunters then would come staggering back with a load of meat, a lot of ivory, and a story. It wasn't the meat that made the difference. It was the story.

It is hard to tell a really gripping tale of how I wrested a wild-oat seed from its husk, and then another, and then another, and then another, and then another, and then I scratched my gnat bites, and Ool said something funny, and we went to the creek and got a drink and watched newts for a while, and then I found another patch of oats. . . . No, it does not compare, it cannot compete with how I thrust my spear deep into the titanic hairy flank while Oob, impaled on one huge sweeping tusk, writhed screaming, and blood spouted everywhere in crimson torrents, and Boob was crushed to jelly when the mammoth fell on him as I shot my unerring arrow straight through eye to brain.

That story not only has Action, it has a Hero. Heroes are powerful. Before you know it, the men and women in the wild-oat patch and their kids and the skills of the makers and the thoughts of the thoughtful and the songs of the singers are all part of it, have all been pressed into service in the tale of the Hero. But it isn't their story. It's his.

When she was planning the book that ended up as *Three Guineas,* Virginia Woolf wrote a heading in her notebook, "Glossary"; she had thought of reinventing English according to a new plan, in order to tell a different story. One of the entries in this glossary is *heroism,* defined as "botulism." And *hero,* in Woolf's dictionary, is "bottle." The hero as bottle, a stringent reevaluation. I now propose the bottle as hero.

Not just the bottle of gin or wine, but bottle in its older sense of container in general, a thing that holds something else.

If you haven't got something to put it in, food will escape you— even something as uncombative and unresourceful as an oat. You put as many as you can into your stomach while they are handy, that being the primary container; but what about tomorrow morning when you wake up and it's cold and raining and wouldn't it be good to have just a few handfuls of oats to chew on and give little Oom to make her shut up, but how do you get more than one stomachful and one handful home? So you get up and go to the damned soggy oat patch in the rain, and wouldn't it be a good thing if you had something to put Baby Oo Oo in so that you could pick the oats with both hands? A leaf a gourd a shell a net a bag a sling a sack a bottle a pot a box a container. A holder. A recipient.

> The first cultural device was probably a recipient. . . . Many theorizers feel that the earliest cultural inventions must have been a container to hold gathered products and some kind of sling or net carrier.

So says Elizabeth Fisher in *Women's Creation* (McGraw-Hill, 1975). But no, this cannot be. Where is that wonderful, big, long, hard thing, a bone, I believe, that the Ape Man first bashed somebody with in the movie and then, grunting with ecstasy at having achieved the first proper murder, flung up into the sky, and whirling there it became a space ship thrusting its way into the cosmos to fertilize it and produce at the end of the movie a lovely fetus, a boy of course, drifting around the Milky Way without (oddly enough) any womb, any matrix at all? I don't know. I don't even care. I'm not telling that story. We've heard it, we've all heard all about all the sticks and spears and swords, the things to bash and poke and hit with, the long, hard things, but we have not heard about the thing to put things in, the container for the thing contained. That is a new story. That is news.

And yet old. Before—once you think about it, surely long before—the weapon, a late, luxurious, superfluous tool; long before the useful knife and ax; right along with the indispensable whacker, grinder, and digger—for what's the use of digging up a lot of potatoes if you have nothing to lug the ones you can't eat home in—with or before the tool that forces energy outward, we made the tool that brings energy home. It makes sense to me. I am an adherent of what Fisher calls the Carrier Bag Theory of human evolution.

This theory not only explains large areas of theoretical obscurity and avoids large areas of theoretical nonsense (inhabited largely by tigers, foxes, and other highly territorial mammals); it also grounds me, personally, in human culture in a way I never felt grounded before. So long as culture was explained as originating from and elaborating upon the use of long, hard objects for sticking, bashing, and killing, I never thought that I had, or wanted, any particular share in it. ("What Freud mistook for her lack of civilization is woman's lack of *loyalty* to civilization," Lillian Smith observed.) The society, the civilization they were talking about, these theoreticians, was evidently theirs; they owned it, they liked it; they were human, fully human, bashing, sticking, thrusting, killing. Wanting to be human too, I sought for evidence that I was; but if that's what it took, to make a weapon and kill with it, then evidently I was either extremely defective as a human being, or not human at all.

That's right, they said. What you are is a woman. Possibly not human at all, certainly defective. Now be quiet while we go on telling the Story of the Ascent of Man the Hero.

Go on, say I, wandering off towards the wild oats, with Oo Oo in the sling and little Oom carrying the basket. You just go on telling how the mammoth fell on Boob and how Cain fell on Abel and how the bomb fell on Nagasaki and how the burning jelly fell on the villagers and how the missiles will fall on the Evil Empire, and all the other steps in the Ascent of Man.

If it is a human thing to do to put something you want, because it's useful, edible, or beautiful, into a bag, or a basket, or a bit of rolled bark or leaf, or a net woven of your own hair, or what have you, and then take it home with you, home being another, larger kind of pouch or bag, a container for people, and then later on you take it out and eat it or share it or store it up for winter in a solider container or put it in the medicine bundle or the shrine or the museum, the holy place, the area that contains what is sacred, and then next day you probably do much the same again—if to do that is human, if that's what it takes, then I am a human being after all. Fully, freely, gladly, for the first time.

Not, let it be said at once, an unaggressive or uncombative human being. I am an aging, angry woman laying mightily about me with my handbag, fighting hoodlums off. However I don't, nor does anybody else, consider myself heroic for doing so. It's just one of those damned things you have to do in order to be able to go on gathering wild oats and telling stories.

It is the story that makes the difference. It is the story that hid my humanity from me, the story the mammoth hunters told about bashing, thrusting, raping, killing, about the Hero. The wonderful, poisonous story of Botulism. The killer story.

It sometimes seems that that story is approaching its end. Lest there be no more telling of stories at all, some of us out here in the wild oats, amid the alien corn, think we'd better start telling another one, which maybe people can go on with when the old one's finished. Maybe. The trouble is, we've all let ourselves become part of the killer story, and so we may get finished along with it. Hence it is with a certain feeling of urgency that I seek the nature, subject, words of the other story, the untold one, the life story.

It's unfamiliar, it doesn't come easily, thoughtlessly to the lips as the killer story does; but still, "untold" was an exaggeration. People have been telling the life story for ages, in all sorts of words and ways. Myths of creation and transformation, trickster stories, folktales, jokes, novels . . .

The novel is a fundamentally unheroic kind of story. Of course the Hero has frequently taken it over, that being his imperial nature and uncontrollable impulse, to take everything over and run it while making stern decrees and laws to control his uncontrollable impulse to kill it. So the Hero has decreed through his mouthpieces the Lawgivers, first, that the proper shape of the narrative is that of the arrow or spear, starting *here* and going straight *there* and THOK! hitting its mark (which drops dead); second, that the central concern of narrative, including the novel, is conflict; and third, that the story isn't any good if he isn't in it.

I differ with all of this. I would go so far as to say that the natural, proper, fitting shape of the novel might be that of a sack, a bag. A book holds words. Words hold things. They bear meanings. A novel is a medicine bundle, holding things in a particular, powerful relation to one another and to us.

One relationship among elements in the novel may well be that of conflict, but the reduction of narrative to conflict is absurd. (I have read a how-to-write manual that said, "A story should be seen as a battle," and went on about strategies, attacks, victory, etc.) Conflict, competition, stress, struggle, etc., within the narrative conceived as carrier bag / belly / box / house / medicine bundle, may be seen as necessary elements of a whole which itself cannot be characterized either as conflict or as harmony, since its purpose is neither resolution nor stasis but continuing process.

Finally, it's clear that the Hero does not look well in this bag. He needs a stage or a pedestal or a pinnacle. You put him in a bag and he looks like a rabbit, like a potato.

That is why I like novels: instead of heroes they have people in them.

So, when I came to write science-fiction novels, I came lugging this great heavy sack of stuff, my carrier bag full of wimps and klutzes, and tiny grains of things smaller than a mustard seed, and intricately woven nets which when laboriously unknotted are seen to contain one blue pebble, an imperturbably functioning chronometer telling the time on another world, and a mouse's skull; full of beginnings without ends, of initiations, of losses, of transformations and translations, and far more tricks than conflicts, far fewer triumphs than snares and delusions; full of space ships that get stuck, missions that fail, and people who don't understand. I said it was hard to make a gripping tale of how we wrested the wild oats from their husks, I didn't say it was impossible. Who ever said writing a novel was easy?

If science fiction is the mythology of modern technology, then its myth is tragic. "Technology," or "modern science" (using the words as they are usually used, in an unexamined shorthand standing for the "hard" sciences and high technology founded upon continuous economic growth), is a heroic undertaking, Herculean, Promethean, conceived as triumph, hence ultimately as tragedy. The fiction embodying this myth will be, and has been, triumphant (Man conquers earth, space, aliens, death, the future, etc.) and tragic (apocalypse, holocaust, then or now).

If, however, one avoids the linear, progressive, Time's-(killing)-arrow mode of the Techno-Heroic, and redefines technology and science as primarily cultural carrier bag rather than weapon of domination, one pleasant side effect is that science fiction can be seen as a far less rigid, narrow field, not necessarily Promethean or apocalyptic at all, and in fact less a mythological genre than a realistic one.

It is a strange realism, but it is a strange reality.

Science fiction properly conceived, like all serious fiction, however funny, is a way of trying to describe what is in fact going on, what people actually do and feel, how people relate to everything else in this vast sack, this belly of the universe, this womb of things to be and tomb of things that were, this unending story. In it, as in all fiction, there is room enough to keep even Man where he belongs, in his place in the scheme of things; there is time enough to gather plenty of wild oats and sow them too, and sing to little Oom, and listen to Ool's joke, and watch newts, and still the story isn't over. Still there are seeds to be gathered, and room in the bag of stars.

HEROES

(1986)

For Elizabeth Arthur and Joy Johannessen

For thirty years I've been fascinated by books about the early ex-
plorations of the Antarctic, and particularly by the books written
by men who were on the expeditions: Scott, Shackleton, Cherry-
Garrard, Wilson, Byrd, and so on, all of them not only men of
courage and imagination but excellent writers, vivid, energetic,
exact, and powerful. As an American I wasn't exposed to the British
idolization of Scott that now makes it so chic to sneer at him, and I
still feel that I am competent to base my judgment of his character,
or Shackleton's, or Byrd's, on their own works and witness, without
much reference to the various biases of biographers.

They were certainly heroes to me, all of them. And as I followed
them step by frostbitten-toed step across the Ross Ice Barrier and
up the Beardmore Glacier to the awful place, the white plateau, and
back again, many times, they got into my toes and my bones and my
books, and I wrote *The Left Hand of Darkness*, in which a Black man
from Earth and an androgynous extraterrestrial pull Scott's sledge
through Shackleton's blizzards across a planet called Winter. And
fifteen years or so later I wrote a story, "Sur," in which a small group
of Latin Americans actually reach the South Pole a year before
Amundsen and Scott, but decide not to say anything about it,
because if the men knew that they had got there first—they are all
women—it wouldn't do. The men would be so let down. "We left no
footprints, even," says the narrator.

Now, in writing that story, which was one of the pleasantest experiences of my life, I was aware that I was saying some rather hard things about heroism, but I had no desire or intention to debunk or devalue the actual explorers of Antarctica. What I wanted was to join them, fictionally. I had been along with them so many times in their books; why couldn't a few of us, my kind of people, housewives, come along with them in my book . . . or even come before them?

These simple little wishes, when they become what people call "ideas"—as in "Where do you get the *ideas* for your stories?"—and when they find themselves in an appropriate nutrient medium such as prose, may begin to grow, to get yeasty, to fizz. Whatever the "idea" of that story was, it has continued to ferment in the dark vats of my mental cellars and is now quite heady, with a marked nose and a complicated aftertaste, like a good '69 Zinfandel.

I wasn't aware of this process until recently, when I was watching the Public Broadcasting series about Shackleton (as well conceived, cast, and produced as the series about Scott and Amundsen was shoddy). There were Ernest Shackleton and his three friends struggling across the abomination of desolation towards the Pole, two days before they had to turn back only ninety-seven miles short of that geometrical *bindu* which they desired so ardently to attain. And the voice-over spoke words from Shackleton's journal: "Man can only do his best. The strongest forces of Nature are arrayed against us." And I sat there and thought, Oh, what nonsense!

That startled me. I had been feeling just as I had always felt for those cold, hungry, tired, brave men, and commiserating them for the bitter disappointment awaiting them—and yet Shackleton's words struck me as disgustingly false, as silly. Why? I had to think it out; and this paper is the process of thinking it out.

"Man can only do his best"—well, all right. They were all men, of course, and a long way from the suffragists back home; they honestly believed that "man" includes women, or would have said they did if they had ever thought about it, which I doubt they ever did. I am sure they would have laughed heartily at the proposal that their expedition include women. But still, Man can only do his best; or, to put it in my dialect, people can only do their best; or, as King Yudhisthira says in the great and bitter end of the *Mahabharata,* "By nothing that I do can I attain a goal beyond my reach." That king whose dog's name is Dharma knows what he is talking about. As did those English explorers, with their clear, fierce sense of duty.

But how about "The strongest forces of Nature are arrayed against us"? Here's the problem. What did you expect, Ernest? Indeed, what did you ask for? Didn't you set it up that way? Didn't you arrange, with vast trouble and expense, that the very strongest "forces of Nature" would be "arrayed against" you and your tiny army?

What is false is the military image; what is foolish is the egoism; what is pernicious is the identification of "Nature" as enemy. We are asked to believe that the Antarctic continent became aware that four Englishmen were penetrating her virgin whiteness and so unleashed upon them the punishing fury of her revenge, the mighty weaponry of wind and blizzard, and so forth and so on. Well, I don't believe it. I don't believe that Nature is either an enemy, or a woman, to humanity. Nobody has ever thought so but Man; and the thought is, to one not Man, no longer acceptable even as a poetic metaphor. Nobody, nothing, "arrayed" any "forces" against Shackleton except Shackleton himself. He created an obstacle to conquer or an enemy to attack; attacked; and was defeated—by what? By himself, having himself created the situation in which his defeat could occur.

Had he reached the Pole he would have said, "I have conquered, I have achieved," in perfectly self-justified triumph. But, forced to retreat, he does not say, "I am defeated"; he blames it on that which is not himself, Nature. If Man wins the battle he starts, he takes the credit for winning, but if he doesn't win, he doesn't lose; "forces arrayed against" him defeat him. Man does not, cannot fail. And Shackleton, speaking for Man, refuses the responsibility for a situation for which he was responsible from beginning to end.

In an even more drastic situation for which he was even more responsible, in his last journal entry Scott wrote:

> We took risks, we knew we took them; things have come out against us, and therefore we have no cause for complaint, but bow to the will of Providence, determined still to do our best to the last.

I have seriously tried to find those words false and silly; I can't do it. Their beauty is no accident.

"Things have come out against us" sounds rather like a projection of fault (like the "forces arrayed against us") but lacks any note of accusation or blame; the underlying image is that of gambling, trusting to luck. "Providence," which is how Scott referred to God, does seem to come in as the "Other," a will opposed to Scott's will as Nature was opposed to Shackleton's; but something you call by the name of Providence is not something you perceive as an opponent or an enemy—indeed, the connotations are maternal: nurturing, sheltering, providing. The man may be speaking like a child, but not like a spoiled child. He takes responsibility for the risks taken, and beyond hope finds duty unalterable: "to do our best to the last." Like Yudhisthira, he knew what "the last" meant. Nothing in me finds this contemptible, and I can't imagine ever finding it contemptible. But I don't know. I have found so many things silly that just a few years ago seemed fine. . . . Time to bottle the wine: if you leave it too long in the wood it sours and is lost. I don't want to go sour. All I want to do is lose the hero myths so that I can find what is worth admiration.

All right: what I admire in Shackleton, at that moment on the Barrier, is that he turned back. He gave up; he admitted defeat; and he saved his men. Unfortunately he also saved his pride by posturing a bit, playing hero. He couldn't admit that his weakness was his strength; he did the right thing, but said the wrong one. So I go on loving Shackleton, but with the slightest shade of contempt for his having boasted.

But Scott, who did nearly everything wrong, why have I no such contempt for Scott? Why does he remain worthy in my mind of that awful beauty and freedom, my Antarctica? Evidently because he admitted his failure completely—living it through to its end, death. It is as if Scott realized that his life was a story he had to tell, and he had to get the ending right.

This statement may be justly seen as frivolous, trivializing. The death of five people isn't "just a story."

But then, what is a story? And what does one live for? To stay alive, certainly; but only that?

In Amundsen's practical, realistic terms, the deaths of Scott and his four companions were unnecessary, preventable. But then, in what terms was Amundsen's polar journey necessary? It had no justification but nationalism/egoism—"Yah! I'm going to get there first!"

When Scott's party stopped for the last time, the rocks they had collected for the Museum of Natural History were still heavy on the sledge. That is very moving; but I will not use the scientific motives of Scott's expedition to justify his polar journey. It was a mere race too, with no goal but winning. It was when he lost the race that it became a real journey to a real end. And this reality, this value to others, lies in the account he kept.

Amundsen's relation of his polar run is interesting, informative, in some respects admirable. Scott's journal is all that and very much more than that. I would rank it with Woolf's or Pepys's diaries, as a personal record of inestimable value, written by an artist.

Scott's temperament was not very well suited to his position as leader; his ambition and intensity drove him to lead, but his inflexibility, vanity, and unpredictability could make his leadership a disaster, for example in his sudden decision to take four men, not three, on the last lap to the Pole, thus oversetting all the meticulous arrangements for supplies. Scott arranged his own defeat, his death, and the death of the four men he was responsible for. He "asked for it." And there were certainly self-destructive elements in his personality. But it would be merely glib to say that he "wanted to fail," and it would miss what I see as the real heroism: what he made of his failure. He took complete responsibility for it. He witnessed truly. He kept on telling the story.

"Unless a grain of wheat fall into the ground and die, it abideth alone; but if it die, it bringeth forth much fruit."

His self-sacrifice was not, I think, deliberate; but his behavior was sacrificial, rather than heroic. And it was as that unheroic creature, a writer, that he gathered, garnered, saved what could be saved from defeat, suffering, and death. Because he was an artist, his testimony turns mere waste and misery into that useful thing, tragedy.

His companion Edward Wilson, whose paintings are perhaps the finest visual record of Antarctica, kept a diary of the polar journey too. Wilson was a far sweeter, more generous man than Scott, and his diary is very moving, but it has not the power of Scott's—it is not a work of art; it records, but it does not ultimately take responsibility for what happens. Self-absorbed, willful, obsessed, controlling, Scott was evidently an artist born. He should never have been entrusted with a polar expedition, no doubt. But he was; and he had so fierce a determination to tell his story to the end that he wrote it even as he lay in the tent on the ice dying of cold, starvation, and gangrene among his dead. And so Antarctica is ours. He won it for us.

PROSPECTS FOR WOMEN
IN WRITING

(1986)

I was invited to sit on a panel called Women in the Arts, at the Conference on Women in the Year 2000, held in Portland in September of 1986. Each panelist was asked to make a ten-minute statement about the prospects for women in her particular field.

It's only been about two hundred years since women gained access to literacy and began to empower themselves with that great power, the written word. And they have written. The works of women acknowledged as "great"—Austen, the Brontës, Dickinson, Eliot, Woolf—make a high road for other women writers to follow, so wide and clear that even the conscious or unconscious misogyny of most critics and teachers of literature hasn't been able to hide or close it.

There is less sexism in book and magazine publishing than in any field I know about. Of course most publishers are men, but most publishers now aren't even human: they're corporations. Many editors and other human beings in publishing are women or unmacho men. And thirty to fifty percent of living authors are women. With talent and obstinacy, then, a woman can and will get her writing published; with talent, obstinacy, and luck, her writing will be widely read and taken notice of. But.

As Tillie Olsen has demonstrated in *Silences,* although thirty to fifty percent of books are written by women, what is called "literature" remains eighty-eight to ninety percent male, decade after decade. No matter how successful, beloved, influential her work was, when a woman author dies, nine times out of ten she gets dropped from the lists, the courses, the anthologies, while the men get kept. If she had the nerve to have children, her chances of getting dropped are higher still. So we get Anthony Trollope coming out the ears while Elizabeth Gaskell is ignored, or endless studies of Nathaniel Hawthorne while Harriet Beecher Stowe is taught as a footnote to history. Most women's writing—like most work by women in any field—is called unimportant, secondary, by masculinist teachers and critics of both sexes; and literary styles and genres are constantly redefined to keep women's writing in second place. So if you want your writing to be taken seriously, don't marry and have kids, and above all, don't die. But if you have to die, commit suicide. They approve of that.

To find out what women writers are up against, if you want the useful blues, read Tillie Olsen, and if you want to get cheerfully enraged, read Joanna Russ's *How to Suppress Women's Writing* or Dale Spender's wonderful *Man Made Language*.

To try to summarize my own experience: The more truly your work comes from your own being, body and soul, rather than fitting itself into male conventions and expectations of what to write about and how to write it, the less it will suit most editors, reviewers, grant givers, and prize committees. But among all those are women and men to whom the real thing, the art, comes first; and you have to trust them. You have to trust yourself. And you have to trust your readers.

The writer only does half the job. It takes two to make a book. Many more women buy and read books than men. And in the last fifteen years there has been an increasing sense of strength and mutual validation among women writers and readers, a resistance to the male control over reading, a refusal to join men in sneering at what women want to write and read. Get hold of *The Norton Anthology of Literature by Women* and read it and then tell me women can't show men how to write and what to write about! The English profs keep sweeping our work under the rug, but that rug is about three feet off the floor by now, and things are coming out from under it and eating the English profs. Housework is woman's work, right? Well, it's time to shake the rugs.

Who's afraid of Virginia Woolf? Every little macho dodo, from Hemingway to Mailer. There is no more subversive act than the act of writing from a woman's experience of life using a woman's judgment. Woolf knew that and said it in 1930. Most of us forgot it and

had to rediscover it all over again in the sixties. But for a whole
generation now, women have been writing, publishing, and reading
one another, in artistic and scholarly and feminist fellowship. If we
go on doing that, by the year 2000 we will—*for the first time ever*—
have kept the perceptions, ideas, and judgments of women alive in
consciousness as an active, creative force in society for more than
one generation. And our daughters and granddaughters won't have
to start from zero the way we did. To keep women's words, women's
works, alive and powerful—that's what I see as our job as writers
and readers for the next fifteen years, and the next fifty.

TEXT, SILENCE, PERFORMANCE

(1986)

This talk was given for Composers Inc., on the campus of the University of California at Berkeley in the fall of 1986. To prepare it for print I have had to truncate it and fiddle it around, since I had to omit most of the readings it was the matrix of (though I left in "She Who" as bait), and since my composer-collaborator Elinor Armer could not join me on the page as she did on stage to talk about the text/music piece we were about to premiere. But to smooth it all down into a proper essay seemed to be in bad faith towards its subject; it was a performance, and so on the page it has some of the queerness and incompleteness of all oral works written down.

The printed word is reproducible. You can type the word "sunrise" or print it in type or on a computer screen or printout, and it's the same word reproduced. If you handwrite the word "sunrise" and then I handwrite it, I've reproduced it, I've copied it, though its identity is maybe getting a little wrinkly and weird around the edges. But if you say "sunrise" and then I say "sunrise," yes, it's the same word we're saying, but we can't speak of reproduction, only of repeating, a very different matter. It matters who said it. Speech is an event. The sunrise itself happens over and over, happens indeed continuously, by way of the Earth turning, but I don't think it is ever legitimate to say, "It's the same sunrise." Events aren't reproducible. To say that the letters O and M "make" the word "OM" is to confuse sign and event, like mistaking a wristwatch for the rotation of the planet. The word "OM" is a sound, an event; it "takes" time to say it; its saying "makes" time. The instrument of that sound is the breath, which we breathe over and over, by way of being alive. Indeed the sound can be reproduced mechanically, but then it has ceased to be, as we say, live. It's not the event, but a shadow of it.

Writing of any kind fixes the word outside time, and silences it. The written word is a shadow. Shadows are silent. The reader breathes back life into that unmortality, and maybe noise into that silence.

People used to be aware that the written word was the visible sign of an audible sign, and they read aloud—they put their breath into it. Apparently if the Romans saw somebody sitting reading silently to themself they nudged each other and sniggered. Abelard and Aquinas moved their lips while they read, like louts with comic books. In a Chinese library you couldn't hear yourself think, any more than you can in a Chinese opera.

So long as literacy was guarded by a male elite as their empowering privilege, most people knew text as event. What we call literature was recitation: the speaking and hearing, by live people gathered together, of a more or less fixed narrative or other formal structure, using repetition, conventional phrases, and a greater or lesser amount of improvisation. That's the *Odyssey*, the *Bhagavad-Gita*, the *Torah*, the *Edda*, all myths, all epics, all folktales, the entire literature of North America, South America, and much of Africa before the White conquests, and still the literature of many cultures and subcultures from New Guinea to the slum streets.

Yet we call the art of language, language as an art, "writing." I'm a writer, right? Literature literally means letters, the alphabet. The oral text, verbal art as event, as performance, has been devalued as primitive, a "lower" form, discarded, except by babies, the blind, the electorate, and people who come to hear people give lectures.

What, in fact, are we doing here—me lecturing, you listening? Something ever so ethnic. We're indulging in orality. It isn't illegal, but it's pretty kinky. It's disreputable, because oral text is held to be "inferior" to written—and written really now means printed. We value the power of print, which is its infinite reproducibility. Print is viral. (Virile is now subsumed in viral.) The model of modern Western civilization is the virus: the pure bit of information, which turns its environment into endless reproductions of itself.

But the word, she squeaks, is not information. What is the information value of the word "fuck"? Of the word "OM"?

Information is, or may be, one value or aspect of the word. There are others. Sound is one of them. Significance does not necessarily imply reference to an absent referent; the event itself may be considered significant: for example, a sunrise; a noise. A word in the first place is a noise. To the computers all aspects of the word other than information are "noise." But we are not computers. We may not be very bright, but we are brighter than computers.

It is high time that I did what I am talking about, so here is a fragment of a story from an oral literature, written in the form in which we usually read such literature.

> Then the great Grizzly Bear took notice of it. She became angry, ran out, and rushed up to the man who was scolding her. She rushed into his house, took him, and killed him. She tore his flesh to pieces and broke his bones. Then she went. Now she remembered her own people and her two children. She was very angry, and she went home.

Franz Boas wrote the story for us that way, in that form, as information—part of the information he was gathering about Tsimshian culture. But before that, in the first place, he wrote it down in Tsimshian as he heard it, as it was spoken, performed for him; and then he did an interlinear word-for-word translation into English. And that translation, arranged in breath-groups, reads like this:

> Then she noticed it,
>   the great Grizzly Bear.
> Then she came,
>   being sick in heart.
> Then quickly she ran out at him,
>   greatly angry.
>
> Then she went where the man was
>   who scolded.
> Then into that place she stood.
>
> Then she took the man.
> Then all over she killed him.
> It was dead,
>   the man.
> All over was finished his flesh.
> Then were broken all his bones.
>
> At once she went.
> She remembered her people,
>   where her two cubs were.
> Then went the great Grizzly Bear.
> Angry she was,
>   and sick at heart.

As Barre Toelken (from whom I took these illuminating passages) says, the literal translation is direct, dramatic, strange.* It has
a pace, a rhythm, that makes you hear it even reading it in silence on
the page. What Boas did with the passage was turn it into prose. As
the fellow in Molière says, "You mean I've been talking prose all my
life?"—but in fact, he hadn't. Prose is an artifact of the technology
of writing. The Tsimshian text, and Boas's first transliteration of it,
is actually not prose, nor poetry, nor drama, but *the notation of a
verbal performance.*

Originally music was recited just as verbal text was (and we still
say "recital" for a solo performance of music). It was performed
from memory, by imitation and rote learning, more or less exactly
repeating an original, with considerable latitude for variations, or

---

* Barre Toelken and Tacheeni Scott, "Poetic Retranslation and the 'Pretty Lan-
guages' of Yellowman," in *Traditional Literatures of the American Indian: Texts and
Interpretations*, ed. Karl Kroeber (Lincoln: University of Nebraska Press, 1981).
This anthology, and the work of Dell Hymes in *"In Vain I Tried to Tell You": Essays in
Native American Ethnopoetics* (Philadelphia: University of Pennsylvania Press, 1981),
of Dennis Tedlock in *The Spoken Word and the Work of Interpretation* (Philadelphia:
University of Pennsylvania Press, 1983) and *Finding the Center: Narrative Poetry of the
Zuñi Indians* (Lincoln: University of Nebraska Press, 1978), and of others concerned with the translation of works in the great oral verbal traditions, were my
only guide into the fascinating and complex subject matter of this talk when I
wrote it, except for Walter J. Ong's *The Presence of the Word: Some Prolegomena for
Cultural and Religious History* (Minneapolis: University of Minnesota Press, 1981).
To enter the subject from Native American verbal art is to bypass all assumptions of
the superiority or primacy of written literature, and the arrogant dismissal of
performance as a secondary, unimportant aesthetic category. This saves one a great
deal of time, which can be wasted in worrying over such statements as this:
"Meanwhile the truth is simple and clear: 'There are many performances of the
same poem—differing among themselves in many ways. A performance is an
event, but the poem itself, if there *is* any poem, must be some kind of enduring
object'" (Elizabeth Fine quoting Roman Jakobson quoting Wimsatt and Beardsley). I think it is fair to say that the longer one considers that statement, the less
clear, the less simple, and the less true it reveals itself to be.

After I had reworked the talk for this volume, I came upon Fine's splendid *The
Folklore Text: From Performance to Print* (Bloomington: Indiana University Press,
1984), which not only led me to Richard Bauman's *Verbal Art as Performance*
(Prospect Heights, Ill.: Waveland Press, 1984) and Arnold Berleant's *The Aesthetic
Field* (Springfield, Ill.: Charles C. Thomas, 1970), but which summarizes and
synthesizes current work and theory in the whole area with genuine clarity and
simplicity, though without claim to final truth. If my piece leads any readers to her
book, or to the wonderful things that are happening to literary theory and practice
in the realms of Native American literature both old and contemporary, it will have
served a good purpose.

else improvised according to strong guiding conventions of structure and technique.

Notation—the writing of music and the means of printing it and now the photoreproduction technology that makes even manuscript infinitely reproducible—had a huge effect on both the composition and the performance of music. Yet there is a lot of music that actively resists or evades notation, including some of the liveliest contemporary music (jazz, synthesizer composition). And written music, in any case, did not replace performance. We don't go to the symphony or the rock concert and each sit there reading a printed score in silence.

But that's exactly what we do in the library.

Why did it happen to words and not to music? A dumb question, but I need an answer to it. Which, I guess, might be that the note is purely a sound, the word impurely a sound. The word is a sound that symbolizes, has significance; though it is not pure information, it is or can function as a sign. Insofar as it is a sign it can be replaced by another sign, equally arbitrary, and this sign can be a visual one. The note, having no symbolic value in itself, no "meaning," can't be replaced by a sign. It can only be indicated by one.

Word spoken and note sung both enter the mind through that whorled and delicate fleshly gateway the ear. Poem written or song written come through that crystalline receiver of quanta the eye, in search of the inner, the mental ear. In music, this eye detour is a convenience, an adjunct only; music goes on being what is sounded and heard. But the written word found a detour past both outer ear and inner ear to nonsensory understanding. A kind of short circuit, a way around the body. Written text can be read as pure sign, as meaning alone. When we started doing that, the word stopped being an event.

I'm not complaining, you know. If it weren't for writing, for books, how could I be a novelist married to a historian? Written language is the greatest single technology of the storage and dissemination of knowledge, which is the primary act of human culture. It gives us all the libraries full of books of science, reference, fact, theory, thought. It gives us newspapers, journals. It gives us interoffice memos, catalogues of obscure forms of potholder and electric tempeh shredder, and the reports of federal committees on deforestation printed on paper that used to be a forest. That's how it is—we're literate. And we're word processors now too, since information theory and the computer are hooked up together. That's dandy. But why do we lock ourselves into one mode? Why either/or? *We* aren't binary. Why have we replaced oral text with written? Isn't there room for both? Spoken text doesn't even take storage room; it's self-recycling and does not require wood pulp. Why have we abandoned and despised the interesting things that happen when the word behaves like music and the author is not just "a writer" but the player of the instrument of language?

The stage: yes. Plays get printed, but their life is still clearly in performance, in the actors' breath, the audience's response. But the drama isn't central to our literature any more. Nor is the aesthetic power of the language of drama central to it, at present. The power and glory of Renaissance plays, or of a writer as recent as Synge, is the language; but for fifty years or more we've been satisfied in the theater by the mere selective imitation of common speech. I wonder if this isn't partly the influence of movies and TV. A play is words, it is nothing but words; in film the words are secondary, the medium is a visual one where the strongest aesthetic values are not verbal at all.

That doesn't mean that words have to be as badly treated as they are in most film and TV drama. The media use words like they were sanitary landfill. Even radio, the aural medium par excellence, where in the early decades there was a lot of real wordplay, mostly uses words only to give the news and weather. Talk shows aren't art, and rock lyrics keep getting more rudimentary. Radio drama has made a small comeback on NPR, and NPR radio readings have led to a demand for cassettes of readings to play during commuter gridlock, but that's still a tiny sideline to book publishing. Our text is still silent.

Where have I *heard* language as art? In some, some few, speeches—Martin Luther King. . . . In some well-told ghost stories at the campfire, and some really funny dirty jokes, and from my mother at eighty telling us her experience in the 1906 earthquake when she was nine. From comedians with a great text, like Bill Cosby's *Chickenheart,* or Anna Russell's version of the *Ring,* aesthetically far superior to Wagner's. From poets reading, live or on tape, and fiction writers performing—prose pros, you might call them. But from amateurs too. People reading aloud to each other. And here's a point I've been aiming at: If you can read silently you can read aloud. It takes practice, sure, but it's like playing the guitar; you don't have to be Doc Watson, you can get and give pleasure just pickin'. And second point: A lot of the stuff we were taught to read silently—Jane! You are moving your lips!—reads better out loud.

Reading aloud is of course the basic test of a kid's book. If you apply it to literary works written for adults reading in the silent-perusal mode—that is, in prose—the results can be positively, or negatively, surprising. An example: The present-tense narrative so much in vogue, particularly in "minimalist" fiction, seems more casual and more immediate than the conventional narrative-past tense; but read aloud, it sounds curiously stilted and artificial; its ultimate effect of distancing the text from the reader becomes clear. Another example: Last spring after reading *Persuasion* to each other, my partner and I decided tentatively and unhopefully to have a bash at *To the Lighthouse*. When Austen wrote, people still read aloud a great deal, and she clearly heard her text and suited its cadences to the voice; but Woolf, so cerebral and subtle and . . . so, we found our only problem was that our reading got impeded by tears, shouts of delight, and other manifestations of intellectual exhilaration and uncontrollable emotion. I will never read Virginia Woolf silently again, if I can help it; you miss half what she was doing.

As for poetry, the Beats brought the breath of life back to it, and then Caedmon Records, with that first Dylan Thomas recording; and these days all poets tell you earnestly that they write to be heard. I've become a bit skeptical. I think some of them write to be printed on the pages of magazines, because their stuff goes kind of stiff, or kind of limp, performed. Other stuff that doesn't look like much lying on the page comes to terrific life embodied in the voice. But since poets become poets by publishing in the magazines, the premium is still on the work that works silently. The poem that works better orally can be dismissed as a "performance piece," with all the usual disparagements of oral texts: primitive, crude, repetitive, naive, etc., etc., etc. Some techniques proper to oral poetry stick out awkwardly in print (just as eye-poetry devices like a series of one-word lines or typographical trickery are useless or worse in performance). The poets who really work in both modes at once, like Ted Hughes or Carolyn Kizer, aren't common (but tend to be looked down upon as "common" by the magazine mandarins). My impression is that at present women are more interested in voice-poetry than men. Women may turn to the living voice, the ephemeral, subversive performance, deliberately to escape the macho-mandarin control over "literature." One of the poems that started me thinking about this is Judy Grahn's "She Who," in *The Work of a Common Woman* (St. Martin's Press, 1978), a poem that

must be read aloud, cannot be read silently: its appearance in print
is like music notation—an indication of performance.

> She Who
> She, she SHE, she SHE, she WHO?
> she - she WHO she - WHO she WHO - SHE?
> She, she who? she WHO? she, WHO SHE?
>
> who who SHE, she - who, she WHO - WHO?
> she WHO - who, WHO - who, WHO - who, WHO - who. . . . .
>
> She. who - WHO, she WHO. She WHO - who SHE?
> who she SHE, who SHE she, SHE - who WHO —
> She WHO?
> She SHE who, She, she SHE
> she SHE, she SHE who.
> *SHEEE*   *WHOOOOOO*

(When I was planning this talk I found, in a book by the Tai Chi
master Da Liu, a description of Taoist breathing: "the sounds *hu*,
shi, . . . blowing and breathing with open mouth . . . evoking harmony." Hear that, Judy?)

With stuff like that around, I began to wonder why I had to work
in silence all my life, as if I were writing in a giant library with a
giant librarian always going *ssshhh*. . . .

My last book, *Always Coming Home*, is about a nonexistent Californian people called the Kesh, who had a lively tradition of both oral
and written literature, never having scrapped one in favor of the
other. Many of the translations from the Kesh in the book (the Kesh
language, incidentally, came into being only after most of the translations from it were made) are texts of performance pieces, nota-
tions of verse, narrative, or drama that properly exists, like music,
as sound. There is a piece of a novel, which, like our novels, exists
primarily in writing to be read in silence, and equally there are
transcriptions of stories told aloud, from the improvised to the fixed
ritual recitation. Most Kesh poetry was occasional—the highest
form, according to Goethe—and much of it was made by what we
call amateurs, people doing poetry as a common skill, the way
people do sewing or cooking, as an ordinary and essential part of
being alive. The quality of such poetry, sewing, and cooking of
course varies enormously. We have been taught that only poetry of
extremely high quality is poetry at all; that poetry is a big deal, and
you have to be a pro to write it, or, in fact, to read it. This is what
keeps a few poets and many, many English departments alive.

That's fine, but I was after something else: the poem not as fancy pastry but as bread; the poem not as masterpiece but as life-work.

I don't believe that such an attitude towards poetry leads, as it might seem to, to any devaluing of the poet's singular gift, or patient craft, or sullen art. After all, Shakespeare wrote when every gent was scribbling sonnets; the common practice of an art indeed may be the surest guarantee of quality in professional practice of it.

A "secondary" professional—a critic or an English professor— might be inclined to say that the standards of nonprofessional poetry are lower. But the Kesh did not use higher and lower as values; nor do I. They used central and less central, to state where their values were, what they prized and praised; and poetry was at the center. So, not surprisingly, it is for me.

But I would certainly agree that the standards must be different. Very different. Insofar as our poetry and its criticism has been "professional," which is to say male-dominated, I am out to subvert it wherever I can. A masculine poetics depends ultimately upon the absence of women, the objectification of Woman and Nature. If Kesh verse does nothing else, at least it spits in the eye of Papa Lacan.

After translating from the Kesh for a couple of years, I came back to English as a First Language—but changed. I had been talking womantalk, and I went on wanting to work with the voice, not the silent word. At the same time, having done a little work with technicians in sound studios, I was greatly impressed with their gifts and arts; and the two interests naturally tended to come together on tape. Audio tape of course is used principally to reproduce, to make infinite copies. But it can be used as an artistic medium in itself, working with the speaking voice, using dynamics, pitch change, doubletracking, cutting, and all the dodges and delicacies of the sound technician's craft and the resources of increasingly refined instruments. Poets can play new games here, just as they did when printing (also a technology of reproduction) was new. Unless the poet can afford the machineries and becomes a technician, the work has to be a collaboration; but then, all performance is collaboration. Poetry as the big solo ego trip is only one version of the art; there are others, equally enjoyable and demanding.

Audio poetry is not, of course, performance: if you buy the tape you have the reproduction, not the event. You have the unmortal shadow. But at least it isn't silent; at least the text was woven with the living voice.

"WHO IS RESPONSIBLE?"

(1987)

In the spring of 1987, Pamela Sargent, Ian Watson, and George Zebrowski asked several writers for a response—to be printed in the Bulletin of the Science Fiction Writers of America—to the following question: "What should science fiction be? Is that what it is? Who is responsible for its current state?"

I was at first hesitant about answering at all, because although I am a science-fiction writer, I am not only a science-fiction writer, and will perhaps never know the field so purely from within as the writers whose entire work is there; so who am I to tell them what's what? But then I realized that this had never bothered me until some people who write about sf began saying that I had "turned my back on science fiction," ratted out, gone mainstream, headed for Fame and Money in the Eastern Literary Establishment, and generally played apostate, all of which had made me a bit self-conscious, as well as a bit cross. Facing that self-consciousness, I decided that though I didn't have a whole lot to say on this particular subject, I'd go ahead and say it, and not let myself be silenced; for although I am not only a science-fiction writer, I am a science-fiction writer, and as such am entitled to the usual passionate feelings about the whole thing.

"What should science fiction be? Is that what it is?"

All my noisiest ego-people, the moralist, the preacher, the legislator, the know-it-all, love an invitation to say what something "should" be, and they drown out the softer voices of my mind, the storyteller, the poet, the feminist, the clown, who aren't all that sure what science fiction should be or even what it is. But all of us in here agree on the third question, "Who is responsible for its current state?" To that I reply unanimously: Nobody's responsible for science fiction, surely, but the people who write it and the people who read it.

Editors, publishers, agents, booksellers, promoters, book clubs, fan organizations, awards boards, reviewers, critics, teachers of literature and of writing, all have immense influence on what is written and read in sf; and editors, publishers, and chain bookstores in particular have a great deal of control over it. But all the same I don't think they're responsible for it. Control is a matter of power-over; it's when you have the power-to that you're responsible.

The market's, marketers', or censors' area of control over what's printed and the writer/reader's area of autonomy and responsibility may overlap happily or conflict destructively. In this country, though the market pressure is enormous and there is indirect censorship, I think the size of our area of power is pretty much up to us (us being the writers and readers). Of course, if we hand over control of our work, at any stage, to them (them being the middlemen), they'll take it, and the area of our autonomous action will shrink. To accept the responsibility of writing and reading not what they tell us is wanted / will sell / other people want / we "should," but what we choose to write and read, is to increase the area of our power, both personal and as members of a community of writers and readers.

At present it seems that many people are allowing market control over sf to dominate other options and values, and correspondingly the feeling of community among sf people seems rather weaker than it was. But whether we choose to write for the market, for the critics, for love, for fans, for survival, or for all of that or none of that or a mixture, I don't see how anybody can be blamed or praised or held responsible for our words but ourselves.

CONFLICT

(1987)

From looking at manuals used in college writing courses, and from listening to participants in writing workshops, I gather that it is a generally received idea that a story is the relation of a conflict, that without conflict there is no plot, that narrative and conflict are inseparable.

Now, that something or other has to happen in a story, I agree (in very general, broad terms; there are, after all, excellent stories in which everything has happened, or is about to happen). But that what happens in a story can be defined as, limited to, conflict, I doubt. And that to assert the dependence of narrative on conflict is to uphold Social Darwinism in all its glory, I sadly suspect.

Existence as struggle, life as a battle, everything in terms of defeat and victory: Man versus Nature, Man versus Woman, Black versus White, Good versus Evil, God versus Devil—a sort of apartheid view of existence, and of literature. What a pitiful impoverishment of the complexity of both!

In E. M. Forster's famous definition (in *Aspects of the Novel*), this is a story:

> The King died and then the Queen died.

And this is a plot:

> The King died and then the Queen died of grief.

In that charming and extremely useful example, where is the "conflict"? Who is pitted against what? Who wins?

Is the first book of *Genesis* a story? Where is the "conflict"?

Has *War and Peace* a plot? Can that plot be in any useful or meaningful way reduced to "conflict," or a series of "conflicts"?

People are cross-grained, aggressive, and full of trouble, the storytellers tell us; people fight themselves and one another, and their stories are full of their struggles. But to say that that *is* the story is to use one aspect of existence, conflict, to include and submerge other aspects which it does not include and does not comprehend.

Romeo and Juliet is a story of the conflict between two families, and its plot involves the conflict of two individuals with those families. Is that all it involves? Isn't *Romeo and Juliet* about something else, and isn't it the something else that makes the otherwise trivial tale of a feud into a tragedy?

I for one will be glad when this gladiatorial view of fiction has run its course. I may then have time to find out how and when the tremendous word "epiphany," which I thought meant the coming of the Holy into the holy place, began to be thrown around in writing courses to mean, I gather, something like the high point of the plot, the crux or *noeud,* the moment when it all comes together, in such stories as have such a moment. This is a pretty hifalutin word for a pretty ordinary narrative event. I wonder if James Joyce is responsible for its cheapening; I seem to recall that he talked about "having epiphanies" in his bathroom. I guess you have to have a fairly high opinion of yourself and your bathroom to talk that way.

"WHERE DO YOU GET YOUR IDEAS FROM?"

(1987)

With thanks to my students in the fiction workshops at Haystack, Clarion West, and Humboldt Community College, in the summer and fall of 1987, whose work and talk enabled me to write this.

Whenever I talk with an audience after a reading or lecture, somebody asks me, "Where do you get your ideas from?" A fiction writer can avoid being asked that question only by practicing the dourest naturalism and forswearing all acts of the imagination. Science-fiction writers can't escape it, and develop habitual answers to it: "Schenectady," says Harlan Ellison. Vonda N. McIntyre takes this further, explaining that there is a mail order house for ideas in Schenectady, to which writers can subscribe for five or ten or (bargain rate) twenty-five ideas a month; then she hits herself on the head to signify remorse, and tries to answer the question seriously. Even in its most patronizing form—"Where do you get all those crazy ideas from?"—it is almost always asked seriously: the asker really wants to know.

The reason why it is unanswerable is, I think, that it involves at least two false notions, myths, about how fiction is written.

First myth: There is a secret to being a writer. If you can just learn the secret, you will instantly be a writer; and the secret might be where the ideas come from.

Second myth: Stories start from ideas; the origin of a story is an idea.

I will dispose of the first myth as quickly as possible. The "secret" is skill. If you haven't learned how to do something, the people who have may seem to be magicians, possessors of mysterious secrets. In a fairly simple art, such as making pie crust, there are certain teachable "secrets" of method that lead almost infallibly to good results; but in any complex art, such as housekeeping, piano-playing, clothes-making, or story-writing, there are so many techniques, skills, choices of method, so many variables, so many "secrets," some teachable and some not, that you can learn them only by methodical, repeated, long-continued practice—in other words, by work.

Who can blame the secret-seekers for hoping to find a shortcut and avoid all the work?

Certainly the work of learning any art is hard enough that it is unwise (so long as you have any choice in the matter) to spend much time and energy on an art you don't have a decided talent for. Some of the secretiveness of many artists about their techniques, recipes, etc., may be taken as a warning to the unskilled: What works for me isn't going to work for you unless you've worked for it.

My talent and inclination for writing stories and keeping house were strong from the start, and my gift for and interest in music and sewing were weak; so that I doubt that I would ever have been a good seamstress or pianist, no matter how hard I worked. But nothing I know about how I learned to do the things I am good at doing leads me to believe that there are "secrets" to the piano or the sewing machine or any art I'm no good at. There is just the obstinate, continuous cultivation of a disposition, leading to skill in performance.

So much for secrets. How about ideas?

The more I think about the word "idea," the less idea I have what it means. Writers do say things like "That gives me an idea" or "I got the idea for that story when I had food poisoning in a motel in New Jersey." I think this is a kind of shorthand use of "idea" to stand for the complicated, obscure, un-understood process of the conception and formation of what is going to be a story when it gets written down. The process may not involve ideas in the sense of intelligible thoughts; it may well not even involve words. It may be a matter of mood, resonances, mental glimpses, voices, emotions, visions, dreams, anything. It is different in every writer, and in many of us it is different every time. It is extremely difficult to talk about, because we have very little terminology for such processes.

I would say that as a general rule, though an external event may trigger it, this inceptive state or story-beginning phase does not come from anywhere outside the mind that can be pointed to; it arises in the mind, from psychic contents that have become unavailable to the conscious mind, inner or outer experience that has been, in Gary Snyder's lovely phrase, composted. I don't believe that a writer "gets" (takes into the head) an "idea" (some sort of mental object) "from" somewhere, and then turns it into words and writes them on paper. At least in my experience, it doesn't work that way. The stuff has to be transformed into oneself, it has to be composted, before it can grow a story.

The rest of this paper will be an attempt to analyze what I feel I am actually working with when I write, and where the "idea" fits into the whole process.

There seem to be five principal elements to the process:

1. The patterns of the language—the sounds of words.

2. The patterns of syntax and grammar; the ways the words and sentences connect themselves together; the ways their connections interconnect to form the larger units (paragraphs, sections, chapters); hence, the movement of the work, its tempo, pace, gait, and shape in time.

(Note: In poetry, especially lyric poetry, these first two kinds of patterning are salient, obvious elements of the beauty of the work—word sounds, rhymes, echoes, cadences, the "music" of poetry. In prose the sound patterns are far subtler and looser and must indeed avoid rhyme, chime, assonance, etc., and the patterns of sentencing, paragraphing, movement and shape in time, may be on such a large, slow scale as to escape conscious notice; the "music" of fiction, particularly the novel, is often not perceived as beautiful at all.)

3. The patterns of the images: what the words make us or let us see with the mind's eye or sense imaginatively.

4. The patterns of the ideas: what the words and the narration of events make us understand, or use our understanding upon.

5. The patterns of the feelings: what the words and the narration, by using all the above means, make us experience emotionally or spiritually, in areas of our being not directly accessible to or expressible in words.

All these kinds of patterning—sound, syntax, images, ideas, feel-ings—have to work together; and they all have to be there in some degree. The inception of the work, that mysterious stage, is perhaps their coming together: when in the author's mind a feeling begins to connect itself to an image that will express it, and that image leads to an idea, until now half-formed, that begins to find words for itself, and the words lead to other words that make new images, perhaps of people, characters of a story, who are doing things that express the underlying feelings and ideas that are now resonating with each other . . .

If any of the processes get scanted badly or left out, in the conception stage, in the writing stage, or in the revising stage, the result will be a weak or failed story. Failure often allows us to analyze what success triumphantly hides from us. I do not recommend going through a story by Chekhov or Woolf trying to analyze out my five elements of the writing process; the point is that in any success-ful piece of fiction, they work in one insoluble unitary movement. But in certain familiar forms of feeble writing or failed writing, the absence of one element or another may be a guide to what went wrong.

For example: Having an interesting idea, working it up into a plot enacted by stock characters, and relying upon violence to replace feeling, may produce the trash-level mystery, thriller, or science-fiction story; but not a good mystery, thriller, or science-fiction story.

Contrariwise, strong feelings, even if strong characters enact them, aren't enough to carry a story if the ideas connected with those feelings haven't been thought through. If the mind isn't working along with the emotions, the emotions will slosh around in a bathtub of wish fulfillment (as in most mass-market romances) or anger (as in much of the "mainstream" genre) or hormones (as in porn).

Beginners' failures are often the result of trying to work with strong feelings and ideas without having found the images to embody them, or without even knowing how to find the words and string them together. Ignorance of English vocabulary and gram-mar is a considerable liability to a writer of English. The best cure for it is, I believe, reading. People who learned to talk at two or so and have been practicing talking ever since feel with some justifica-tion that they know their language; but what they know is their spoken language, and if they read little, or read schlock, and haven't written much, their writing is going to be pretty much what

their talking was when they were two. It's going to require considerable practice. The attempt to play complicated music on an instrument which one hasn't even learned the fingering of is probably the
commonest weakness of beginning writers.

A rarer kind of failure is the story in which the words go career-
ing around bellowing and plunging and kicking up a lot of dust,
and when the dust settles you find they never got out of the corral.
They got nowhere, because they didn't know where they were going.
Feeling, idea, image, just got dragged into the stampede, and no
story happened. All the same, this kind of failure sometimes strikes
me as promising, because it reveals a writer reveling in pure language—letting the words take over. You can't go on that way, but it's
not a bad place to start from.

The novelist-poet Boris Pasternak said that poetry makes itself
from "the relationship between the sounds and the meanings of
words." I think that prose makes itself the same way, if you will allow
"sounds" to include syntax and the large motions, connections, and
shapes of narrative. There is a relationship, a reciprocity, between
the words and the images, ideas, and emotions evoked by those
words: the stronger that relationship, the stronger the work. To
believe that you can achieve meaning or feeling without coherent,
integrated patterning of the sounds, the rhythms, the sentence
structures, the images, is like believing you can go for a walk without
bones.

Of the five kinds of patterning that I have invented or analyzed
here, I think the central one, the one through which all the others
connect, is the imagery. Verbal imagery (such as a simile or a
description of a place or an event) is more physical, more bodily,
than thinking or feeling, but less physical, more internal, than the
actual sounds of the words. Imagery takes place in "the imagination," which I take to be the meeting place of the thinking mind
with the sensing body. What is imagined isn't physically real, but it
feels as if it were: the reader sees or hears or feels what goes on in the
story, is drawn into it, exists in it, among its images, in the imagination (the reader's? the writer's?) while reading.

This illusion is a special gift of narrative, including the drama.
Narration gives us entry to a shared world of imagination. The
sounds and movement and connections of the words work to make
the images vivid and authentic; the ideas and emotions are embodied in and grow out of those images of places, of people, of events,
deeds, conversations, relationships; and the power and authenticity

of the images may surpass that of most actual experience, since in the imagination we can share a capacity for experience and an understanding of truth far greater than our own. The great writers share their souls with us—"literally."

This brings me to the relationship of the writer to the reader: a matter I again find easiest to approach through explainable failure. The shared imaginative world of fiction cannot be taken for granted, even by a writer telling a story set right here and now in the suburbs among people supposed to be familiar to everybody. The fictional world has to be created by the author, whether by the slightest hints and suggestions, which will do for the suburbs, or by very careful guidance and telling detail, if the reader is being taken to the planet Gzorx. When the writer fails to imagine, to *image*, the world of the narrative, the work fails. The usual result is abstract, didactic fiction. Plots that make points. Characters who don't talk or act like people, and who are in fact not imaginary people at all but mere bits of the writer's ego got loose, glibly emitting messages. The intellect cannot do the work of the imagination; the emotions cannot do the work of the imagination; and neither of them can do anything much in fiction without the imagination.

Where the writer and the reader collaborate to make the work of fiction is perhaps, above all, in the imagination. In the joint creation of the fictive world.

Now, writers are egoists. All artists are. They can't be altruists and get their work done. And writers love to whine about the Solitude of the Author's Life, and lock themselves into cork-lined rooms or droop around in bars in order to whine better. But although most writing is done in solitude, I believe that it is done, like all the arts, for an audience. That is to say, with an audience. All the arts are performance arts, only some of them are sneakier about it than others.

I beg you please to attend carefully now to what I am not saying. I am not saying that you should think about your audience when you write. I am not saying that the writing writer should have in mind, "Who will read this? Who will buy it? Who am I aiming this at?"—as if it were a gun. No.

While *planning* a work, the writer may and often must think about readers; particularly if it's something like a story for children, where you need to know whether your reader is likely to be a five-year-old or a ten-year-old. Considerations of who will or might read the piece are appropriate and sometimes actively useful in planning it, thinking about it, thinking it out, inviting images. But once you start writing, it is fatal to think about anything but the writing. True work is done for the sake of doing it. What is to be done with it afterwards is another matter, another job. A story rises from the springs of creation, from the pure will to be; it tells itself; it takes its own course, finds its own way, its own words; and the writer's job is to be its medium. What a teacher or editor or market or critic or Alice will think of it has to be as far from the writing writer's mind as what breakfast was last Tuesday. Farther. The breakfast might be useful to the story.

Once the story is written, however, the writer must forgo that divine privacy and accept the fact that the whole thing has been a performance, and it had better be a good one.

When I, the writer, reread my work and settle down to reconsider it, reshape it, revise it, then my consciousness of the reader, of collaborating with the reader, is appropriate and, I think, necessary. Indeed I may have to make an act of faith and declare that they will exist, those unknown, perhaps unborn people, my dear readers. The blind, beautiful arrogance of the creative moment must grow subtle, self-conscious, clear-sighted. It must ask questions, such as: Does this say what I thought it said? Does it say all I thought it did? It is at this stage that I, the writer, may have to question the nature of my relationship to my readers, as manifested in my work. Am I shoving them around, manipulating them, patronizing them, showing off to them? Am I punishing them? Am I using them as a dump site for my accumulated psychic toxins? Am I telling them what they better damn well believe or else? Am I running circles around them, and will they enjoy it? Am I scaring them, and did I intend to? Am I interesting them, and if not, hadn't I better see to it that I am? Am I amusing, teasing, alluring them? Flirting with them? Hypnotizing them? Am I giving to them, tempting them, inviting them, drawing them into the work *to work with me*—to be the one, the Reader, who completes my vision?

Because the writer cannot do it alone. The unread story is not a story; it is little black marks on wood pulp. The reader, reading it, makes it live: a live thing, a story.

A special note to the above: If the writer is a socially privileged person—particularly a White or a male or both—his imagination may have to make an intense and conscious effort to realize that people who don't share his privileged status may read his work and will not share with him many attitudes and opinions that he has been allowed to believe or to pretend are shared by "everybody." Since the belief in a privileged view of reality is no longer tenable outside privileged circles, and often not even within them, fiction written from such an assumption will make sense only to a decreasing, and increasingly reactionary, audience. Many women writing today, however, still choose the male viewpoint, finding it easier to do so than to write from the knowledge that feminine experience of reality is flatly denied by many potential readers, including the majority of critics and professors of literature, and may rouse defensive hostility and contempt. The choice, then, would seem to be between collusion and subversion; but there's no use pretending that you can get away without making the choice. Not to choose, these days, is a choice made. All fiction has ethical, political, and social weight, and sometimes the works that weigh the heaviest are those apparently fluffy or escapist fictions whose authors declare themselves "above politics," "just entertainers," and so on.

The writer writing, then, is trying to get all the patterns of sounds, syntax, imagery, ideas, emotions, working together in one process, in which the reader will be drawn to participate. This implies that writers do one hell of a lot of controlling. They control all their material as closely as they can, and in doing so they are trying to control the reader, too. They are trying to get the reader to go along helplessly, putty in their hands, seeing, hearing, feeling, believing the story, laughing at it, crying at it. They are trying to make innocent little children cry.

But though control is a risky business, it need not be conceived in confrontational terms as a battle with and a victory over the material or the reader. Again, I think it comes down to collaboration, or sharing the gift: the writer tries to get the reader working with the text in the effort to keep the whole story all going along in one piece in the right direction (which is my general notion of a good piece of fiction).

In this effort, writers need all the help they can get. Even under the most skilled control, the words will never fully embody the vision. Even with the most sympathetic reader, the truth will falter and grow partial. Writers have to get used to launching something beautiful and watching it crash and burn. They also have to learn when to let go control, when the work takes off on its own and flies, farther than they ever planned or imagined, to places they didn't know they knew. All makers must leave room for the acts of the spirit. But they have to work hard and carefully, and wait patiently, to deserve them.

OVER THE HILLS
AND A GREAT WAY OFF

(1988)

My husband and I have known Barbara since 1968, when we and our children spent a sabbatical year in her son's house in Islington. At that time she also lived in London; after her husband's death, she moved to the Berkshire village of Inkpen, where, on our next sabbatical, we often stayed with her and went with her on long walks on the Berkshire and Wiltshire Downs, to Stonehenge, to the other great henge, Avebury, and to the Vale of the White Horse. Life in the lovely, lonely Inkpen house began to be difficult for a woman in her seventies, and so she moved recently to a sunny little house in Oxford. She is "English Granny" to our three grown children, who have all been to stay with her. It was our turn: we went to England in September to see Barbara. England, too; London, of course—a land and a city we love to return to; but at the heart of it is the person, the dear friend, the wellspring. And we'd been promising for years to "do" Dorset and Somerset with her.

What we didn't know was that much of that journey, all new country to us, would be for her a returning to the source. Chideock was where her family went, summers, for their seacoast holiday, when she was a little child. She had climbed Golden Cap, the highest headland of England's south coast, exactly fifty years before, in 1937, with her young husband and her baby son. She had tramped the long dike paths of Dorchester's great Iron Age fort, Maiden Castle, with a granddaughter. She knew the roads and the byroads, and how to find hidden Toller Fratrum and its tiny, ancient barnyard church. For her, the journey was return; and therefore for us, all its intensity of unknownness was doubled with a shared nostalgia, a familiar tenderness, which was again redoubled by the soft, rainy, breezy, gleaming weathers of autumn in the west of England, so like the autumn of our Oregon so much farther west.

I kept this journal while we drove, or before sleep, so that we might return again to these places, with Barbara, in words and memory—just as I took photographs along the way. Like photographs, a diary doesn't explain, it just reacts; but I don't think much needs explaining to those unfamiliar with the countryside, except perhaps the Cerne Giant, in whose village we stayed three nights. He is a huge figure cut into the side of a steep hill; the hill is chalk covered with grass, so he is outlined white on green, and has been since the Dark Ages. He is, unmistakably and tremendously, a fertility symbol. And perhaps I should assure you that though I am a fiction writer, I didn't make up a single one of the names of villages. You can find them all on a map, as I do sometimes, to remind myself that they are there, and that we were there, and might go back— with Barbara.

Friday, September 4. In the car. Barbara drives; Charles navigates; I stare and scribble.

We left Oxford about noon and are now on the A34 south, coming into rolling uplands dotted with trees in their varying distances. Fields grey-green or stubble-ocher. Sunlight and big sea clouds.

A bare-armed boy in a black singlet, herding calves by a haystack: his red-gold hair, white skin—the white is strange.

Now heading towards Hungerford and Bristol among brown and yellow plowlands paling into chalk streaks. Oaks and beeches, alone or in rows and groves.

A silvery quality to the green of this country, in this season.

Now off the artery onto the quieter Hungerford road; and through poor Hungerford haunted by the specters of the mass murder here last summer—the honest, familiar, curving street of shops where people want to buy cheese and letter paper and shoelaces, not to be slaughtered.

Into Wiltshire on the high road past Prosperous. Past pretty Shalbourne in its vale, shepherded by its small, square, grey church. Our road follows a ridgetop, steep swaling off to the left and up again to another long ridge. And now we're on an even smaller road, *down* between hedgerows—*up* onto the open downs—a sheep biting its ankle. Great, long, pale Wiltshire distances.

Down now into little thatch-browed, whitewashed, bright-gardened Collingbourne Ducis. Weeds sprouting from a long grey thatch. We discuss Barbara's friend Edmund's list of eligible wives, which did not include Barbara, she having crossed herself off before being asked, which annoyed Edmund considerably. We discuss the ugly way so many people dress themselves in London.

Red poppies, and black fighter planes, and white chalk.

We pass Stonehenge now, driving on the Amesbury Road, which I walked with my brother Karl in 1951. We had never been in England before, everything was new; we were twenty-four and twenty-one. We took the bus from Salisbury to Amesbury village so that we could come to Stonehenge on foot, because it seemed the right way to come to Stonehenge, and it was. We walked and walked, talking Housman and Borrow and Hardy, for we were very literary brats, and we kept seeing this little thing way off on a great downside, like a flock of sheep maybe, or stumps of trees, or more like stumps of teeth, really, giant's teeth, a ring . . . Is that *it*? Is that *them*? And so I first came walking among them, among those great presences, in the bright morning.

And then again, with Charles, in '54, the year we married. And other times, always walking out from Amesbury so that we could see the sheep become the teeth become the stones, so that we could walk back over the millennia. In '69 we walked it with the kids; the youngest was only four years old and never did approve of long hikes. He was bribed all the way out with the promise of a new Matchbox car, a red one; he got it, and played with it on the Altar stone, *vrrrooom, vrrooommmm* . . .

And then when we stayed with Barbara in '75, that Christmas, she took us over to Stonehenge on the evening of the winter solstice. If the druids had been there, they were gone. Everyone was gone. There was a long, golden, winter light on the stones, a light frost, a great and ancient silence on the high downs. Barbara took photographs of that honey light, which seemed to shine out of the stones themselves.

A couple of years after that, they put a steel fence around Stonehenge because too many people came and camped and trampled and chipped and trashed the stones. We said then we wouldn't go back. You learn to say goodbye to places: to keep them in your heart and go on, as we do now.

Down and up again . . . a big, hard-bitten farm on the Warminster road, a man in the field throwing lumps of fire to spread the field-burning blaze. A Tank Crossing sign; helicopters yammering. This is all military country.

Down down down between high gold slopes where they're making hay and into Chitterne village in its vale and up up up again to sheep against the sky. And the land is growing lumpy—a long barrow, then a round barrow on a chalky ridge—the old bones showing through.

Warminster, a grey stone and brick town, rather linear and grim.

We have stopped for lunch and are sitting in a field in a tiny village/farm just this side of Somerset. We sit on Barbara's mac and munch cheese, and a lonesome horse watches us from up the hill. We all pee in the hedgerow.

On again, into Frome of the many-splendored gardens, where a sign says Fish and Chips and Chinese Food. Out of Frome, and ridge-running across the long green land that drops to either side, intersected with dark hedgerows, dark trees. The green is vivid now, wet green.

Heavy Plant Crossing. I imagine giant artichokes lumbering across the road . . .

Beer Garden and Children's Play Area, in Shepton Mallet, and then Cannard's Grave Inn—a place for serious drinking.

A sheep under a round green hill scratches its stomach with a hind hoof thoughtfully.

And now we're at our bed-and-breakfast for tonight, West Holme Farm in North Wootton, having been greeted by kids, cats, dogs, and made welcome. Barbara's room is a long way down the hall from ours, a shining-floored, narrow hall, with windows, and steps up, and steps down, and little angle-turns. The farmhouse was built in fits and starts from the fifteenth to the nineteenth centuries; turn a corner and you're Elizabethan . . . Our room has two low-set, deep-set square windows, one looking out on rough red-tile roofs, green-mossed, and a rainy green ridge beyond them; the other on young Friesians (Holsteins to Charles and me), some of the hundred head of cattle this farm runs, black and glossy white, grazing for wind-falls among the apple trees of Avalon.

For this is the Vale of Apples, this is Arthurian country, legendary land. When we first talked with Barbara about coming here, back a dozen years ago, we had been reading up on King Arthur, who and when he might have been in history, and where he might have gone in the old West Country. By now we've all forgotten all the facts we read, but not the legends. They're not forgettable, and Malory, Tennyson, and White are with us here.

Barbara finds her way from the Victorian Era to the Elizabethan Age to tell us that it's stopping raining and we can be off to Glastonbury. On the way we get our first glimpse of Glastonbury Tor, bare, abrupt, dark, topped with a broken tower, rising like an island over the rainy fields. An island it was; for all these farmlands were bog, marsh, and lake. The Iron Age town of Glastonbury was wealthy and famous, protected by water on all sides, an island within the greater island, England. So to the rich Glastonbury of Roman times St. Joseph of Arimathea came, so goes the tale, and climbed that other hill just above the town, Weary-All Hill, and planted a hawthorn by the church he founded. The church grew, building and rebuilding itself over the centuries (like West Holme Farm) till its fall and ruin when Henry VIII broke the power of the monks; but the descendant of St. Joseph's tree still flourishes, and bears its tiny roses in the dead of winter, at Christmastime—a faithful miracle, a not uncommon genetic oddity in hawthorns.

So we walked the ruins of Glastonbury Abbey all the afternoon, wandering in sky-ceilinged chapels, through apple orchards, past the pond, seeking that holy thorn the whole time, and finally finding it right back where we started from: a venerable little patriarch of a tree, crouching by the wall near the entrance gate.

Out to the farm then, to wash and change, and back to the Methodist chapel turned house and workshop where the potters Liz Raeburn and Rod Lawrence live, and entertain us with their beautiful three-year-old son Haydon, whisky, dinner, good talk, and good pots. We discussed the Rajneeshees, a far cry from eastern Oregon. Drove back to the farm in the country night, and slept in pure silence, until the wind came up again and wuthered in a baritone organ tone around the house, and the rain came in great soft gusts.

Saturday, September 5. I am sitting now on the curve of the staircase up to the Chapter House of Wells Cathedral, the second most beautiful staircase in the world, surely, after the one in the Laurentian Library in Florence. The choir is practicing; music rings along the high spaces defined by stone. The smell of stone, grey stone with a hint of rose-beige. Little stone faces high and low look down out of the old centuries.

We got very rained-on eating sandwiches at a deli across from the west face of Wells Cathedral, and hurried to find Pac-A-Macs in town. Mine is baby-green, Charles's baby-blue, Women's XL Size, Made in China; keep English rain off very well. Then back through

the tors-and-vales once-was-swamp to Pilton, and to the Old
Vicarage, our new B&B. Our large room looks down upon the
vicar's church, the spire on one corner of the square church tower
about level with the window. We walked the deep lanes of the village
to high fields above it, before dinner; it is a steep town, with a deep
stream. There are some good monsters on the south church wall. A
silky bear-colored cat came in to visit and slept on my shirts in my
suitcase, and fowls and a rabbit and two children wander and hop
about the big back garden. But it is a vicar's cold house, compared
with last night's sweet, buttery, cidery farm.

An enormous dinner at the Apple Tree on the Glastonbury road.

Sunday, September 6. Barbara's back, which has moods, was in a good
mood, and we all wanted to be outside. So we went back to Glastonbury and walked up the tor, starting from Chilkwell Street, where
we left the car. A lovely windy walk. At the top it came on to rain and
blow, and dark rain-mist ate up all the west and south of the
immense countryside of green strip fields and dark green hedgerows and ridges and levels and red roofs and round tor-sides. It
stopped raining as we went down the other side, and we went to the
Holy Well, or Chalice Well, which is only holy as all springs are: a
lovely red iron-water running into wading pools, healing pools, in
delightful small gardens cut into the side of the tor, under the high
skyline.

Lunch with Dora Raeburn, Liz's mother and Barbara's old friend,
and her friend Anita, and Liz, Rod, and Haydon, in the house semi-
attached to the chapel house. "Cholls! Cholls!" Haydon cries, impe-
rious; he likes Charles. He sits on Charles's lap, sucking his thumb,
and dreamily fingers Charles's dewlap; when he sits on his grandmother's lap, he uses her earlobe the same way.

In all these places vast cats are to be seen, cats the size of small
pumas.

Monday, September 7. We set off from hilly Pilton in the mild, rainy
late morning along winding byways to Pylle. I am writing in the
back seat of the car. Past Evercreech and onto the Fosseway, long
and Roman-straight, which takes us down onto the Somerset Levels,
the lowlands low. Left past cows to Hornblotton among apples. Go
in square zigs around every farm's flat fields across Cary Moor to
North Barrow, and then up and down and round about, Charles

guiding us by the half-inch map, to North Cadbury, South Cadbury and its great Iron Age fort, past Pauncefoot, Sutton Montis, Queen Camel . . . We stop to see St. Thomas à Becket Church, which seems to be frequented mostly by sheep, and then on, out of Somerset into Dorset, at last!

Over a beacon hill, down big, deep hills past dark woods, to Sherborne. A busy town with a confusing car park and a fine, steep High Street; everyone looks somewhat as if they had voted for Margaret Thatcher and were pleased at the result; many Volvos. A pleasant woman popped out of an office to set us on the right way to Sherborne Abbey. We fortified ourselves with egg and cress sandwiches at a tea shop and then did the abbey, which I found handsome but not endearing. Visited Barbara's publisher friend at Alpha Books, once we found it, then blundered around Robin Hood's barn back to the elusive car park. Round about again to find the Dorchester Road, and finally found it.

Please Take Your Litter Home. Is this addressed to the vast cats?

Cyril Tite, Car Breaker. For young cars that need a firm hand on the reins, I guess?

In deep country, through thick beech and oak woods, over a hilltop, all twisty stone walls, to Up Cerne—which consists of a Great House and its properties. A man in tweeds came stalking along the road with his stick and snubbed us as we stood looking at the view, which he referred to as "My View." (Later we found that the place is owned by a bunch of Austrian businessmen who come there only to shoot grouse or something, and he was a complete fake, which is nice.) Then we drove on down, past Giant Hill, where we got a fine afternoon view of the giant, to Cerne Abbas. Our B&B is the Sound o' Water—named from a William Barnes poem—on Duck Street, by the little quiet-running Cerne, in this bright, quiet hill village. Flint, brick, and stone in courses; half-timbering. The small church, mostly tower, has striped courses, and strange faces peer from corners all over it. A cool, bright evening. We found dinner, good plaice and good beer, at the Red Lion. Going to sleep, an owl crying, wailing, in the big woods of beech and oak that stand all round the streets.

Tuesday, September 8. Waking in the morning to "Tak' *two* coos, Taffy . . . Tak' *two* coos, Taffy . . . Tak'—" What do our western mourning doves say? It's not quite the same sentence, but I can't recall it, hearing this.

I was up at seven to bathe in the radiantly clean, moss-green and violet bathroom in the sunny, clear, cool September morning. A good English breakfast and then back to the little church to photograph the stone faces in better light. On to St. Austin's Well, a spring in old stone basins under huge lime trees, behind the church, below the graveyard. Then we followed the path up onto Giant Hill, misled at first by sheep trails; up by the fence, for the Giant has to be fenced in, like Stonehenge, because "we are too many." Wonderful combes and hillsides enlarging as we climb. On along the hilltop past the fence through thistly bits to where you can walk freely about the tumuli and small earthworks of a village and field system of the Iron Age or earlier, and see all about the beautiful hills: Wancombe Hill and Rowdon Hill and down into strange-shaped Yetcombe Bottom. (Kiddle's Bottom, the map shows, is farther south.) Then we come on back down the other side of the Giant, and can see him a little, the chalk lines along the hill slopes. Back below him, through the beech and sycamore woods, into town.

We bought crackers and tomatoes and cheese and Rybena and picnicked on Black Hill in a green field under a blue sky.

On to Dorchester, to Maiden Castle, that great work of hands. We circumambulated it first by car—unintentionally, trying to find the way to it—then on foot, deliberately. Sun and wind and the immense earthworks. Four thousand years. Sheep have been replaced by archaeologists, not an improvement. But you can still be quite alone, watching the hawk hunting.

Back via the valley of the Piddle. We stopped for the church in Piddlehinton; we passed the Piddle Valley Microwave store in Piddletrenthide; and came on across Kiddle's Bottom right up onto a high chalk ridge that took us straight to Cerne Abbas, which now feels very much like home to the leg-weary who have walked so far back today in time.

Wednesday, September 9. I woke this morning to a rather thin, middle-aged male voice in my mind saying the following poem:

The Earthworks of Mai-Dun

Men hurry to hurt and kill.
Great nations fall.
Still the hawk hangs still
On the wind above the wall.

It sounds very like Thomas Hardy, but not in top form.

At breakfast, when we told Mr. Simmonds, our kind host, where we were planning to go, he said, "An upalong downalong day," and so it is as I ride in the back of the car—to Toller Fratrum. This is a magical place, no more than a farm, a big farm not even a village, but the farm has a chapel with a font carved in the Dark Ages, and the barn was where the brothers ate, the refectory; the beautiful farmhouse is early seventeenth century. The hills rise up all around in sun and silence.

And on to Toller Porcorum, wonderfully named, with its staunch Dorset church standing, as the guide booklet points out, on seven feet of buried villagers—the mound that raises church and churchyard above the village lanes. More excellent openmouthed "gurgoils" staring down from the grey walls. Inside the church, numerous crewelwork pigs.

And on upalong downalong to wild, lonesome, hilly Powerstock under a Stone Age fort past and through dark oak forests, acorns for the Toller Porcorum pigs—wild boars for kings to hunt. Through a tunnel cut in sandstone and roofed with tree branches and vines, smelling earthy, rocky, dark, and then out and up onto the big hills again, past Pymore and past Dottery, to the sea. Thalassa, Thalassa! cries Barbara.

We lunched on the beach of Chideock Sea Town, all ruddy tawny flints and agates—and oddly some obsidian—and Barbara did Tai Chi down at the waves' edge. Then we made the ascent of Golden Cap, the high head that dominates that coast; Barbara had climbed it last in 1937, so it was a golden anniversary. We could see east past Eype, pronounced Eep, to Portland Bill curving out grandly, and west past Lyme Regis to the far blue coasts.

We went back up to Moore's Dorset Bakery, where Barbara used to buy Dorset knobs in 1912 or so, but the silly people "only bake knobs in the winter now"; so we settled for some butter cookies, cursing. Then back in the car past Swyre and Puncknowle, through Littlebredy, red thatched house in deep gloomy vale, huge stone H-shaped barn with a high slate roof and a stone-walled yard crammed jammed full of lowing black and white cattle. Up again. The rivers run clear, clear, a clear stream runs through Sydling St. Nicholas. They are field-burning, the air dims.

Home to Sound o' Water and a good whisky and a long wait for dinner at the Red Lion. The owls called again in the night, two and then three of them, a pure, quavering, falling cry and reply.

Thursday, September 10. At breakfast, Doug Simmonds sang for us his beautiful song of the old man that lived on Chesil Beach under a boat. He showed us his garden, lovely, half encircled by the little clear Cerne. Charles and I had been up at seven to walk up to see the Giant from the road once more, and back round by the Cerne to endearing Cerne Abbas church.

By eleven, I am writing in the car, in the green tunnel of trees that leads you out of Cerne Abbas up past Yetcombe Bottom—and now the last long view right down Yetcombe to the village and the square tower of the church and the rooks wheeling and playing in the high air.

On along up ridge and down dale, through Duntish, past Mappowder and Lydden Ho. Many farm trucks, lorries, I mean, very strong-smelling of sweet muck. A village called King's Stag among oaks, and a deer park, the spotted deer grazing easy among big, wide-spaced oaks and horse chestnuts. Past Lydlinch on the River Lydden, and we have never yet found out what a linch is. Sturminster Newton, a fine market town on a hill. The streams and sky all look like Constable today—a streak of silver aspens brightens the wind. Level green pastures for a while. Now we climb and climb steep slopes up to steep-streeted Shaftesbury, and so back into Wiltshire. Dorset, fare thee well.

The hilly wooded lands open out wider and wider now. Fewer hedgerows. After Noyle we are in the wide-open rolling chalk-pale plowlands of Wilts. Golden-fleeced sheep on the high hills. An army van: Caution Abnormal Load.

We go high-flying along an A road, vast rolling dun-gold greeny-brown pale plain all round, puffy receding clouds above, honey sunlight on hay rolls and sheep flocks.

It's clouding up quite fast.

We turn off to Avebury—what luck, to see Avebury again! A picnic on the outer dike, and then a quick run around the great Circles of the Stones, while Barbara rests in the car. Caught by pelting rain at the stones that I call the King and Queen at the end of the outer row, we huddled against the Queen in our baby-blue and baby-green Pac-A-Macs, and she sheltered us. We then refuged in the National Trust shop and bought a tea-cozy sheep and a Kendalls Mint Cake, and came out to silvery running sunshine and cloud-shadows, and photographed like mad. I sit now in the car in Marlborough High Street to write this, while Barbara and Charles grocery-shop.

Then up, up, up the Berkshire Downs across the high, wide, autumnal land, across the old Ridgeway, to the downs' end and overlook above the whole Valley of the Thames: flat and full of business of mankind all the way to the hazy horizon.

> Over the hills and a great way off,
> The wind will blow your top-knot off.

And so back to Oxford, to Barbara's house.

THE FISHERWOMAN'S
DAUGHTER

(1988)

*I read the first version of this paper at Brown University and at Miami
University in Ohio, and revised it heavily to read at Wesleyan College in
Georgia. Then I wrote it all over again to read at Portland State
University. I have a feeling I read it somewhere else, but can't reconstruct
where. When I went to Tulane to be a Mellon Fellow—to be precise, a
quarter of a Mellon—I rewrote it again, and that version, which I
pretended was definitive, appeared in Tulane's series of Mellon papers,
under the title "A Woman Writing." Asked to give the talk in a benefit
series in San Francisco, I decided to include more about my mother, whose
writing life was lived in the Bay Area; and that led to another full
revision.*

*In preparing the manuscript of this book, I came to the immense folder
containing the five—in places identical, in places widely differing—
typescripts of the talk; and I thought, "If I have to rewrite that thing once
more I will die." So I merely included the latest version, without reread-
ing it. My ruthless editor would have none of that. "Pusillanimous
woman," she said, "what about all the bits you left out?" "What about
them?" I snarled. "I think if we just put them together it will work," said
she. "Show me," said I, craftily. So she did. I hope it does.*

*What pleases me most about the piece, after so much work on it, is that I
can look on it at last as a collaboration. The responses from the various
audiences I read it to, both questions in the lecture hall and letters
afterward, guided and clarified my thinking and saved me from many
follies and omissions. The present re-collation and editing has given me
back the whole thing—not shapely and elegant, but a big crazy quilt. And
that was my working title for it when I first began gathering material:
"Crazy Quilt." That name hints again at collaboration, which is what I
saw myself as doing as I pieced together the works and words of so many
other writers—ancestors, strangers, friends.*

" 'So of course,' wrote Betty Flanders, pressing her heels rather deeper in the sand, 'there was nothing for it but to leave.' "

That is the first sentence of Virginia Woolf's *Jacob's Room.*[1] It is a woman writing. Sitting on the sand by the sea, writing. It's only Betty Flanders, and she's only writing a letter. But first sentences are doors to worlds. This world of Jacob's room, so strangely empty at the end of the book when the mother stands in it holding out a pair of her son's old shoes and saying, "What am I to do with these?"— this is a world in which the first thing one sees is a woman, a mother of children, writing.

On the shore, by the sea, outdoors, is that where women write? Not at a desk, in a writing room? Where does a woman write, what does she look like writing, what is my image, your image, of a woman writing? I asked my friends: "A woman writing: what do you see?" There would be a pause, then the eyes would light up, seeing. Some sent me to paintings, Fragonard, Cassatt, but mostly these turned out to be paintings of a woman reading or with a letter, not actually writing or reading the letter but looking up from it with unfocused eyes: Will he never never return? Did I remember to turn off the pot roast? . . . Another friend responded crisply, "A woman writing is taking dictation." And another said, "She's sitting at the kitchen table, and the kids are yelling."

And that last is the image I shall pursue. But first let me tell you my own first answer to my question: Jo March. From the immediacy, the authority, with which Frank Merrill's familiar illustrations of *Little Women*[2] came to my mind as soon as I asked myself what a woman writing looks like, I know that Jo March must have had real influence upon me when I was a young scribbler. I am sure she has influenced many girls, for she is not, like most "real" authors, either dead or inaccessibly famous; nor, like so many artists in books, is she set apart by sensitivity or suffering or general superlativity; nor is she, like most authors in novels, male. She is close as a sister and common as grass. As a model, what does she tell scribbling girls? I think it worthwhile to follow the biography of Jo March the Writer until we come to that person of whom, as a child and until quite recently, I knew almost nothing: Louisa May Alcott.

We first meet Jo as a writer when sister Amy vengefully burns her manuscript, "the loving work of several years. It seemed a small loss to others, but to Jo it was a dreadful calamity." How could a book, several years' work, be "a small loss" to anyone? That horrified me. How could they ask Jo to forgive Amy? At least she nearly drowns her in a frozen lake before forgiving her. At any rate, some chapters later Jo is

> very busy in the garret . . . seated on the old sofa, writing busily, with her papers spread out on a trunk before her. . . . Jo's desk up here was an old tin kitchen . . .

—the *OED* says, "New England: a roasting pan." So Jo's room of her own at this stage is a garret furnished with a sofa, a roasting pan, and a rat. To any twelve-year-old, heaven.

> Jo scribbled away till the last page was filled, when she signed her name with a flourish. . . . Lying back on the sofa she read the manuscript carefully through, making dashes here and there, and putting in many exclamation points, which looked like little balloons; then she tied it up with a smart red ribbon and sat a minute looking at it with a sober, wistful expression, which plainly showed how earnest her work had been.

I am interested here by the counterplay of a deflating irony—the scribbling, the dashes, the balloons, the ribbon—and that wistful earnestness.

Jo sends her story to a paper, it is printed, and she reads it aloud to her sisters, who cry at the right places. Beth asks, "Who wrote it?"

> The reader suddenly sat up, cast away the paper, displaying a flushed countenance, and with a funny mixture of solemnity and excitement, replied, in a loud voice, "Your sister."

The March family makes a great fuss, "for these foolish, affectionate people made a jubilee of every little household joy"—and there again is deflation, a writer's first publication reduced to a "little household joy." Does it not debase art? And yet does it not also, by refusing the heroic tone, refuse to inflate art into something beyond the reach of any "mere girl"?

So Jo goes on writing; here she is some years later, and I quote at length, for this is the central image.

> Every few weeks she would shut herself up in her room, put on her scribbling suit, and "fall into a vortex," as she expressed it, writing away at her novel with all her heart and soul, for till that was finished she could find no peace. Her "scribbling suit" consisted of a black woollen pinafore on which she could wipe her

pen at will, and a cap of the same material, adorned with a cheerful red bow. . . . This cap was a beacon to the inquiring eyes of her family, who during these periods kept their distance, merely popping in their heads semi-occasionally to ask, with interest, "Does genius burn, Jo?" They did not always venture even to ask this question, but took an observation of the cap, and judged accordingly. If this expressive article of dress was drawn low upon the forehead, it was a sign that hard work was going on; in exciting moments it was pushed rakishly askew; and when despair seized the author it was plucked wholly off and cast upon the floor. At such times the intruder silently withdrew; and not until the red bow was seen gayly erect upon the gifted brow, did anyone dare address Jo.

She did not think herself a genius by any means; but when the writing fit came on, she gave herself up to it with entire abandon, and led a blissful life, unconscious of want, care, or bad weather, while she sat safe and happy in an imaginary world, full of friends almost as real and dear to her as any in the flesh. Sleep forsook her eyes, meals stood untasted, day and night were all too short to enjoy the happiness which blessed her only at such times, and made these hours worth living, even if they bore no other fruit. The divine afflatus usually lasted a week or two, and then she emerged from her vortex, hungry, sleepy, cross, or despondent.

This is a good description of the condition in which the work of art is done. This is the real thing—domesticated. The cap and bow, the facetious turns and the disclaimers, deflate without degrading, and allow Alcott to make a rather extraordinary statement: that Jo is doing something very important and doing it entirely seriously and that there is nothing unusual about a young woman's doing it. This passion of work and this happiness which blessed her in doing it are fitted without fuss into a girl's commonplace life at home. It may not seem much; but I don't know where else I or many other girls like me, in my generation or my mother's or my daughters', were to find this model, this validation.

Jo writes romantic thrillers and they sell; her father shakes his head and says, "Aim at the highest and never mind the money," but Amy remarks, "The money is the best part of it." Working in Boston as a governess-seamstress, Jo sees that "money conferred power: money and power, therefore, she resolved to have; not to be used for herself alone," our author's author hastily adds, "but for those whom she loved more than self. . . . She took to writing sensation stories." Her first visit to the editorial office of the *Weekly Volcano* is handled lightly, but the three men treat her as a woman who has come to sell herself—true Lévi-Straussians, to whom what a woman does is entirely subsumed in woman as commodity. Refusing shame, Jo writes on, and makes money by her writing; admitting shame, she does not "tell them at home."

> Jo soon found that her innocent experience had given her but few glimpses of the tragic world which underlies society; so, regarding it in a business light, she set about supplying her deficiencies with characteristic energy. . . . She searched newspapers for accidents, incidents, and crimes; she excited the suspicions of public librarians by asking for works on poisons; she studied faces in the street, and characters good, bad, and indifferent all about her. . . . Much describing of other people's passions and feelings set her to studying and speculating about her own—a morbid amusement, in which healthy young minds do not voluntarily indulge—

but which one might think appropriate, even needful, to the young novelist? However, "wrongdoing always brings its own punishment, and when Jo most needed hers, she got it."

Her punishment is administered by the Angel in the House, in the form of Professor Bhaer. Knowing that she is soiling her pure soul, he attacks the papers she writes for: "I do not like to think that good young girls should see such things." Jo weakly defends them, but when he leaves she rereads her stories, three months' work, and burns them. Amy doesn't have to do it for her any more; she can destroy herself. Then she sits and wonders: "I almost wish I hadn't any conscience, it's so inconvenient!" A cry from the heart of Bronson Alcott's daughter. She tries a pious tale and a children's story, which don't sell, and gives up: she "corked up her inkstand."

Beth dies, and trying to replace her, Jo tries "to live for others"— finally driving her mother to say, "Why don't you write? That always used to make you happy." So she does, and she writes both well and successfully—until Professor Bhaer returns and marries her, evidently the only way to make her stop writing. She has his two boys to bring up, and then her two boys, and then all those Little Men in the next volume; at the end of *Little Women,* in the chapter called "Harvest Time," she says, "I haven't given up the hope that I may write a good book yet, but I can wait."

The harvest seems indefinitely deferred. But, in Rachel Blau Du Plessis' phrase,[3] Jo writes beyond the ending. In the third volume,

Jo's Boys, she has gone back in middle age to writing, and is rich and famous. There is realism, toughness, and comedy in the descriptions of her managing the household, mothering the teenagers, writing her chapters, and trying to avoid the celebrity hunters. In fact this, like the whole story of Jo the Writer, is quite close to Louisa Alcott's own story, with one large difference. Jo marries and has children. Lu did not.

And yet she undertook the responsibility for a family, some of whom were as improvident and self-centered as any baby. There is a heartbreaking note in her journal[4] for April 1869, when she was suffering a "bad spell" of mercury poisoning (the calomel given her to cure fever when she was a nurse in the Civil War made her sick the rest of her life):

> Very poorly. Feel quite used up. Don't care much for myself, as rest is heavenly, even with pain; but the family seems so panic-stricken and helpless when I break down, that I try to keep the mill going. Two short tales for L., $50; two for Ford, $20; and did my editorial work, though two months are unpaid for. Roberts wants a new book, but am afraid to get into a vortex lest I fall ill.

Alcott used the same word Jo used for her passions of writing; here are a couple of journal passages comparable to the "vortex" passage in *Little Women*.

> August 1860—"Moods" [a novel]. Genius burned so fiercely that for four weeks I wrote all day and planned nearly all night, being quite possessed by my work. I was perfectly happy, and seemed to have no wants.

> February 1861—Another turn at "Moods," which I remodelled. From the 2d to the 25th I sat writing, with a run at dusk; could not sleep, and for three days was so full of it I could not stop to get up. Mother made me a green silk cap with a red bow, to match the old green and red party wrap, which I wore as a "glory cloak." Thus arrayed sat in a grove of manuscripts, "living for immortality" as May said. Mother wandered in and out with cordial cups of tea, worried because I couldn't eat. Father thought it fine, and brought his reddest apples and hardest cider for my Pegasus to feed upon. . . . It was very pleasant and queer while it lasted. . . .

And it is pleasant to see how the family whose debts she slaved to pay off, and which she strove so to protect and keep in comfort, tried to protect and help her in return.

Like so many women of her century, then, Lu Alcott had a family, though she did not marry. "Liberty is a better husband than love to many of us," she wrote, but in fact she had very little liberty, in the sense of freedom from immediate, personal responsibilities. She even had a baby—her sister May's. Dying from complications of childbirth, May asked the beloved older sister, then forty-eight, to bring up little Lu; which she did until her death eight years later.

All this is complex, more complex, I think, than one tends to imagine; for the Victorian script calls for a clear choice—either books or babies for a woman, not both. And Jo *seems* to make that choice. I was annoyed at myself when I realized that I had forgotten Jo's survival as a writer—that my memory, except for one nagging scrap that led me to look up *Jo's Boys* at last, had followed the script. That, of course, is the power of the script: you play the part without knowing it.

Here is a classic—a scriptural—description of a writing woman, the mother of children, one of whom is just now in the process of falling down the stairs.

> Mrs Jellyby was a pretty, very diminutive, plump woman, of from forty to fifty, with handsome eyes, though they had a curious habit of seeming to look a long way off. . . . [She] had very good hair, but was too much occupied with her African duties to brush it. . . . We could not help noticing that her dress didn't nearly meet up the back, and that the open space was railed across with a latticework of stay-laces—like a summer-house.
>
> The room, which was strewn with papers and nearly filled by a great writing-table covered with similar litter, was, I must say, not only very untidy, but very dirty. We were obliged to take notice of that with our sense of sight, even while, with our sense of hearing, we followed the poor child who had tumbled downstairs: I think into the back kitchen, where somebody seemed to stifle him. But what principally struck us was a jaded and unhealthy-looking, though by no means plain girl, at the writing-table, who sat biting the feather of her pen, and staring at us. I suppose nobody ever was in such a state of ink.[5]

I will, with difficulty, restrain myself from reading you the rest of *Bleak House*. I love Dickens and will defend his Mrs. Jellyby and her correspondence with Borrioboola-Gha as an eternal send-up of those who meddle with foreign morals while remaining oblivious to the misery under their nose. But I observe also that he uses a woman to make this point, probably because it was, and is, safe: few readers would question the assumption that a woman should put family before public responsibility, or that if she does work outside the "private sphere" she will be neglectful of her house, indifferent to the necks of her children, and incompetent to fasten her clothing. Mrs. Jellyby's daughter is saved from her enforced "state of ink" by marriage, but Mrs. Jellyby will get no help from her husband, a man so inert that their marriage is described as the union of mind and matter. Mrs. Jellyby is a joy to me, she is drawn with so much humor and good nature; and yet she troubles me, because behind her lurks the double standard. Nowhere among Dickens' many responsible, intelligent women is there one who does real artistic or intellectual work, to balance Mrs. Jellyby and reassure us that it isn't what she does but how she does it that is deplorable. And yet the passage just quoted is supposed to have been written by a woman—the character Esther Summerson. Esther herself is a problem. How does she write half Dickens' novel for him while managing Bleak House and getting smallpox and everything else? We never catch her at it. As a woman writing, Esther is invisible. She is not in the script.

There may be a sympathetic portrait of a woman writer with children in a novel written by a man. I have read versions of this paper in Rhode Island, Ohio, Georgia, Louisiana, Oregon, and California, and asked each audience please to tell me if they knew of any such. I wait in hope. Indeed, the only sympathetic picture of a woman novelist in a man's novel that I know is the protagonist of *Diana of the Crossways*. Meredith shows her writing novels for her living, doing it brilliantly, and finding her freedom in her professionalism. But, self-alienated by a disastrous infatuation, she begins to force her talent and can't work—the script apparently being that love is incidental for a man, everything for a woman. At the end, well off and happily married, she is expecting a baby, but not, it appears, a book. All the same, Diana still stands, nearly a century later, quite alone at her crossways.

Invisibility as a writer is a condition that affects not only characters but authors, and even the children of authors. Take Elizabeth Barrett Browning, whom we have consistently put to bed with a spaniel, ignoring the fact that when she wrote *Aurora Leigh* she was the healthy mother of a healthy four-year-old—ignoring, in fact, the fact that she wrote *Aurora Leigh*, a book about being a woman writer, and how difficult one's own true love can make it for one.

Here is a woman who had several children and was a successful

novelist, writing a letter to her husband about a hundred and fifty
years ago, or maybe last night:

> If I *am* to write, I must have a room to myself, which shall be *my*
> room. All last winter I felt the need of some place where I could
> go and be quiet. I could not [write in the dining room] for there
> was all the setting of tables and clearing up of tables and dress-
> ing and washing of children, and everything else going on, and
> . . . I never felt comfortable there, though I tried hard. Then if I
> came into the parlor where you were, I felt as if I were interrupt-
> ing you, and you know you sometimes thought so too.[6]

What do you mean? Not at all! Silly notion! Just like a woman!

Fourteen years and several more children later, that woman wrote
Uncle Tom's Cabin—most of it at the kitchen table.

A room of one's own—yes. One may ask why Mr. Harriet Beecher
Stowe got a room to himself to write in, while the woman who wrote
the most morally effective American novel of the nineteenth century got the kitchen table. But then one may also ask why she
accepted the kitchen table. Any self-respecting man would have sat
there for five minutes and then stalked out shouting, "Nobody can
work in this madhouse, call me when dinner's ready!" But Harriet, a
self-respecting woman, went on getting dinner with the kids all
underfoot *and* writing her novels. The first question, to be asked
with awe, is surely, How? But then, Why? *Why* are women such
patsies?

The quick-feminist-fix answer is that they are victims of and/or
accomplices with the patriarchy, which is true but doesn't really get
us anywhere new. Let us go to another woman novelist for help. I
stole the Stowe quotation (and others) from Tillie Olsen's *Silences,* a
book to which this paper stands in the relation of a loving but
undutiful daughter—Hey, Ma, that's a neat quotation, can I wear it?
This next one I found for myself, in the *Autobiography* of Margaret
Oliphant, a fascinating book, from the generation just after Stowe.
Oliphant was a successful writer very young, married, had three
kids, went on writing, was left a widow with heavy debts and the
three kids plus her brother's three kids to bring up, did so, went on
writing. . . . When her second book came out, she was still, like Jo
March, a girl at home.

> I had a great pleasure in writing, but the success and the three
> editions had no particular effect upon my mind. . . . I had

nobody to praise me except my mother and [brother] Frank, and their applause—well, it was delightful, it was everything in the world—it was life—but it did not count. They were part of me, and I of them, and we were all in it.[7]

I find that extraordinary. I cannot imagine any male author saying anything like that at all. There is a key here—something real that has been neglected, been hidden, been denied.

> . . . The writing ran through everything. But then it was also subordinate to everything, to be pushed aside for any little necessity. I had no table even to myself, much less a room to work in, but sat at the corner of the family table with my writing-book, with everything going on as if I had been making a shirt instead of writing a book. . . . My mother sat always at needlework of some kind, and talked to whoever might be present, and I took my share in the conversation, going on all the same with my story, the little groups of imaginary persons, these other talks evolving themselves quite undisturbed.

How's that for an image, the group of imaginary people talking in the imaginary room in the real room among the real people talking, and all of it going on perfectly quiet and unconfused. . . . But it's shocking. She can't be a real writer. Real writers writhe on solitary sofas in cork-lined rooms, agonizing after *le mot juste*—don't they?

> My study, all the study I have ever attained to, is the little second drawing-room where all the life of the house goes on . . .

—you recall that she was bringing up six children?—

> . . . and I don't think I have ever had two hours undisturbed (except at night when everybody is in bed) during my whole literary life. Miss Austen, I believe, wrote in the same way, and very much for the same reason; but at her period the natural flow of life took another form. The family were half ashamed to have it known that she was not just a young lady like the others, doing her embroidery. Mine were quite pleased to magnify me and to be proud of my work, but always with a hidden sense that it was an admirable joke . . .

—perhaps artists cast off their families and go to the South Sea Islands because they want to be perceived as heroes and their families think they are funny?—

...a hidden sense that it was an admirable joke, and no idea
that any special facilities or retirement was necessary. My mother
would have felt her pride much checked, almost humiliated, if
she had conceived that I stood in need of any artificial aids of
that description. That would at once have made the work unnatural to her eyes, and also to mine.

Oliphant was a proud Scotswoman, proud of her work and her
strength; yet she wrote nonfiction potboilers rather than fight her
male editors and publishers for better pay for her novels. So, as she
says bitterly, "Trollope's worst book was better paid than my best."
Her best is said to be *Miss Marjoribanks,* but I have never yet been
able to get a copy of it; it was disappeared, along with all her other
books. Thanks to publishers such as Virago we can now get
Oliphant's *Hester,* a stunning novel, and *Kirsteen* and a few others,
but they are still taught, so far as I know, only in women's studies
courses; they are not part of the Canon of English Literature,
though Trollope's potboilers are. No book by a woman who had
children has ever been included in that august list.

I think Oliphant gives us a glimpse of why a novelist might not
merely endure writing in the kitchen or the parlor amidst the
children and the housework, but might endure it willingly. She
seems to feel that she profited, that her writing profited, from the
difficult, obscure, chancy connection between the art work and the
emotional/manual/managerial complex of skills and tasks called
"housework," and that to sever that connection would put the writing itself at risk, would make it, in her word, unnatural.

The received wisdom of course is just the opposite: that any
attempt to combine art work with housework and family responsibility is impossible, unnatural. And the punishment for unnatural
acts, among the critics and the Canoneers, is death.

What is the ethical basis of this judgment and sentence upon the
housewife-artist? It is a very noble and austere one, with religion at
its foundation: it is the idea that the artist must sacrifice himself to
his art. (I use the pronoun advisedly.) His responsibility is to his
work alone. It is a motivating idea of the Romantics, it guides the
careers of poets from Rimbaud to Dylan Thomas to Richard Hugo,
it has given us hundreds of hero figures, typical of whom is James
Joyce himself and his Stephen Dedalus. Stephen sacrifices all
"lesser" obligations and affections to a "higher" cause, embracing
the moral irresponsibility of the soldier or the saint. This heroic

stance, the Gauguin Pose, has been taken as the norm—as natural to the artist—and artists, both men and women, who do not assume it have tended to feel a little shabby and second-rate.

Not, however, Virginia Woolf. She observed factually that the artist needs a small income and a room to work in, but did not speak of heroism. Indeed, she said, "I doubt that a writer can be a hero. I doubt that a hero can be a writer." And when I see a writer assume the full heroic posture, I incline to agree. Here, for example, is Joseph Conrad:

> For twenty months I wrestled with the Lord for my creation . . . mind and will and conscience engaged to the full, hour after hour, day after day . . . a lonely struggle in a great isolation from the world. I suppose I slept and ate the food put before me and talked connectedly on suitable occasions, but I was never aware of the even flow of daily life, made easy and noiseless for me by a silent, watchful, tireless affection.[8]

A woman who boasted that her conscience had been engaged to the full in such a wrestling match would be called to account by both women and men; and women are now calling men to account. What "put food" before him? What made daily life so noiseless? What in fact was this "tireless affection," which sounds to me like an old Ford in a junkyard but is apparently intended as a delicate gesture towards a woman whose conscience was engaged to the full, hour after hour, day after day, for twenty months, in seeing to it that Joseph Conrad could wrestle with the Lord in a very relatively great isolation, well housed, clothed, bathed, and fed?

Conrad's "struggle" and Jo March / Lu Alcott's "vortex" are descriptions of the same kind of all-out artistic work; and in both cases the artist is looked after by the family. But I feel an important difference in their perceptions. Where Alcott receives a gift, Conrad asserts a right; where she is taken into the vortex, the creative whirlwind, becoming part of it, he wrestles, struggles, seeking mastery. She is a participant; he is a hero. And her family remain individuals, with cups of tea and timid inquiries, while his is depersonalized to "an affection."

Looking for a woman writer who might have imitated this heroic infantilism, I thought of Gertrude Stein, under the impression that she had used Alice Toklas as a "wife" in this utilitarian sense; but that, as I should have guessed, is an anti-lesbian canard. Stein certainly took hero-artist poses and indulged an enormous ego, but she played fair; and the difference between her domestic partnership and that of Joyce or Conrad is illuminating. And indeed, lesbianism has given many artists the network of support they need—for there *is* a heroic aspect to the practice of art; it is lonely, risky, merciless work, and every artist needs some kind of moral support or sense of solidarity and validation.

The artist with the least access to social or aesthetic solidarity or approbation has been the artist-housewife. A person who undertakes responsibility both to her art and to her dependent children, with no "tireless affection" or even tired affection to call on, has undertaken a full-time double job that can be simply, practically, destroyingly impossible. But that isn't how the problem is posed— as a recognition of immense practical difficulty. If it were, practical solutions would be proposed, beginning with childcare. Instead the issue is stated, even now, as a moral one, a matter of ought and ought not. The poet Alicia Ostriker puts it neatly: "That women should have babies rather than books is the considered opinion of Western civilization. That women should have books rather than babies is a variation on that theme."[9]

Freud's contribution to this doctrine was to invest it with such a weight of theory and mythology as to make it appear a primordial, unquestionable fact. It was of course Freud who, after telling his fiancée what it is a woman wants, said that what we shall never know is what a woman wants. Lacan is perfectly consistent in following him, if I as a person without discourse may venture to say so. A culture or a psychology predicated upon man as human and woman as other cannot accept a woman as artist. An artist is an autonomous, choice-making self: to be such a self a woman must unwoman herself. Barren, she must imitate the man—imperfectly, it goes without saying.*

---

* A particularly exhilarating discussion of this issue is the essay "Writing and Motherhood" by Susan Rubin Suleiman, in *The (M)other Tongue: Essays in Feminist Psychoanalytic Interpretation,* edited by Garner, Kahane, and Springnether (Ithaca: Cornell University Press, 1985). Suleiman gives a short history of the nineteenth-century books-or-babies theory and its refinement in the twentieth century by such psychologists as Helene Deutsch, remarking that "it took psychoanalysis to transform moral obligation into a psychological 'law,' equating the creative impulse with the procreative one and decreeing that she who has a child feels no need to write books." Suleiman presents a critique of the feminist reversal of this theory (she who has a book feels no need to have children) and analyzes current French feminist thinking on the relationship between writing and femininity/motherhood.

Hence the approbation accorded Austen, the Brontës, Dickinson, and Plath, who though she made the mistake of having two children compensated for it by killing herself. The misogynist Canon of Literature can include these women because they can be perceived as incomplete women, as female men.

Still, I have to grit my teeth to criticize the either-books-or-babies doctrine, because it has given real, true comfort to women who could not or chose not to marry and have children, and saw themselves as "having" books instead. But though the comfort may be real, I think the doctrine false. And I hear that falseness when a Dorothy Richardson tells us that other women can have children but nobody else can write *her* books. As if "other women" could have had *her* children—as if books came from the uterus! That's just the flip side of the theory that books come from the scrotum. This final reduction of the notion of sublimation is endorsed by our chief macho dodo writer, who has announced that "the one thing a writer needs to have is balls." But he doesn't carry the theory of penile authorship to the extent of saying that if you "get" a kid you can't "get" a book and so fathers can't write. The analogy collapsed into identity, the you-can't-create-if-you-procreate myth, is applied to women only.

I've found I have to stop now and say clearly what I'm not saying. I'm not saying a writer ought to have children, I'm not saying a parent ought to be a writer, I'm not saying any woman *ought* to write books *or* have kids. Being a mother is one of the things a woman can do—like being a writer. It's a privilege. It's not an obligation, or a destiny. I'm talking about mothers who write because it is almost a taboo topic—because women have been told that they *ought not* to try to be both a mother and a writer because both the kids and the books will *pay*—because it can't be done—because it is unnatural.

This refusal to allow both creation and procreation to women is cruelly wasteful: not only has it impoverished our literature by banning the housewives, but it has caused unbearable personal pain and self-mutilation: Woolf obeying the wise doctors who said she must not bear a child; Plath who put glasses of milk by her kids' beds and then put her head in the oven.

A sacrifice, not of somebody else but of oneself, is demanded of women artists (while the Gauguin Pose demands of men artists only that they sacrifice others). I am proposing that this ban on a woman artist's full sexuality is harmful not only to the woman but to the art.

There is less censure now, and more support, for a woman who wants both to bring up a family and work as an artist. But it's a small degree of improvement. The difficulty of trying to be responsible, hour after hour day after day for maybe twenty *years,* for the well-being of children and the excellence of books, is immense: it involves an endless expense of energy and an impossible weighing of competing priorities. And we don't know much about the process, because writers who are mothers haven't talked much about their motherhood—for fear of boasting? for fear of being trapped in the Mom trap, discounted?—nor have they talked much about their writing as in any way connected with their parenting, since the heroic myth demands that the two jobs be considered utterly opposed and mutually destructive.

But we heard a hint of something else from Oliphant; and here (thanks, Tillie) is the painter Käthe Kollwitz:

> I am gradually approaching the period in my life when work comes first. When both the boys were away for Easter, I hardly did anything but work. Worked, slept, ate, and went for short walks. But above all I worked.
>
> And yet I wonder whether the "blessing" isn't missing from such work. No longer diverted by other emotions, I work the way a cow grazes.

That is marvelous—"I work the way a cow grazes." That is the best description of the "professional" at work I know.

> Perhaps in reality I accomplish a little more. The hands work and work, and the head imagines it's producing God knows what, and yet, formerly, when my working time was so wretchedly limited, I was more productive, because I was more sensual; I lived as a human being must live, passionately interested in everything. . . . Potency, potency is diminishing.[10]

This *potency* felt by a woman is a potency from which the Hero-Artist has (and I choose my words carefully) cut himself off, in an egoism that is ultimately sterile. But it is a potency that has been denied by women as well as men, and not just women eager to collude with misogyny.

Back in the seventies Nina Auerbach wrote that Jane Austen was able to write because she had created around her "a child-free space." Germ-free I knew, odor-free I knew, but child-free? And Austen? who wrote in the parlor, and was a central figure to a lot of nieces and nephews? But I tried to accept what Auerbach said, because although my experience didn't fit it, I was, like many women, used to feeling that my experience was faulty, not right—that it was *wrong*. So I was probably wrong to keep on writing in what was then a fully child-filled space. However, feminist thinking evolved rapidly to a far more complex and realistic position, and I, stumbling along behind, have been enabled by it to think a little for myself.

The greatest enabler for me was always, is always, Virginia Woolf. And I quote now from the first draft of her paper "Professions for Women,"[11] where she gives her great image of a woman writing.

> I figure her really in an attitude of contemplation, like a fisher-woman, sitting on the bank of a lake with her fishing rod held over its water. Yes that is how I see her. She was not thinking; she was not reasoning; she was not constructing a plot; she was letting her imagination down into the depths of her conscious-ness while she sat above holding on by a thin but quite necessary thread of reason.

Now I interrupt to ask you to add one small element to this scene. Let us imagine that a bit farther up the bank of the lake sits a child, the fisherwoman's daughter. She's about five, and she's making peo-ple out of sticks and mud and telling stories with them. She's been told to be very quiet please while Mama fishes, and she really is very quiet except when she forgets and sings or asks questions; and she watches in fascinated silence when the following dramatic events take place. There sits our woman writing, our fisherwoman, when—

> suddenly there is a violent jerk; she feels the line race through her fingers.
>
> The imagination has rushed away; it has taken to the depths; it has sunk heaven knows where—into the dark pool of extraor-dinary experience. The reason has to cry "Stop!" the novelist has to pull on the line and haul the imagination to the surface. The imagination comes to the top in a state of fury.
>
> Good heavens she cries—how dare you interfere with me—how dare you pull me out with your wretched little fishing line? And I—that is, the reason—have to reply, "My dear you were going altogether too far. Men would be shocked." Calm yourself I say, as she sits panting on the bank—panting with rage and disappointment. We have only got to wait fifty years or so. In fifty years I shall be able to use all this very queer knowledge that

you are ready to bring me. But not now. You see I go on, trying to
calm her, I cannot make use of what you tell me—about womens
bodies for instance—their passions—and so on, because the
conventions are still very strong. If I were to overcome the
conventions I should need the courage of a hero, and I am not
a hero.

I doubt that a writer can be a hero. I doubt that a hero can be a
writer.

. . . Very well, says the imagination, dressing herself up again
in her petticoat and skirts, we will wait. We will wait another fifty
years. But it seems to me a pity.

It seems to me a pity. It seems to me a pity that more than fifty
years have passed and the conventions, though utterly different, still
exist to protect men from being shocked, still admit only male
experience of women's bodies, passions, and existence. It seems to
me a pity that so many women, including myself, have accepted this
denial of their own experience and narrowed their perception to fit
it, writing as if their sexuality were limited to copulation, as if they
knew nothing about pregnancy, birth, nursing, mothering, puberty,
menstruation, menopause, except what men are willing to hear,
nothing except what men are willing to hear about housework,
childwork, lifework, war, peace, living, and dying as experienced in
the female body and mind and imagination. "Writing the body," as
Woolf asked and Hélène Cixous asks, is only the beginning. We have
to rewrite the world.

White writing, Cixous calls it, writing in milk, in mother's milk. I
like that image, because even among feminists, the woman writer
has been more often considered in her sexuality as a lover than in
her sexuality as pregnant-bearing-nursing-childcaring. Mother still
tends to get disappeared. And in losing the artist-mother we lose
where there's a lot to gain. Alicia Ostriker thinks so. "The advantage
of motherhood for a woman artist," she says—have you ever heard
anybody say that before? the *advantage* of motherhood for an
artist?—

The advantage of motherhood for a woman artist is that it puts
her in immediate and inescapable contact with the sources of
life, death, beauty, growth, corruption. . . . If the woman artist
has been trained to believe that the activities of motherhood are
trivial, tangential to the main issues of life, irrelevant to the great
themes of literature, she should untrain herself. The training is
misogynist, it protects and perpetuates systems of thought and

feeling which prefer violence and death to love and birth, and it
is a lie.

. . . "We think back through our mothers, if we are women,"
declares Woolf, but through whom can those who are themselves
mothers . . . do their thinking? . . . we all need data, we need
information, . . . the sort provided by poets, novelists, artists,
from within. As our knowledge begins to accumulate, we can
imagine what it would signify to all women, and men, to live in a
culture where childbirth and mothering occupied the kind of
position that sex and romantic love have occupied in literature
and art for the last five hundred years, or . . . that warfare has
occupied since literature began.[12]

My book *Always Coming Home* was a rash attempt to imagine such a
world, where the Hero and the Warrior are a stage adolescents go
through on their way to becoming responsible human beings,
where the parent-child relationship is not forever viewed through
the child's eyes but includes the reality of the mother's experience.
The imagining was difficult, and rewarding.

Here is a passage from a novel where what Woolf, Cixous, and
Ostriker ask for is happening, however casually and unpreten-
tiously. In Margaret Drabble's *The Millstone*,[13] Rosamund, a young
scholar and freelance writer, has a baby about eight months old,
Octavia. They share a flat with a friend, Lydia, who's writing a novel.
Rosamund is working away on a book review:

> I had just written and counted my first hundred words when I
> remembered Octavia; I could hear her making small happy
> noises. . . .
> I was rather dismayed when I realized she was in Lydia's room
> and that I must have left the door open, for Lydia's room was
> always full of nasty objects like aspirins, safety razors and bottles
> of ink; I rushed along to rescue her and the sight that met my
> eyes when I opened the door was enough to make anyone quake.
> She had her back to the door and was sitting in the middle of the
> floor surrounded by a sea of torn, strewed, chewed paper. I
> stood there transfixed, watching the neat small back of her head
> and her thin stalk-like neck and flowery curls: suddenly she gave
> a great screech of delight and ripped another sheet of paper.
> "Octavia," I said in horror, and she started guiltily, and looked
> round at me with a charming deprecating smile: her mouth, I
> could see, was wedged full of wads of Lydia's new novel.
> I picked her up and fished the bits out and laid them carefully

on the bedside table with what was left of the typescript; pages 70 to 123 seemed to have survived. The rest was in varying stages of dissolution: some pages were entire but badly crumpled, some were in large pieces, some in small pieces, and some, as I have said, were chewed up. The damage was not, in fact, as great as it appeared at first sight to be, for babies, though persistent, are not thorough: but at first sight it was frightful. . . . In a way it was clearly the most awful thing for which I had ever been responsible, but as I watched Octavia crawl around the sitting room looking for more work to do, I almost wanted to laugh. It seemed so absurd, to have this small living extension of myself, so dangerous, so vulnerable, for whose injuries and crimes I alone had to suffer. . . . It really was a terrible thing . . . and yet in comparison with Octavia being so sweet and so alive it did not seem so very terrible. . . .

Confronted with the wreckage, Lydia is startled, but not deeply distressed:

. . . and that was it, except for the fact that Lydia really did have to rewrite two whole chapters as well as doing a lot of boring sellotaping, and when it came out it got bad reviews anyway. This did succeed in making Lydia angry.

I have seen Drabble's work dismissed with the usual list of patronizing adjectives reserved for women who write as women, not imitation men. Let us not let her be disappeared. Her work is deeper than its bright surface. What is she talking about in this funny passage? Why does the girl-baby eat not her mother's manuscript but another woman's manuscript? Couldn't she at least have eaten a manuscript by a man?—no, no, that's not the point. The point, or part of it, is that babies eat manuscripts. They really do. The poem not written because the baby cried, the novel put aside because of a pregnancy, and so on. Babies eat books. But they spit out wads of them that can be taped back together; and they are only babies for a couple of years, while writers live for decades; and it is terrible, but not very terrible. The manuscript that got eaten *was* terrible; if you know Lydia you know the reviewers were right. And that's part of the point too—that the supreme value of art depends on other equally supreme values. But that subverts the hierarchy of values; "men would be shocked. . . ."

In Drabble's comedy of morals the absence of the Hero-Artist is a strong ethical statement. Nobody lives in a great isolation, nobody sacrifices human claims, nobody even scolds the baby. Nobody is going to put their head, or anybody else's head, into an oven: not the mother, not the writer, not the daughter—these three and one who, being women, do not separate creation and destruction into *I create / You are destroyed,* or vice versa. Who are responsible, take responsibility, for both the baby and the book.*

But I want now to turn from fiction to biography and from general to personal; I want to talk a bit about my mother, the writer.

Her maiden name was Theodora Kracaw; her first married name was Brown; her second married name, Kroeber, was the one she used on her books; her third married name was Quinn. This sort of many-namedness doesn't happen to men; it's inconvenient, and yet its very cumbersomeness reveals, perhaps, the being of a woman writer as not one simple thing—the author—but a multiple, complex process of being, with various responsibilities, one of which is to her writing.

Theodora put her personal responsibilities first—chronologically. She brought up and married off her four children before she started to write. She took up the pen, as they used to say—she had the most amazing left-handed scrawl—in her mid-fifties. I asked her once, years later, "Did you want to write, and put it off intentionally, till you'd got rid of us?" And she laughed and said, "Oh, no, I just wasn't *ready*." Not an evasion or a dishonest answer, but not, I think, the whole answer.

She was born in 1897 in a wild Colorado mining town, and her mother boasted of having been *born* with the vote—in Wyoming,

---

* My understanding of this issue has been much aided by Carol Gilligan's *In a Different Voice* (Cambridge: Harvard University Press, 1982), as well as by Jean Baker Miller's modestly revolutionary *Toward a New Psychology of Women* (Boston: Beacon Press, 1976). Gilligan's thesis, stated very roughly, is that our society brings up males to think and speak in terms of their rights, females in terms of their responsibilities, and that conventional psychologies have implicitly evaluated the "male" image of a hierarchy of rights as "superior" (hierarchically, of course) to the "female" image of a network of mutual responsibilities. Hence a man finds it (relatively) easy to assert his "right" to be free of relationships and dependents, à la Gauguin, while women are not granted and do not grant one another any such right, preferring to live as part of an intense and complex network in which freedom is arrived at, if at all, mutually. Coming at the matter from this angle, one can see why there are no or very few "Great Artists" among women, when the "Great Artist" is defined as inherently superior to and not responsible towards others.

which ratified woman suffrage along with statehood—and rode a
stallion men couldn't ride; but still, the Angel in the House was very
active in those days, the one whose message is that a woman's needs
come after everybody else's. And my mother really came pretty close
to incarnating that Angel, whom Woolf called "the woman men wish
women to be." Men fell in love with her—all men. Doctors, garage
mechanics, professors, roach exterminators. Butchers saved sweet-
breads for her. She was also, to her daughter, a demanding, approv-
ing, nurturing, good-natured, loving, lively mother—a first-rate
mother. And then, getting on to sixty, she became a first-rate writer.

She started out, as women so often do, by writing some books for
children—not competing with men, you know, staying in the
"domestic sphere." One of these, *A Green Christmas,* is a lovely book
that ought to be in every six-year-old's stocking. Then she wrote a
charming and romantic autobiographical novel—still on safe,
"womanly" ground. Next she ventured into Native American territory with *The Inland Whale;* and then she was asked to write the story
of an Indian called Ishi, the only survivor of a people massacred by
the North American pioneers, a serious and risky subject requiring
a great deal of research, moral sensitivity, and organizational and
narrative skill.

So she wrote it, the first best seller, I believe, that University of
California Press ever published. *Ishi* is still in print in many languages, still used, I think, in California schools, still deservedly
beloved. It is a book entirely worthy of its subject, a book of very
great honesty and power.

So, if she could write that in her sixties, what might she have
written in her thirties? Maybe she really "wasn't ready." But maybe
she listened to the wrong angel, and we might have had many more
books from her. Would my brothers and I have suffered, have been
cheated of anything, if she had been writing them? I think my aunt
Betsy and the household help we had back then would have kept
things going just fine. As for my father, I don't see how her writing
could have hurt him or how her success could have threatened him.
But I don't know. All I do know is that once she started writing (and
it was while my father was alive, and they collaborated on a couple of
things), she never stopped; she had found the work she loved.

Once, not long after my father's death, when *Ishi* was bringing
her the validation of praise and success she very much needed, and
while I was still getting every story I sent out rejected with monoto-
nous regularity, she burst into tears over my latest rejection slip and

tried to console me, saying that she wanted rewards and success for me, not for herself. And that was lovely, and I treasured her saying it then as I do now. That she didn't really mean it and I didn't really believe it made no difference. Of course she didn't want to sacrifice her achievement, her work, to me—why on earth should she? She shared what she could of it with me by sharing the pleasures and anguishes of writing, the intellectual excitement, the shoptalk—and that's all. No angelic altruism. When I began to publish, we shared that. And she wrote on; in her eighties she told me, without bitterness, "I wish I had started sooner. Now there isn't time." She was at work on a third novel when she died.

As for myself: I have flagrantly disobeyed the either-books-or-babies rule, having had three kids and written about twenty books, and thank God it wasn't the other way around. By the luck of race, class, money, and health, I could manage the double-tightrope trick—and especially by the support of my partner. He is not my wife; but he brought to marriage an assumption of mutual aid as its daily basis, and on that basis you can get a lot of work done. Our division of labor was fairly conventional; I was in charge of house, cooking, the kids, and novels, because I wanted to be, and he was in charge of being a professor, the car, the bills, and the garden, because he wanted to be. When the kids were babies I wrote at night; when they started school I wrote while they were at school; these days I write as a cow grazes. If I needed help he gave it without making it into a big favor, and—this is the central fact—he did not ever begrudge me the time I spent writing, or the blessing of my work.

That is the killer: the killing grudge, the envy, the jealousy, the spite that so often a man is allowed to hold, trained to hold, against anything a woman does that's not done in his service, for him, to feed his body, his comfort, his kids. A woman who tries to work against that grudge finds the blessing turned into a curse; she must rebel and go it alone, or fall silent in despair. Any artist must expect to work amid the total, rational indifference of everybody else to their work, for years, perhaps for life: but no artist can work well against daily, personal, vengeful resistance. And that's exactly what many women artists get from the people they love and live with.

I was spared all that. I was free—born free, lived free. And for years that personal freedom allowed me to ignore the degree to which my writing was controlled and constrained by judgments and assumptions which I thought were my own, but which were the internalized ideology of a male supremacist society. Even when subverting the conventions, I disguised my subversions from myself. It took me years to realize that I chose to work in such despised, marginal genres as science fiction, fantasy, young adult, precisely because they were excluded from critical, academic, canonical supervision, leaving the artist free; it took ten more years before I had the wits and guts to see and say that the exclusion of the genres from "literature" is unjustified, unjustifiable, and a matter not of quality but of politics. So too in my choice of subjects: until the mid-seventies I wrote my fiction about heroic adventures, high-tech futures, men in the halls of power, men—men were the central characters, the women were peripheral, secondary. Why don't you write about women? my mother asked me. I don't know how, I said. A stupid answer, but an honest one. I did not know how to write about women—very few of us did—because I thought that what men had written about women was the truth, was the true way to write about women. And I couldn't.

My mother could not give me what I needed. When feminism began to reawaken, she hated it, called it "those women's libbers"; but it was she who had steered me years and years before to what I would and did need, to Virginia Woolf. "We think back through our mothers," and we have many mothers, those of the body and those of the soul. What I needed was what feminism, feminist literary theory and criticism and practice, had to give me. And I can hold it in my hands—not only *Three Guineas,* my treasure in the days of poverty, but now all the wealth of *The Norton Anthology of Literature by Women* and the reprint houses and the women's presses. Our mothers have been returned to us. This time, let's hang on to them.

And it is feminism that has empowered me to criticize not only my society and myself but—for a moment now—feminism itself. The books-or-babies myth is not only a misogynist hang-up, it can be a feminist one. Some of the women I respect most, writing for publications that I depend on for my sense of women's solidarity and hope, continue to declare that it is "virtually impossible for a heterosexual woman to be a feminist," as if heterosexuality were heterosexism; and that social marginality, such as that of lesbian, childless, Black, or Native American women, "appears to be necessary" to form the feminist. Applying these judgments to myself, and believing that as a woman writing at this point I have to be a feminist to be worth beans, I find myself, once again, excluded—disappeared.

The rationale of the exclusionists, as I understand it, is that the material privilege and social approbation our society grants the

heterosexual wife, and particularly the mother, prevent her solidarity with less privileged women and insulate her from the kind of
anger and the kind of ideas that lead to feminist action. There is
truth in this; maybe it's true for a lot of women; I can oppose it only
with my experience, which is that feminism has been a life-saving
necessity to women trapped in the wife/mother "role." What do the
privilege and approbation accorded the housewife-mother by our
society in fact consist of? Being the object of infinite advertising?
Being charged by psychologists with total answerability for children's mental well-being, and by the government with total
answerability for children's welfare, while being regularly equated
with apple pie by sentimental warmongers? As a social "role," motherhood, for any woman I know, simply means that she does everything everybody else does plus bringing up the kids.

To push mothers back into "private life," a mythological space
invented by the patriarchy, on the theory that their acceptance of
the "role" of mother invalidates them for public, political, artistic
responsibility, is to play Old Nobodaddy's game, by his rules, on his
side.

In *Writing Beyond the Ending,* Du Plessis shows how women novelists write about the woman artist: they make her an ethical force, an
activist trying "to change the life in which she is also immersed."[14]
To have and bring up kids is to be about as immersed in life as
one can be, but it does not always follow that one drowns. A lot of us
can swim.

Again, whenever I give a version of this paper, somebody will pick
up on this point and tell me that I'm supporting the Superwoman
syndrome, saying that a woman *should* have kids write books be
politically active and make perfect sushi. I am not saying that. We're
all asked to be Superwoman; I'm not asking it, our society does that.
All I can tell you is that I believe it's a lot easier to write books while
bringing up kids than to bring up kids while working nine to five
plus housekeeping. But that is what our society, while sentimentaliz-
ing over Mom and the Family, demands of most women—unless it
refuses them any work at all and dumps them onto welfare and says,
Bring up your kids on food stamps, Mom, we might want them for
the army. Talk about superwomen, those are the superwomen.
Those are the mothers up against the wall. Those are the marginal
women, without either privacy or publicity; and it's because of them
more than anyone else that the woman artist has a responsibility to
"try to change the life in which she is also immersed."

And now I come back round to the bank of that lake, where the

fisherwoman sits, our woman writer, who had to bring her imagination up short because it was getting too deeply immersed. . . . The
imagination dries herself off, still swearing under her breath, and
buttons up her blouse, and comes to sit beside the little girl, the
fisherwoman's daughter. "Do you like books?" she says, and the child
says, "Oh, yes. When I was a baby I used to eat them, but now I can
read. I can read all of Beatrix Potter by myself, and when I grow up
I'm going to write books, like Mama."

"Are you going to wait till your children grow up, like Jo March
and Theodora?"

"Oh, I don't think so," says the child. "I'll just go ahead and do it."

"Then will you do as Harriet and Margaret and so many Harriets
and Margarets have done and are still doing, and hassle through the
prime of your life trying to do two full-time jobs that are incompatible with each other in practice, however enriching their interplay
may be both to the life and the art?"

"I don't know," says the little girl. "Do I have to?"

"Yes," says the imagination, "if you aren't rich and you want kids."

"I might want one or two," says reason's child. "But why do women
have two jobs where men only have one? It isn't reasonable, is it?"

"Don't ask me!" snaps the imagination. "I could think up a dozen
better arrangements before breakfast! But who listens to me?"

The child sighs and watches her mother fishing. The fisherwoman, having forgotten that her line is no longer baited with the
imagination, isn't catching anything, but she's enjoying the peaceful hour; and when the child speaks again she speaks softly. "Tell
me, Auntie. What is the one thing a writer has to have?"

"I'll tell you," says the imagination. "The one thing a writer has to
have is not balls. Nor is it a child-free space. Nor is it even, speaking
strictly on the evidence, a room of her own, though that is an
amazing help, as is the goodwill and cooperation of the opposite
sex, or at least the local, in-house representative of it. But she
doesn't have to have that. The one thing a writer has to have is a
pencil and some paper. That's enough, so long as she knows that she
and she alone is in charge of that pencil, and responsible, she and
she alone, for what it writes on the paper. In other words, that she's
free. Not wholly free. Never wholly free. Maybe very partially.
Maybe only in this one act, this sitting for a snatched moment being
a woman writing, fishing the mind's lake. But in this, responsible; in
this, autonomous; in this, free."

"Auntie," says the little girl, "can I go fishing with you now?"

Notes

1. Virginia Woolf, *Jacob's Room* (New York: Harcourt Brace Jovanovich, n.d.), p. 7.

2. The edition of *Little Women* I used was my mother's and is now my daughter's. It was published in Boston by Little, Brown, undated, around the turn of the century, and Merrill's fine drawings have also been reproduced in other editions.

3. Rachel Blau Du Plessis, *Writing Beyond the Ending: Narrative Strategies of Twentieth-Century Women Writers* (Bloomington: Indiana University Press, 1985).

4. Louisa May Alcott, *Life, Letters, and Journals* (Boston: Roberts Brothers, 1890). The passages quoted are on pp. 203, 122, and 125.

5. Charles Dickens, *Bleak House* (New York: Thomas Y. Crowell, n.d.), p. 41.

6. Harriet Beecher Stowe, 1841, quoted in Tillie Olsen, *Silences* (New York: Dell, Laurel Editions, 1983), p. 227.

7. This and the subsequent connected passages are from the *Autobiography and Letters of Mrs. Margaret Oliphant*, edited by Mrs. Harry Coghill (Leicester: Leicester University Press, The Victorian Library, 1974), pp. 23, 24.

8. Joseph Conrad, quoted in Olsen, p. 30.

9. Alicia Ostriker, *Writing Like a Woman*, Michigan Poets on Poetry Series (Ann Arbor: University of Michigan Press, 1983), p. 126.

10. Käthe Kollwitz, *Diaries and Letters*, quoted in Olsen, pp. 235, 236.

11. The talk, known in its revised form as "Professions for Women" and so titled in the Essays, was given on January 21, 1931, to the London National Society for Women's Service, and can be found complete with all deletions and alternate readings in Mitchell Leaska's editing of Woolf's *The Pargiters* (New York: Harcourt Brace Jovanovich, 1978).

12. Ostriker, p. 131.

13. Margaret Drabble, *The Millstone* (New York: NAL, Plume Books, 1984), pp. 122–23. Also published under the title *Thank You All Very Much*.

14. Du Plessis, p. 101.

REVIEWS

1977–1986

As I went through my manuscripts in preparing this volume, I was surprised at what a very odd lot of books I was asked, and agreed, to review. I suppose it is because I am myself a genre-buster that I get invited to discuss books that don't fit neatly into the pigeonholes; certainly these are often the books I can best appreciate.

This section contains the only pieces I have ever published under a nom de plume. Some persons who shall be nameless, including myself, co-edited a brief-lived (two issues) journal of reviews of science fiction, called Venom. We felt that sf reviewing had become awfully milquetoasty; it was hard to tell the reviews from the blurbs—everything the greatest, the biggest, the best. Venom was to be an antidote ("Mithridates, he died old"). The precondition for becoming a reviewer for Venom was that you do a killer review of one of your own books, to be published in the magazine. Then you could cut loose on somebody else. So that nobody could know which were the suicides and which were the murders, you had to use a nom de plume. Mine was Mom de Plume.

THE DARK TOWER
by C. S. Lewis
(1977)

For eighty or ninety years a school of writing has flourished that might be called the Inside Club. Although its favored territory begins at the gates of the British public school, outsiders are quite welcome if they have very good brains and can adopt the manner. One reason why T. S. Eliot was sympathetic to Kipling, I suspect, was that he recognized another occasional visitor to the Club—a visitor of genius, to be sure, but his sympathy was perhaps less for the genius than for the manner, that easy, urbane manner which says, never in words, We are on the inside; we *know*. None of the Bloomsbury crowd ever even visited the Club, for a rebellious conscience disbars one automatically. The writing of detective fiction, on the other hand, is almost an entree; mysteries lend themselves all too well to the snobbery of superior knowledge. Mysteries of any kind: including the great mystery, the object of religion. Christianity itself can be taken as an exclusive club, those who know inside, the heathens in the outer dark. By breeding, education, profession, and conviction, C. S. Lewis was a resident member of the Inside Club, and unlike Eliot or Kipling, he seldom ventured out into the dark. He generally speaks from the position of knowing just a bit more than the reader knows. Modestly, of course, and entertainingly, with splendid imagination and wit. But there is a hollow sound, as of tinkling cymbals, in the background.

These tales—one previously unpublished long fragment, three short fantasy pieces, and the unfinished "After Ten Years"—are none of them Lewis at his best; but there are some fine passages. The opening of "After Ten Years," a torment of crowding, cramped muscles, sweat, fear, lust, daydream— Where are these men? In a ship? In a prison? Slowly, with beautiful slowness, one realizes that

C. S. Lewis, *The Dark Tower and Other Stories*, edited by Walter Hooper (New York: Harcourt Brace Jovanovich, 1977).

they are waiting out the night "in the narrow streets of Troy," inside the belly of the wooden horse. This is a superb beginning, and the story of Menelaus's reunion with a middle-aged Helen, if completed, might have fulfilled its promise—if Lewis had treated Helen as a human being. But would he have done so? The indications are that he was going to split her into two stereotypes, heartless beauty and soulless eidolon, the Witch and the Drudge, and would never have arrived at the woman, Helen.

The spitefulness shown towards women in these tales is remarkable. "The Shoddy Lands" is as startling in its cruelty as in its originality; it is, on several levels, a truly frightening story. But the authentic Inside Club tone is at its braying clearest in "Ministering Angels," a humorous piece. Two women volunteer to bring sexual solace to a team of male scientists on Mars. One is a decrepit whore and the other—"Its hair was very short, its nose very long, its mouth very prim, its chin sharp, and its manner authoritative. The voice revealed it as, scientifically speaking, a woman." The true horror of the creature is revealed a page later: "She's a lecturer at a redbrick university." However petty, this is hate. The depth of it is proved in the final paragraph, where the Christian member of the team blissfully contemplates the conversion and salvation of the decrepit whore but never gives a thought to the soul of the "lecturer at a redbrick university."

There's a good deal of hatred in Lewis, and it is a frightening hatred, because this gentle, brilliant, lovable, devout man never saw the need even to rationalize it, let alone apologize for it. He was self-righteous in his faith. That may be permissible to a militant Christian; but it is not permissible to a highly intelligent, highly educated man to be self-righteous in his opinions and his prejudices. Only membership in the Inside Club gives that sanction.

J. R. R. Tolkien, Lewis's close friend and colleague, certainly shared many of Lewis's views and was also a devout Christian. But it all comes out very differently in his fiction. Take his handling of evil: his villains are orcs and Black Riders (goblins and zombies: mythic figures) and Sauron, the Dark Lord, who is never seen and has no suggestion of humanity about him. These are not evil men but embodiments of the evil *in* men, universal symbols of the hateful. The men who do wrong are not complete figures but complements: Saruman is Gandalf's dark-self, Boromir Aragorn's; Wormtongue is, almost literally, the weakness of King Theoden. There remains the wonderfully repulsive and degraded Gollum.

But nobody who reads the trilogy hates, or is asked to hate, Gollum. Gollum is Frodo's shadow; and it is the shadow, not the hero, who achieves the quest. Though Tolkien seems to project evil into "the others," they are not truly others but ourselves; he is utterly clear about this. His ethic, like that of dream, is compensatory. The final "answer" remains unknown. But because responsibility has been accepted, charity survives. And with it, triumphantly, the Golden Rule. The fact is, if you like the book, you love Gollum.

In Lewis, responsibility appears only in the form of the Christian hero fighting and defeating the enemy: a triumph, not of love, but of hatred. The enemy is not oneself but the Wholly Other, demoniac. This projection leaves the author free to be cruel, and cruelty is the dominant tone of several of these stories. Ransom, the hero of Lewis's trilogy, appears in the major work of the volume, "The Dark Tower." His few remarks are in the true Club manner, very modest, very know-it-all. Give me Gollum any day.

Lewis must be called a science-fiction writer if only for the central scenes of the first volume of his trilogy, *Out of the Silent Planet*. These descriptions of Martian landscapes and inhabitants are grand: vivid, emotionally powerful, genuinely unearthly. Science fiction has been imitating them ever since. There are hints of that visionary strength in "The Dark Tower," but weakened by embarrassingly naive sexual overtones; he is not in control of his material. Nobody who draws upon deep unconscious material can be blamed for getting swamped by it at times; and this is one of Lewis's nearest approaches to a venture into the outer (or inner?) dark. But it's not science fiction. Though it is a time-travel story, the rationalization is drawn from the English Ladies of the Trianon and from J. W. Dunne's *An Experiment with Time*—occultism, not science. I am afraid that Lewis's feeling about science is expressed by a character on page 48: "And who ever heard of a new scientific discovery which didn't show that the real universe was even fouler and meaner and more dangerous than you had supposed?" So much for Galileo and Einstein; so much for Konrad Lorenz among the greylag geese. The speaker adds, "I never went in much for religion, but I begin to think Dr. Ransom was right."

Lewis never finished the story. He read the first chapters to his friends, then laid it aside for good. Walter Hooper, his biographer, who found the manuscript and published it—with excellent notes— surely did so from the purest motives of scholarship and admiration; but I begin to think Mr. Hooper was wrong.

CLOSE ENCOUNTERS, STAR WARS,
AND THE TERTIUM QUID
(1978)

A dark screen. The title, *Close Encounters of the Third Kind,* appears in silence. The sound begins very, very softly; rises slowly; explodes into a roaring fortissimo—and stays there during the rest of the movie.

The light is often at top brightness too, but it is almost impossible to make the light from a projector painful; and anyhow, we have eyelids. But no earlids. The light is used with variety and a great deal of beauty. The sound is used with brutality.

Very seldom can one understand a complete sentence. Words are mumbled and slurred off, Method-style, shouted or screamed into dust storms, wind storms, helicopter backwash, yelled simultaneously in French and English, redoubled and self-effaced by loudspeaker echo. A few lines come through clear, and they are effective:

"*I* didn't *want* to see it."

"Yes, I saw you going up in the air, did you see me running after you?"

And my favorite, whispered: "*Mince alors . . .*"

Just enough comes through to convince the middle-aged moviegoer in the fourth row extreme left (does Pauline Kael ever have to sit in the fourth row extreme left?) that she isn't going deaf and that the unintelligibility is deliberate. Perhaps it is used to disguise the banality of most of the dialogue. Certainly there were moments in *Star Wars* when one prayed in vain for unintelligibility. . . . Possibly the high proportion of noise to meaning *has* a meaning. But I am afraid that it serves merely to augment the hysterical tension established in the opening scene and never relaxed thereafter.

Why, after all, does there have to be a dust storm in the Sonora Desert just then? Why does everyone rush about screaming in three languages? The discovery of mysteriously just-abandoned World

War II planes might very well take place quietly, eerily; and deserts aren't noisy, crowded places, as a rule. But no. The wind and all the performers have to howl in unison.

When humans and aliens finally communicate, it is by musical tones. In that one scene the noise gimmickry all comes together; it is at last a genuine climax. If it rose to true music, it would be a great moment.

But even then it would not justify the rest of the soundtrack, which uses noise to whip up emotion, the same trick that's so easy to do with electronically amplified instruments: decibellicosity. Exposed to aggression by loud noise, the body must continually resist its own fight/flight reaction, thus building up an adrenaline high, thus feeling surges of unfocused emotion, increased pulse rate, etc.—thrills and chills. No harm. Same kick as a rollercoaster. But a rollercoaster doesn't pretend to have a message.

On the other hand ... *Star Wars,* which rather ostentatiously pretends not to have any message, may be even tricksier.

The end of *Star Wars* kept bothering me after I saw it the first time. I kept thinking, such a funny silly beautiful movie, why did George Lucas stick on that wooden ending, a high-school graduation, with prizes for good citizenship? But when I saw it again I realized it wasn't high school but West Point: a place crawling with boots and salutes. Aren't there any civilians in this Empire, anyhow? Finally a friend who knows films explained to me that the scene is a nostalgic evocation or imitation of Leni Riefenstahl's famous film of the 1936 Olympics, with the German winners receiving a grateful ovation from the Thousand-Year Reich. Having dragged Dorothy and Toto and that lot around the cosmos a bit, Lucas cast about for another surefire golden oldie and came up with Adolf Hitler.

Anyhow, what the hell is nostalgia doing in a science-fiction film? With the whole universe and all the future to play in, Lucas took his marvelous toys and crawled under the fringed cloth on the parlor table, back into a nice safe hideyhole, along with Flash Gordon and the Cowardly Lion and Huck Skywalker and the Flying Aces and the Hitler Jugend. If there's a message there, I don't think I want to hear it.

There are gorgeous moments in *Star Wars,* especially on the desert planet (before everybody gets into uniform): the little desert people, the caravan, the behemoth, the town, R2D2 lost, and so on. Through the impasto of self-indulgence and the comic-book compulsion to move-move-move, there breaks a childlike, radical, precise gesture of the imagination: and you glimpse what a science-fiction movie might be like, when they get around to making one.*

Close Encounters has science-fictional elements—the space ship is even more splendid than the ones in *Star Wars*—but it seems to me essentially an occultist movie. It's much more amiable than the endless nasties about little girls possessed by devils; it's definitely on the side of the angels. But the arrival of benevolent aliens in saucers is a theme science fiction hasn't dealt with, except facetiously, for at least a generation. Fiction writers got out long ago, leaving the field to believers, faddists, amateur photographers, psychologists, and the Air Force. Saucerism has a lot to do with religion, as Jung pointed out, but nothing at all to do with either science or science fiction.

Indeed, the movie seemed almost entirely irrational. Perhaps, being middle-aged and seeing it from a highly oblique angle, I missed some explanations. I ought to see it again before saying this; but my impression is that the plot abounds in giant loopholes, as the universe abounds in black holes. How does the U.S. government know *when* to expect the aliens? Why do they have a troop of—well, exchange students, I guess—all dressed up in red pantsuits (one woman, or was it two, in the whole troop) ready to go aboard the saucer? How do they know they'll be wanted? What the dickens is François Truffaut doing there? And if he's there, amidst all the security officers and dead sheep, why aren't there any Mexicans or Chinese or Russians or Canadians or Peruvians or Samoans or Swahili or Thai? Why does the United States get to hog the cosmic show? Why does— Oh, well. Shoot. Why do you spoil it, asking questions? everybody snarls at me.

Well, because both movies come on as science fiction, or as "sci fi," anyhow; and I was brought up to believe that science fiction, whatever its shortcomings in the way of character, catharsis, and grammar, was supposed to try to be intellectually coherent: to have an idea and to follow it through. Neither of these movies would know an idea if they fell over it (which, of course, given their subject matter, they frequently do). *Star Wars* is all action and *Close Encounters* is all emotion, and both are basically mindless.

The emotional bias interests me somewhat more—it's a greater artistic risk to take. In *Close Encounters* sometimes the emotions do

---

*They did get around to making two, so far (1988)—*Time Bandits* and *Brother from Another Planet.*

move. Children are genuinely important throughout it, and so there is a deep resonance for a moment when the aliens first appear, childlike, gracile, almost fetal forms bathed in pure light. But then Spielberg blows it with a disastrous close-up. His hand is so heavy! Nobody is allowed to do anything, even load a camera, quietly or easily; all movements are frenetic, violent, as if the characters were being pursued by giant sharks. Yet the actors are so good they establish personality and believable response against all the odds. You begin to feel with them, to go along with them . . . and then another load of hysteria gets dumped on and the volume gets turned up another notch.

The end, for instance. I think we're supposed to be sort of misty-eyed; but what about? I want to be clear about what I'm misty about. Is it because they didn't blow us up? Because we didn't blow them up? Because the hero's doing what he wanted and going off in a really gorgeous supersaucer? But what happened to the other guys (and gal) in red pantsuits? They don't seem to be going into the saucer with him. And why does the heroine express her emotion by suddenly ignoring her beautiful kid and shooting a full twenty-four-shot roll of snapshots, color slides no doubt, of the hero's exodus? There she is, smiling through her tears, pressing the shutter again—and again—and again—and again— Is that an adequate dramatic expression of human emotion at a peak experience? Is it even appropriate? I find it pitiful: and, since this is a movie, grotesquely self-conscious. It happened, because it's on film. . . .

Well, it's real pretty. And some day they'll make a science-fiction movie. Meanwhile, I think I'll go back and see *Dersu Uzala* for the third time. Because that is a movie about a world and a time none of us will ever see; about aliens; about fear, and love; and because it lets us see that the universe really is endless, and terrible, and beautiful.

SHIKASTA
by Doris Lessing
(1979)

Doris Lessing takes risks but does not play games. One does not turn to her books for humor or wit or playfulness, nor will one find in them any game-playing in the sense of one-upping, faking, posturing. In her introductory remarks to *Shikasta* she states with characteristic straightforwardness what she sees as the modern novelist's debt to science fiction. Not even taking refuge in the respectability of "speculative fiction," she presents her book as science fiction, and I shall review it as such, gratefully; for science fiction has wasted far too much time apologizing to the pretentious and explaining itself to the willfully ignorant.

If I had read *Shikasta* without knowing who wrote it, I do not think I would have guessed it to be the work of an established author writing with some awkwardness in a new mode. I am afraid I would have said: A first novel, typically earnest and overambitious, badly constructed, badly edited, showing immense promise; when this writer has learned the art, we'll have a first-ranker. . . . Novel-making is novel-making, whether imagination or observation dominates, and given Lessing's experience with the fiction of ideas and with near-future settings, the unshapeliness of *Shikasta* is surprising; the rambling title is only too descriptive. To be sure, the subject is no less than a history of human life on earth, past, present, and future, not the sort of thing novelists who play safe, winners of fictional parlor games, are likely to attempt. Lessing mentions Olaf Stapledon in her introduction, and in scope the book—especially as the first of a series—indeed vies with *Last and First Men;* but the almost obsessive organization, the unity of Stapledon's thought, is wanting. The majesty of the vision is fitful. Sometimes it is majestic, sometimes it is little more than a pulp Galactic Empire with the

Doris Lessing, *Canopus in Argos—Archives. Re: Colonised Planet 5. Shikasta. Personal, Psychological, Historical Documents Relating to Visit by Johor (George Sherban) Emissary (Grade 9). 87th of the Period of the Last Days* (New York: Alfred A. Knopf, 1979).

Goodies fighting the Baddies. Then again it goes off into allegory, like C. S. Lewis, for a while; and there are moments—the bad moments, for me—when it all seems to have been inspired by the Velikovsky–Von Däniken school of, as it were, thought.

The aesthetic incoherence is not due to the plurality of viewpoints, but it may be connected to Lessing's use of the alien viewpoint: most of the events are recounted by an extraterrestrial witness. This is of course one of the basic devices of science fiction (and of prescientific ironic tales), but familiar as the technique is, it requires very great care. Only intense and continual imaginative effort by the author can keep the "alien" voice from sounding human, all too human—thus subverting the estrangement that is the goal of the technique, and so disastrously shrinking, instead of expanding, the universe. This is what has happened in those dreary backwaters of science fiction where the heroes fight the dirty (Commies) (Capitalists) from Aldebaran. Lessing commits no such political imbecilities; the trouble lies more with ethics, I think. The morality voiced by her aliens seems less universal than sectarian, and at times Canopus in Argos sounds strangely like a pulpit in Geneva.

The villains of the piece, from a planet called Shammat, part of the Empire of Puttiora, remain offstage. Though Shammat is the author of evil on earth, all the agents of evil we meet in the book are human beings. But the agents of good we meet are not human; they come from Canopus. One is left in doubt whether mankind has any moral being at all; perhaps we are all puppets of either Shammat or Canopus. In any case, the logic of the book is inescapable: humanity is incapable of doing good on its own, without direct and continual prompting by Benevolences from Outer Space. (The behavior of these guardian angels I personally find, on the evidence given, paternalistic, imperialist, authoritarian, and male supremacist. The latter trait is particularly galling; they claim to be bisexual, but if you notice, they always impregnate human women and never permit themselves to be impregnated by human men.) The picture, then, is, or resembles, one currently very popular indeed, that of the chariots of the gods, or *dei ex machina;* and the message is: In us there is no truth or power. All great events on earth result from decisions made elsewhere; all our inventions were given us by extraterrestrials; all our religions feebly reflect the glory of an unhuman Founder. We have done, and can do, unaided and by ourselves, nothing. Except, perhaps—this is not clear—evil.

To find this projective ethic stated by a considerable writer, no hack or crank, is disquieting to me. Though *Shikasta* is not a Christian book, I think it is a Calvinist one: it affirms the radical irresponsibility of mankind. Salvation not by works but by grace alone, not by the soul's effort but by intercession/intervention—for a few, the chosen, the elect: the rest consigned to damnation by judgment/holocaust/apocalypse. The theme has recently been common in pseudoscience and of course is a cornerstone of fundamentalism. Its roots I suppose are in the Near East. It turns up in the West in hard centuries, whenever people seek the counsels of despair. It has no claim to universality, however, since it remains unsympathetic and essentially unintelligible to the great majority of people. It is not a position sympathetic to most artists, either, since it leaves no room in the world for tragedy, or for charity.

There is much self-hatred in *Shikasta*—hatred of the feminine, the middle-class, the national, the White, the Western, the human—which all comes to a head in the strange episode of the Trial, late in the story, and there perhaps self-destructs. But there is no catharsis; the ethic of guilt forbids it. A brief utopian coda rings false to my ear—the usual Luddite prigs sharing everything with nary a cross word. And all through these final sections the protagonist, Johor, in his last incarnation as George, stalks about bearing the White Man's Burden until you want to kick him. We never meet the Shammatians, we never meet the Sirians, and the Canopans are twits. But the humans . . . There is the story of Rachel; the story of Lynda; the story of "Individual 6"—the exact, brilliant, compassionate, passionate portrayal of human minds driven out of "sanity," forced on beyond. In such passages, Lessing is incomparable. Does she need to write science fiction to achieve them? Would there not be more place for them in a conventional novel?

She seems to have little real interest in the alien as such, little pleasure in it. Invention is an essential ingredient of science fiction, and she lacks or scants it, letting theory and opinion override the humble details that make up creation (primary or secondary). Canopus and the Canopans remain dead words, a world without a landscape, characters without character. No games, no play. The Canopans are angels, messengers of God, but Lessing's concept of the divine excludes that Trickster who creates and destroys. No Coyote, no Loki, no Hermes. Life is real, life is earnest, and Shiva is not allowed to dance in this universe. Like Solzhenitsyn, like the late Victorians, Lessing denies the value of pure invention, permitting

only the "meaningful." The work will be not a mystery but a morality. And so it is. And yet—

Every now and then she stops moralizing and looks around at the
world she has got herself into; and at such times there is no doubt at
all why she is there, or that she belongs there. She does not write
conventional fiction because she does not have a conventional mind.
She is not a realist at all. Nor is she a fantasist. The old distinctions
are useless and must be discarded. Before the critics can do that, we
novelists must get on past them ourselves, clear past. It is not easy;
no wonder Lessing moves awkwardly. But she moves forward. I
would not wish to dwell upon things like SOWF, or substance-of-we-
feeling—is the phrase or its acronym worse?—but maybe we had to
go through SOWF to get to Zone 6. Zone 6—which is Hades, and
the landscape of the Tibetan *Book of the Dead,* and certain remote
territories of the unconscious mind, and the Borderland, and
more—is magnificent in conception and in imagery.

Intellectual fiction, the novel of ideas, all too often slides down
into the novel of opinions. Science fiction gone self-indulgent rants
and preaches, with no more right to, despite its vast subject matter,
than any other kind of art. Lessing's opinions, her diatribes against
"science" and "politics" and so forth, are very nearly the ruin of the
novel. But beneath and beyond the opinions, not fully under her
control, perhaps even disobeying her conscious intent, is the creative spirit that can describe a terrorist's childhood with the authority of a Dostoyevsky, or imagine the crowded souls crying at the
gates of life—and the lurching, lumbering, struggling book is
redeemed, is worth reading, is immortal diamond.

TWO FROM "VENOM"
(1980)

A fat clod and a girl who can't make up her mind how to spell her name get into these woods and go back and forth and back and forth and back and forth until you want to scream, and then they go back and forth some more. Nobody in *The Beginning Place* can make up their mind about anything, not even what time of day it is. When they meet a dragon they can't even make up their mind what *sex* it is. In order to leave a village populated exclusively by exquisitely boring Archetypes, they finally start going straight forth, but as usual they can't make up their minds which way is forth, so it turns out to be back, after all. The climax of this thrilling narrative is when they find out that the way to get downtown is to take the bus. Recommended to persons with mild inner-ear disturbances and those who want very badly to be branch reference librarians.

* * *

In the first place, *The Book of the Dun Cow* isn't *The Book of the Dun Cow*. *The Book of the Dun Cow* is a twelfth-century Irish manuscript about a cattle raid—an appallingly primitive epic that you can find, if you're lucky, in a beautiful English translation by the poet Thomas Kinsella, *The Tain*. Read it and decide if things have changed much in Ireland. Why did Walter Wangerin Jr. use the title for his book, which has nothing to do with Ireland ancient or modern? There is an allegorical dun cow in his book, but you can write a book with a whale in it without calling it *Moby Dick*. I guess he just liked the sound of it, and what it really is isn't supposed to matter. Like Joan Didion writing *The Book of Common Prayer*. Kinda cute and like tasteless and I mean like who *cares* about those *old* books anyhow.

So this book which isn't *The Book of the Dun Cow* is about this

Ursula K. Le Guin, *The Beginning Place* (New York: Harper & Row, 1980); Walter Wangerin Jr., *The Book of the Dun Cow* (New York: Harper & Row, 1978).

Rooster (which shows that it's American; if it was a British bird it would be a Cock, te-he, quoth she). The Rooster is Good. There is also an Evil Rooster. One is on God's side—guess which one. The other is on the side of a mighty black serpent who lives under the earth. If this sounds familiar, please keep in mind that we are not discussing *The Book of Common Prayer* by Joan Didion or anyone else. Because he is evil, God damns the serpent, forcing him to live underground. No, no, dummy, the *serpent* is evil, not God. How do I know? Because the author says so. And because the serpent crawls and smells bad and lives in the dark. But God *made* him live there, so it's not *his* fault— Shuddup. The serpent is BAD, and God is GOOD, and you take that on faith. You'd better, because when we finally get a reason, here it is: the serpent's evil plan:

> [The serpent] would roar almighty challenges to the Lord God Himself. He would spew chaos among the stars; and he would whirl his tail with such power that when it hit the earth, that planet would be cracked from its fixed position at the center of things to spin like nonsense going nowhere. . . . He himself would make of his earth prison a puny mockery. *He* would make it little among the planets and nothing among the suns. *He* would snatch purpose from its being, giving it a loose, erratic, mean- ingless course to travel. *He* would surround it with cold, empty space. And *he* would cancel heaven from above it.

I told you he was BAD. Like Copernicus. Like Galileo. Like Newton, like Einstein—BAD right to the core.

I'll bet that smelly serpent even thinks women are people. Nobody else in the book does. Females are beyootiful, dootiful, divinely inspired at times, and God made them to Help Men. (God help those who help themselves!) Leaders, of course, are male. All leaders. Even when we're talking about ants (this is an animal fable, not the Old Testament), the Leader of the Ants has to be a Man Ant. Yep.

The hero has a coop full of hens, but his relations with the hens are kind of glided over. Then he falls in love with the beyootiful, dootiful, and divinely inspired heroine hen, and she bears his chil- dren. Guess which sex. Would a hero and a heroine have *female chicks*?

The book is so sloppy it's hard to talk about. Almost worse than Joan Didion. (I said almost.) For instance, there's a "Language of Power," which is Latin. Latin has indeed been a language of power, first secular, then religious, which makes its use in an outside-world-time fable either grossly tendentious or grossly inept, unless it is used with great care. If there's one thing about languages of power that we might all agree on, it's that they *have* to be used right. Right? Well, my Latin's not so hot, but I know that the adjective *potens* would have a plural, something like *potentes,* so that the phrase "crows potens," to mean powerful cockadoodles, doesn't hold together. And the allegorical dog's name, Mundo Cani, sounds like that Italian movie *Mondo Cane* but seems to mean "dog-world," in the ablative case, for some reason. If the author meant "dog of the world," I think it would be Mundi Canis. But I don't know what he meant. He doesn't seem to care. Faith is all you need. On page 157 he says, "Be it known that neither Basil nor Paprika nor any other Turkey had a sense of smell." On page 159 he says, "But Turkeys have a most impartial sense of smell." *Credo quia absurdum!*

Inside this silly, sexist, sentimental, specious book there's a good thing: a subversive weasel, struggling to get out. The weasel is true and funny. The rest is Cream-of-Christian cant.

—MOM DE PLUME

FREDDY'S BOOK
and
VLEMK THE BOX-PAINTER
by John Gardner
(1980)

Freddy's Book is a brilliant novel about a sixteenth-century Swedish knight who, with the Devil's assistance, helps Gustav Vasa gain the throne and then, with a Bishop's assistance, kills the Devil. Going strictly by internal evidence, one might suppose *Freddy's Book* to be the work of the offspring of an illicit but delightful union between Ingmar Bergman and Isak Dinesen; but it was written by John Gardner (who, characteristically, insists that it was written by Freddy).

They say that inside every fat man is a thin man trying to get out. Inside John Gardner, whose jacket photographs show what looks like a very sizable fellow, there must be a really enormous man trying to get out, and succeeding. The narrator of the fine Gothic tale that introduces the main story is a tall and bulky professor, who meets (in strange circumstances) Freddy, a giant, who has written a book about an eight-foot Swedish knight. All this height and girth might seem a bit obsessive, but it is in fact enjoyable. We have had lots of books about little creeps, and after all Mr. Sammler is not the only inhabitant of his planet. It should also be observed that the Devil is even larger, very much larger, than the other big fellows in *Freddy's Book*. He is one of the largest and most convincing devils to be found in modern literature; he is very stupid and very subtle; and his eventual murder at the hands and bone knife of the knight is an event of great dramatic power and originality, and of most devious and echoing implications. The tale left me mystified and satisfied to the highest degree. Who could ask for anything more?

John Gardner, *Freddy's Book*, illustrated by Daniel Biamonte (New York: Alfred A. Knopf, 1980); *Vlemk the Box-Painter*, illustrated by Catherine Kanner (Northridge, Calif.: Lord John Press, 1979).

Freddy's Book is illustrated in darkly appropriate black and white by Daniel Biamonte. Catherine Kanner's illustrations to *Vlemk the Box-Painter* are elegant and intelligent but vitiated by Beardsleyism. One must wonder why so many illustrators of fantasy seem scarcely to use their powers of fantasy, the concrete visual imagination that is their birthright as artists, but limit themselves to the style and mannerisms of Beardsley, Rackham, Nielsen, and other late-Victorian and Edwardian minor artists. A tradition there must be, but why might it not start from Dürer, or Rembrandt, or Géricault, or Klee? Why must fantasy characters and fantasy places always be drawn so clean pretty shiny and twee? Is there no dirt in Middle Earth?

So I arrive grumpily at *Vlemk,* which is what I think one must call a minor work. It has charm and interest; it plays in narrative form with some of the ideas discussed in Gardner's *On Moral Fiction* and with some other ideas all its own; but it does not seem to arrive anywhere. It remains in between. It sets off in a manner suited to adult or child, that straightforward narrative mode of the tale told aloud: "Once a man and wife lived in a vinegar jug by the sea," "There was once a king of the Sakya clan," "There once was a man who made pictures on boxes. . . ." But the matter is intended for a highly sophisticated readership, and so the folktale manner soon sounds affected; nor is it consistently maintained.

In the same way, the setting, the time/place where it happens, is neither here nor there. In *On Moral Fiction* Gardner makes it plain that "truth of place" is something he can cheerfully dispense with, going so far as to say that "truth is useful in realistic art but is much less necessary to the fabulous." Alas, I could not disagree more strongly. Effective works of fantasy are distinguished by their often relentless accuracy of detail, by their exactness of imagination, by the coherence and integrity of their imagined worlds—by, precisely, their paradoxical truthfulness. (I assert this not only of *The Lord of the Rings* or *Le Petit Prince* but of *Beowulf,* in the latter case the "truth of place" being not visual but psychological.) An infallible sign of amateur or careless fantasy writing is the blurred detail, the fudged artifact, the stupid anachronism that proclaims, "This is just a fantasy, folks, so it doesn't really matter." It matters more in fantasy than anywhere else, since in fantasy we stand on no common mundane ground but have only the fantasist to trust. The writer is our only space ship, and all our hippogriff. If the fantasist's truth fails us—*ffft.* So I found most grievous Gardner's coy or careless references to garbage men and biologists in his stock Generic Medieval setting. And why does the box-painter take thirty mortal pages to carry the talking picture to the princess? Because if he did it sooner, if, in other words, he behaved like a human being, it would subvert the allegory. But why make the story a bloody allegory? It's a lovely idea, the fierce little miniature portrait that talks back. If only Gardner had told it with faith in its reality, if only he had honored his fable with confidence in its truth! This need not have been a minor work.

But everybody, no matter how major, is allowed their minor works; and anyhow we may all rejoice that we've got *Freddy's Book* and its inexhaustible author, Gardner Son of Grendel's Mother.

THE MARRIAGES BETWEEN ZONES THREE, FOUR, AND FIVE
by Doris Lessing
(1980)

With a sigh that she refused to deepen into a groan, she again saw him as her fellow prisoner, and marvelling that this taut, grief-marked man could be the gross and fleshy Ben Ata of their first days, she enclosed him, as he did her, and their lovemaking was all a consoling and a reassurance. When his hand felt for their child, now responding quite vigorously to their lovemaking, as if wishing to share in it—as if it were the promise of a festival—it was with respect and a promise not to an extension of himself, or of her, but a salute to the possibilities of them both; a considered and informed salute, at that, for Al·Ith, feeling the delicately contained strength of those enquiring fingers, knew that the potentialities he acknowledged were for the unknown and the unexpected, as well as for familiar delight. For this union of incompatibles could not be anything less than a challenge.

A challenge it is, and a reward. The second of the *Canopus in Argos* series of novels is a finer-grained and stronger book than *Shikasta*, the first. *The Marriages* may be read for the pure pleasure of reading it, a tale unencumbered by metaphysical machinery. The Canopans and Sirians, the superhuman powers of good and evil of *Shikasta*, stay offstage this time. The manipulations of the Sirians are only hinted at; the powers of good, here known as the Providers, emit directives by Voice (like Joan of Arc's Voices) and, entertainingly, by beating an invisible drum. The Providers—I kept thinking of Scott's Antarctic crew, who referred to Providence, upon which they depended quite consciously if not always successfully, as "Provvy"—the Providers command Al·Ith, ruler of Zone Three, and Ben Ata, ruler of Zone Four, to marry. Both obey the order not

Doris Lessing, *The Marriages Between Zones Three, Four, and Five* (New York: Alfred A. Knopf, 1980).

259

happily but unquestioningly. Theirs not to reason why. (Why not?)
Once they meet, however, the two human beings begin to behave
very humanly indeed, and what might have been a fable enacted by
wooden puppets twitching on the strings of allegory becomes a
lively and lovable novel. A novel in the folktale mode, bordering on
the mythic.

The theme is one of the major themes of both myth and novel:
marriage. Lessing's treatment of it is complex and flexible, passionate and compassionate, with a rising vein of humor uncommon in
her work, both welcome and appropriate. Marriage in all modes.
Marriage sensual, moral, mental, political. Marriage of two people,
an archetypally sensitive lady and an archetypally tough soldier.
Marriage of female and male; of masculine and feminine; of intu-
itional and sensational; of duty and pleasure. Marriage of their two
countries, which reflect all these opposites and more, including the
oppositions wealth/poverty, peace/war. And then suddenly a marriage with Zone Five is ordered, a second marriage, a tertium quid,
startling and inevitable.

It may be worth noting that this series of oppositions does not
overlap very far with the old Chinese system of opposites, the yin
and yang. At female/male and perhaps at intuitional/sensational
they coincide; otherwise Lessing simply omits the dark, wet, cold,
passive, etc., the whole yin side of the Tai Chi figure. Her dialectic of
marriage takes place almost wholly in terms of yang. Its process
therefore is Hegelian, struggle and resolution, without the option of
a maintained balance (the marriage cannot last). This is illustrative
of the extreme Westernness of Lessing's ethic and metaphysic. The
Canopus books propose a cosmic viewpoint: but it turns out to be so
purely European an explanation of human destiny that anyone
even slightly familiar with other religious or philosophical systems
must find it inadequate, if not presumptuous. In her introduction to
Shikasta, referring to "the sacred literatures of all races and nations,"
Lessing said, "It is possible we make a mistake when we dismiss
them as quaint fossils from a dead past." Possible, indeed. Who but
a bigot or an ignoramus would do so? Lessing is neither, but the
parochialism is disturbing.

The landscapes and societies of Zones Three, Four, and Five (and,
most tantalizingly, Two) are sketched, not detailed. One cannot live
in these lands, as one can in Middle Earth. These are the countries
of parable, intellectual nations which one can only visit in a closed
car; but the scenery is vastly interesting, and one may wish one could

at least stop and get out. The quick-paced plot is kept distanced by several devices: by use of the folktale ambience of faraway lands once upon a time; by frequent reference, in a kind of stop-frame effect, to paintings of the events recounted; and by having the tale told by an elderly male Chronicler of Zone Three.

At first the protagonists also appear at a distance, a bit larger than life, all of a piece, heroic. Perhaps the Ben Hur lurking in the name Ben Ata is even deliberate (though I wish the Alice trying to lisp her way out of Al·Ith were not so audible). As the two enter upon their difficult marriage, however, and are driven through all the changes of fear, patience, lust, rage, liking, masochism, ecstasy, jealousy, rebellion, dependence, friendship, and the rest, they become smaller, more distinct, more complicated. They get older. Their heroism is no longer easy, it has become painful, it has become real. By having the courage to use these great stock characters, the Queen and the King, and to take them seriously as people, Lessing has presented a personal drama of general significance, skillfully and without falsification. Her portrait of a marriage is perfectly clear-sighted and admirably inconclusive. Moralist that she is, she makes no judgment here. Character is destiny: her characters make themselves a human destiny, far more impressive than any conceivable pseudo-divine Five-Year Plan for the good of Zones Three to Five. They might even have risen to tragedy, had the author not opened heaven's trapdoor to them to prevent that chance.

Though accurate, that last sentence is probably unfair. After all, *The Marriages* aspires to myth, not to tragedy. Zone Two is certainly an unconventional and attractive heaven, or stage on the way to heaven; one may be content to leave Al·Ith to it at last. Perhaps it is only mean-mindedness that makes me distrust Zone One, fearing that it will turn out to be not simply better but Perfectly Good, and therefore longing to find something wrong with it: just as we discovered, gradually, guided gently by our author, what was wrong with the utopian Zone Three, that now quite familiar country where nobody is possessive or destructive or macho or has bad taste in furniture.

The Manichaean-Calvinistic hierarchy, the closed system implied by the structure and the more vatic bits of *Shikasta*, seems here to give way to an open source of relative values—a way, a human way. Or does Lessing not agree with the Chronicler who tells her tale so well? I think she does.

We chroniclers do well to be afraid when we approach those parts of our histories (our natures) that deal with evil, the depraved, the benighted. Describing, we become. . . .

I tell you that goodness—what we in our ordinary daylight selves call goodness: the ordinary, the decent—these are nothing without the hidden powers that pour forth continually from their shadow sides. . . .

In those high places there is a dark side, and who knows but that it may be very dark. . . .

But the tale is not a fearful one. It is kindly, careful, cheerful. Its teller, knowing the darkness, faces the light.

KALILA AND DIMNA
retold by Ramsay Wood
(1980)

In order to be happy with a place or a person or a book, some of us need to know where we are and where we stand, while others are perfectly content to float free. Floaters will enjoy this book more than standers. As an old stander, I felt frustrated by the breezy sketchiness of the information granted us (by Doris Lessing in a friendly introduction and by the author in a brief afterword) concerning what, exactly, the book is. A translation, one gathers, of part of—of what? Well, one can't say exactly, because it turns out not to be a translation at all, but a collation, reworking, and modernification of various earlier translations of—of what? Well, at this point I went to the library (a good place to make a stand) and established to my own satisfaction that *Kalila and Dimna* and the *Fables of Bidpai* and the *Tales of Pilpay* and all the rest are versions of a single original: a very old Sanskrit collection of stories, the *Panchatantra*, upon which translations and variations have grown and overgrown like vines on an ancient temple in the forests of India. Two hundred versions, over the centuries, in over fifty languages, says my library source; twenty English translations alone in the century 1788–1888, says Lessing. Many of the stories are now familiar—to Buddhists, Hindus, Moslems, Christians—as folktales, and probably many of them started out as folktales; but the *Panchatantra* and its Persian, Arabian, and other recensions are not folklore but literature. The book was a "Mirror for Princes"—a lively manual of political advice, Machiavellian in its realism and psychological astuteness, making and marking its points by animal fables.

Dull books do not become global millennial best sellers. (Our great animal fable is Orwell's *Animal Farm*, a worthy continuation of the tradition.) The stories are trenchant, funny, charming, cruel.

Kalila and Dimna: Selected Fables of Bidpai, retold by Ramsay Wood, illustrated by Margaret Kilrenny (New York: Alfred A. Knopf, 1980).

Part of the success of this collection surely lies in the way the stories are presented, an exquisitely tormenting Chinese box technique, which Ramsay Wood has preserved. The frame story involves a King and a Wise Man. When we are quite deep into the story of these two, the Wise Man says, "O King! permit me to illustrate my point with the tale of the Bull and the Lion," and starts telling it. Just as we are getting really interested in the fate of the Bull, a Jackal says to the Lion, "O Lion, do you remember the story of the Mice that ate the Iron?" and starts telling it, and just as we're really into that one—and on it goes. The most rigid and determined stander must consent to float free while this ramification of suspense from suspense proceeds. It provides a salutary exercise of intellect and spirit for both kings and commoners. Recent practitioners of forms of the Chinese box narrative technique include Italo Calvino, Gene Wolfe, and Russell Hoban, all masters of sudden corner-turnings, intricate proliferation, and the final (or semifinal) reward—when the Iron, the Mice, the Lion, the Jackal, the Bull, the Wise Man, and the King are all brought back rapidly in order in the most brilliantly satisfying fashion. In this, Ramsay Wood follows his originals closely, and slips with skill in and out of stories as elegantly interfolded as the petals of a rose.

The vitality of the stories and the fascination of the narrative plan kept me going, but the language made the going hard. It is not so much a free-floating style as a mishmash of mannerisms, few of which have any aesthetic relation to the matter, and some of which are in gross contrast to it. Effects intended to be light and humorous fall dead. A rat named Zirac lives in a town called Mahila in the cell of a monk called Charlie. The Charlie sort of thing may be meant to generalize the reference of the tale by disorienting expectation, but to me it merely cheapens the tone. Translations of the Eastern classics have tended to be stuffy, but there's no need to rush to the other extreme and be twerpy. Edgerton's laborious 1924 reconstruction of the original *Panchatantra*, intended for scholars, not for the common reader, calls the monk Tuft-Ears, and another monk, whom Wood calls merely "Charlie's friend," appears as Fat-Paunch, with a footnote saying the name really translates "Big Buttocks." All this is a good deal funnier than Charlie, and also reminds us that being rude about the clergy is a very ancient art.

The worst trouble with tone is in the dialogue:

> "Come along, Lady Pinfeathers," he menaced gruffly. "We'll leave Zirac to make himself at home while you and I get some

chow ready. I'll hunt for it and you can be the pretty waitress.
Heh heh! . . ."

This kind of stuff goes on for pages. And "he menaced gruffly" is
symptomatic of another tendency in Wood's prose, towards the
purple pulpish:

> The afternoon sun blazed low in the sky, its light raking across
> the landscape and scattering all detail into glinting brilliance. A
> zephyr caressed the iridescent kiang tips, swaying them back
> and forth, one into another, in brief, shimmering waves.

Seldom have so many present participles achieved so little. Here, for
contrast, is a bit from the stuffy old Edgerton version:

> [The lion] laid upon him his right hand, plump, round, and
> long, and adorned with claws like thunderbolts in place of orna-
> ments, and said courteously, "Peace be with you. . . ."

Now, that's how animals talk! Ramsay Wood seems to lack faith in
his material, to believe that it needs "brightening up" or "interpreting for the modern reader," as they say. It doesn't. It's good, strong
stuff. It tastes a lot better without 7-Up.

The illustrations by Margaret Kilrenny have all the wit and grace
one could desire, and their exact and delicate reference to their
sources in Eastern art is a delight. Only the first two books of the
Panchatantra's five are presented here; if you publish the rest, O
Publisher! please let us have more of these lovely drawings.

UNFINISHED BUSINESS
by Maggie Scarf
(1980)

All of us feel down sometimes, but some of us get down and can't come up again. Depression is the only clinically recognized psychic illness that is frequently fatal: it ends all too often in suicide. There are forty to sixty-five million depressives in the United States. Two-thirds of them, the consistent large majority of diagnosed cases, are women. Housewives and wage earners alike, home-and-babies or office-and-career, it makes no difference: a person taught by her society to perceive herself as a born loser is going to find it hard to feel like a winner. Maggie Scarf's *Unfinished Business* is a big book on a big subject: depression in women.

What is depression?

"I keep making decisions and then disassembling them. . . ." That's Brenda, one of the many voices in the book, women interviewed at clinics and hospitals. "Feeling as if I'm in mourning for something without having any notion what that something is. . . ." That's Diana.

"If one conceives of life as a kind of continuous thread," says Scarf, "then depression is a place of snarling, of tangling, of stoppage . . . a signal of adaptive failure." The symptoms include inability to experience pleasure, impaired ability to think and remember, indecisiveness, irritability, fatigue (or frenzied activity), sleep problems, impotence or frigidity, sadness, and lack of interest in anything outside one's self and one's pain. "The mood state itself is a filter of experience, allowing nothing cheerful or gratifying to come through."

These are only indications; Scarf does not "define" depression and then color in the outlines. The whole book is a definition, and the picture she gives of depression grows out of and remains rooted

Maggie Scarf, *Unfinished Business: Pressure Points in the Lives of Women* (New York: Doubleday & Co., 1980).

in individual case studies and in her discussions of theories and therapies. These discussions are of a breadth and equanimity rather unusual in the field. While making her own inclinations clear, Scarf leaves us free to think. No instant certainties are offered. This is a work of popular psychology, written in accessible journalistic prose without technical jargon; it's for Us, not for Them. But it isn't "pop psych." Opinion is not uttered but presented for examination. The book is eminently judicious, in that it makes very few judgments. And it is admirably good-natured. It isn't always easy to keep your cool in the bullet-riddled area between the Male-as-Norm bastions of traditional psychology and the Male-as-Enemy outposts of radical feminism, but Maggie Scarf never loses her head. She can even cope with Freud's famous statement "What we shall never know is what a woman really wants." Some women, including this reviewer, automatically foam at the mouth at the fatuousness of the remark, its bland arrogation of cognition to men—for who, after all, are "we"? Again and again, the male is human, the woman is deviant. But Scarf mildly calls the statement "rather ironical," and goes on: "What I am trying to do is actually turn the question from a semi-mocking one to a perfectly serious one—to ask what it is that, when *lacking* in a woman's life, can lead to states of depression? What do women, at the various stages of their lives, require in order to live?"

Well, cheers for *that* question—cheers and praise.

The subtitle, *Pressure Points in the Lives of Women,* is misleading if it makes the book sound like another predictable-crises manual. The "stages of their lives" are simply the six decades from the teens to seventy, each exemplified by one or several portrait-interviews, each voice, each woman, a voice from the darkness: Loss, Mourning, Terror, Despair, Anger, Loneliness. The first great loss in the adolescent's life is that of her childhood. She must trade baby security for adult independence, and if love fails along the way, she may perceive the process not as liberation but as abandonment, and be left to cope with life not in hope and trust but in grief and fear. At each phase of life this pattern may arise or recur. And always the achievement of self-reliance, of a self that can freely be and do in the world, is hampered by the cultural bias that encourages a woman to ask, "What do *they* want of me?" and frowns upon her asking, "What do *I* want to do, to be?"

For me, the weakest part of the book is the section on women over fifty. Scarf is very funny about doctors who consider old age—in women, not in men—abnormal and curable; but her argument against the "hormone replacement therapy" school seems to lead her into some sweeping denials. She refuses to connect depression with menopausal hormone changes in any way. Evidence supports her in that depression is not statistically any more frequent in the years from forty-five to fifty-five than before or after. The convenient stereotype of the moody bitchy crazy menopausal woman—give her Valium, it's all hormones—is out. But since she has connected depression directly with hormone changes at puberty and after childbirth, I wonder why Scarf dismisses hormones so absolutely at menopause, not even considering hormone fluctuation (as opposed to loss), nor mentioning the often careless prescription of oral hormones, including the Pill, as a possible cause of depressive states. The one case study for the fifties is curiously atypical; after hearing about the woman's childhood, you can only admire her for getting to age fifty-two at all. In the sixties, again only one case study, and again some proselytizing—for ECT, electroshock. I found the discussion of this hot subject cursory, compared to the full, solid discussions of drugs used to treat depression. And "Mrs. Garvey"—all the others are on a first-name basis, only this one is distanced—seems dull, insipid, a typical little old lady, seen with so little empathy that Scarf twice admits to "feeling strange" when asking her about her mother. But aren't grandmothers allowed to be daughters? And if ECT is so safe for Mrs. Garvey, and so helpful, despite the fact that nobody can say what it does, why not use it on depressives of forty or thirty or fifteen? But Scarf doesn't suggest that, leaving me with an unhappy impression that she thinks ECT is fine for *old* depressives. Why? Because the old depressives are right, at last? Because what they knew all along, waking alone in the black pit of 2:00 a.m., is true—*they don't matter any more*?

Scarf has not the sensitive ear of such interviewers as Ronald Blythe; all her informants tend to sound alike, sharing her own rather flat casual style. But this is a minor flaw in a book of real weight and integrity. Depression is an immensely complex subject, and the patience and comprehensiveness of Maggie Scarf's handling are perfectly appropriate. Depression may be a depressing subject, but the voices of women from the darkness are very moving, and *Unfinished Business* is, in its firmness and intelligence and charity, an invigorating, hope-giving book.

ITALIAN FOLKTALES
by Italo Calvino
(1980)

Prowling among dictionaries, I discovered that the word "fairy" is *fata* in Italian and that it derives, like the word "fate," from the Latin verb *fari,* "to speak." Fate is "that which is spoken." The Fates that once presided over human life dwindled away in fairies, fairy god-mothers, inhabitants of fairytales.

The English word "fable" and the Italian *fiaba* or *favola,* a story, "a narrative or statement not founded on fact," as the *Shorter Oxford* puts it, descend from the Latin *fabula,* which derives from that same verb, *fari,* "to speak." To speak is to tell tales.

The predestined spindle has pricked her thumb; here lies the Sleeping Beauty in the silent castle. The prince arrives. He kisses her. Nothing happens.

So the prince comes back again next day, and the next day too, and his love is

> so intense that the sleeping maiden gave birth to twins, a boy and a girl, and you never saw two more beautiful children in your life. They came into the world hungry, but who was to nurse them if their mamma lay there like a dead woman? They cried and cried, but their mother didn't hear them. With their tiny mouths they began seeking something to suck on, and that way the boy child happened to find his mother's hand and began sucking on the thumb. With all that sucking, the spindle tip lodged under the nail came out, and the sleeper awakened. "Oh, me, how I've slept!" she said, rubbing her eyes.

The two children are named Sun and Moon, and Sleeping Beauty's mother-in-law tries to have them served up stewed for the prince's supper, but he hears the silver bells sewn on his wife's seven

Italo Calvino, *Italian Folktales,* translated by George Martin (New York: Harcourt Brace Jovanovich, 1980).

skirts ringing, and saves everybody—except the mother-in-law—
and they live happily ever after, in Calabria.

To find the moral, the message, the meaning of a folktale, to
describe its "uses," even so circuitously as Bruno Bettelheim has
done, is a risky business; it is like stating the meaning of a fish, the
uses of a cat. The thing you are talking about is alive. It changes and
is never quite what you thought it was, or ought to be.

One of the innumerable delights of *Italian Folktales* is its mixture
of the deeply familiar with the totally unexpected.

Most of the basic "story-types," of which Calvino says there are
about fifty represented here, are more or less familiar to members
of the English folk literary tradition. The themes that recur in all
Western folktales run through these; we meet the youngest son of
the king, the wicked stepmother, the stupid giant, the helpful animals, the magic boots, the house of the winds, the well that leads to
another world: people and places we all recognize, archetypal forms
of our perception of life, according to Jung, embodiments of ideas
as basic to our subjective existence as the ideas of extension, right/
left, reversal, are to our existence in space. But the recombinations
of these themes are mostly not familiar. This is much more than
Cinderella served up with *salsa di pomodora*. The tales are endlessly
surprising. And their mood is quite different from the elegance of
the French *contes*, the iconic splendors of Russian *skazki*, the forest
darknesses of German *Märchen*. Often they resemble the British
tales of the Joseph Jacobs collections in their dry and zany humor,
but they have more sunlight in them. Some are wonderfully beautiful. "The natural cruelties of the folktale give way to the rules of
harmony," as Calvino says in his introduction.

> Although the notion of cruelty persists along with an injustice
> bordering on inhumanity as part of the constant stuff of stories,
> although the woods forever echo with the weeping of maidens or
> of forsaken brides with severed hands, gory ferocity is never
> gratuitous; the narrative does not dwell on the torment of the
> victim, not even under pretense of pity, but moves swiftly to a
> healing solution.

Italo Calvino's part in this book is not that of the eminent author
condescending to honor a collection of popular tales with an introduction—anything but. Essentially the book is to Italian literature
what the Grimms' collection is to German literature. It is both the
first and the standard. And its particular glory is that it was done,

not by a scholar-specialist, but by a great writer of fiction. The author of *The Baron in the Trees* and *Invisible Cities* used all his skills to bring together the labors of collectors and scholars from all the regions of Italy, to translate the tales out of dialects into standard Italian, and to retell them:

> I selected from mountains of narratives . . . the most unusual, beautiful, and original texts. . . . I enriched the text selected from other versions and whenever possible did so without altering its character or unity, and at the same time filled it out and made it more plastic. I touched up as delicately as possible those portions that were either missing or too sketchy.

With absolute sureness of touch Calvino selected, combined, rewove, reshaped, so that each tale and the entire collection would show at its best, clear and strong, without obscurity or repetition. As a teller of tales he had, of course, both the privilege and the responsibility to do so. He assumed his privilege without question and fulfilled his responsibility magnificently. One of the best storytellers alive telling us some of the best stories in the world—what luck!

Fiabe italiane was first published in Italy in 1956. My children grew up with a selected edition of them, *Italian Fables* (Orion Press, 1959). The book was presented for children, without notes, in a fine translation by Louis Brigante, just colloquial enough to be a joy to read aloud, and with line drawings by Michael Train that reflected the wit and spirit of the stories. Perhaps a reading-aloud familiarity with the cadences of this earlier translation has prejudiced my ear; anyhow I find George Martin's version heavier, often pedestrian, sometimes downright ugly. I don't hear the speaking voice of the storyteller in it, or feel the flow and assurance of words that were listened to by the writer as he wrote them. Nor does the occasional antique woodcut in the present edition add much to the stories. But the design of the book is handsome and generous, entirely appropriate to the work, which includes for the first time in English all the tales, as well as Calvino's complete introduction, and his notes (edited by himself for this edition) on each story. The notes illuminate his unobtrusive scholarship and explain his refashionings of the material, and the introduction contains some of the finest things said on folklore since Tolkien—such throwaway lines as:

> No doubt the moral function of the tale, in the popular conception, is to be sought not in the subject matter but in the very nature of the folktale, in the mere fact of telling and listening.

Come and listen, then. Come hear how a girl named Misfortune found her Fate on the seashore of Sicily:

> At the oven, Misfortune found the old woman, who was so foul, blear-eyed, and smelly that the girl was almost nauseated. "Dear Fate of mine, will you do me the honor of accepting—" she began, offering her the bread.
> "Away with you! Begone! Who asked you for bread?" And she turned her back on the girl.

But Misfortune persists in showing goodwill towards this nasty hag, and so we find how Fate may turn to Fairy by the magic of Fable.

> The Fate, who was growing tamer, came forward grumbling to take the bread. Then Misfortune reached out and grabbed her and proceeded to wash her with soap and water. Next she did her hair and dressed her up from head to foot in her new finery. The Fate at first writhed like a snake, but seeing herself all spick-and-span she became a different person entirely. "Listen to me, Misfortune," she said. "For your kindness to me, I'm making you a present of this little box," and she handed her a box as tiny as those which contain wax matches.

And what do you think Misfortune found in the little box?

PEAKE'S PROGRESS
by Mervyn Peake
(1981)

Classification, the distinguishing of styles and relationships, is essential to literary criticism, but some writers are members of a class that contains no other member. Such troublemakers, who won't quite fit in anywhere, tend to get left out of the textbooks and ignored in the discussions. Critical neglect may be overcompensated by uncritical praise from reader-devotees, which gives the critics ground to gibe at the "cultists," whose praise then grows shriller. The major fantasists are all mavericks, and all of them, including Carroll and Tolkien, have traveled at least part of this descending gyre of neglect-defense-contempt-adulation. So have such great unclassifiable novels as *Finnegans Wake* and *Kim*. Though American Lit people ought to be used to mavericks, they don't seem to be able to lay a rope on Austin Tappan Wright. An illustrious name in the egregious non-company of those who don't belong is that of Mervyn Peake; and now, possibly to the annoyance of the critics, certainly to the delight of his readers, *Peake's Progress* has appeared to exhibit the maverick genius in all his superb gaits and paces—storyteller, playwright, poet, illustrator.

If one has read no Mervyn Peake, the first of his books to read surely is *Titus Groan*, and the second *Gormenghast*. The third book of the trilogy, *Titus Alone*, written in the terrible shadow of the illness that killed the author, is not the place to start. Some of the minor pieces and juvenilia in this collection will best please those who already love Peake; but it is full of pleasures, and the unwary dipper-in might well get caught—by Captain Slaughterboard, perhaps, or a lurking Figure of Speech—and emerge only to go in hot search of the trilogy. A great debt of gratitude is owing to Maeve

Peake's Progress: Selected Writings and Drawings of Mervyn Peake, edited by Maeve Gilmore (London: Overlook Press, 1981).

Gilmore for the hard and delicate task she has performed in gathering these scattered pieces of prose, verse, and drawing from the author's whole life, and to John Watney (author of a fine biography of Peake) for his sensitive introduction. My only disappointment with the book is that it is not a selection from the very best work Peake did. To one who has not read the novels or seen Peake's magnificent illustrations to *Treasure Island, The Rime of the Ancient Mariner, Alice in Wonderland,* the narrative pieces and drawings in this volume will give an idea of his versatility and marvelous originality, but not a full realization of his solid and enduring achievement. But the poetry in *Peake's Progress* is another matter.

> It has no right—no right at all
> To soar above the orchard wall,
> With chilblains on its knees.

In this sort of thing Peake belongs firmly to a classifiable tradition—a maverick tradition, of course: English nonsense verse, that maddest flower of Albion. He was a master of nonsense to equal Edward Lear. His play *The Wit to Woo,* here included, is in verse, which lends its Wildean capers a singular and batty beauty:

> PERCY (*bursting out of cupboard door*):
>   No, no, no!
>   I cannot breathe in there—the mothballs, Kite!
>   Ah, let me gulp a little air again—
>   A little air—a little of that space
>   That gentle Einstein curved for our amusement. . . .

Wit, style, humor, daring, are never common qualities; Peake has them all. But the treasure of *Peake's Progress* is several serious poems of extraordinary power and brilliance, chief among them the narrative "Rhyme of the Flying Bomb." A conscious heir of Coleridge and a contemporary of Dylan Thomas wrote this poem; hard to classify he may be, but a critic who ignores Mervyn Peake henceforth may be accused of ignorance. The poem is heartbreakingly and unforgettably illustrated by the man who wrote it—twelve years after, when he could not hold the pen for more than a few moments at a time, and had to be reminded what he was drawing.

In those twenty pages alone the book earns permanence. There is also the strange "Reverie of Bone" and a selection of love poems and war poems. "London, 1941" ends with these lines:

Across a world of sudden fear and firelight
She towers erect, the great stones at her throat,
Her rusted ribs like railings round her heart;
A figure of dry wounds—of winter wounds—
O mother of wounds; half masonry, half pain.

I know no other poem so fit to stand with Henry Moore's drawings
of London in the Blitz.

THE SENTIMENTAL AGENTS
by Doris Lessing
(1983)

Doris Lessing's *Canopus in Argos* series has had some queer reviews. Some academic critics, unwilling to recognize experiment in content rather than form, dismiss her greatest experimental venture as "mere science fiction," not to be taken seriously. But among science-fiction readers and reviewers, where the books might have been greeted with intelligent interest, the attitude seems to be: Lessing is not One of Us, therefore we will not take her seriously. Some feminist critics denounce her for departing from the single issue of feminism. And then there are her adorers, for whom she can do no wrong. None of these reviewers does her novels justice.

Neither will I. I am much too angry at her. But perhaps this review will move a reader to begin or to continue the series, of which *The Sentimental Agents* is the fifth book—and that's what I'm after. Doris Lessing deserves to be read! How many novelists are there writing now who can make you really angry? How many refuse triviality, self-imitation, and the safe line, whether it panders to the know-it-all snob or the know-nothing slob? How many novelists take any risks at all? If you are thirsty for the dry taste of courage, try Lessing.

But don't start with this one. Start with the first of the series, *Shikasta*, or the second, *The Marriages Between Zones Three, Four, and Five* (which I think very much the best so far). In this latest one, all the faults and few of the strengths of Lessing's style survive the ordeal of an effort at satirical playfulness by the most humorless major writer alive. She takes the themes of Orwell's brief, beautiful *Animal Farm* and clomps around all over them page after page, so gracelessly and so tastelessly that one ends up cheering for the targets of her satire. She sets up feeble men of straw and knocks

Doris Lessing, *The Sentimental Agents* (New York: Alfred A. Knopf, 1983).

them over, braying, "Look! What fools! What knaves!" She loads every die she throws; she propagandizes steadily throughout a novel the intent of which is to satirize propaganda; she preaches against preaching and rants about ranting. The keenest novelistic observer of the political human being since the Koestler of *Darkness at Noon*, she generalizes marvelously, but as soon as she embodies the idea in a character, she overmanipulates, and all we see is a puppet kicking on strings. She bravely discards verisimilitude and even probability, but she discards compassionate insight along with them, replacing it not with irony but with judgmentalism. We must endure even her judgments on music; on a planet somewhere across the universe, we are informed that Tchaikovsky is a complainer and that the tune of "We Shall Overcome" is dismal. Finally, her confusion of emotion with sentimentality is a moral disaster.

And all this is presented as the wisdom of Canopus. I have not found much wisdom in the apparent heroes of the saga, Johor and the other agents of Canopus. They are arrogant, anthropocentric, authoritarian, forever smiling pityingly, forever talking down to everybody else, bearing the galactic version of the White Man's Burden with stifled but audible moans of self-pity through a universe populated by lesser breeds without the law. . . . And they are immortal. They are as self-righteous as the tiresome old Laputans of Robert Heinlein's novels, though less talkative. In fact, when it comes to real information, they stop talking. They smile pityingly.

Can it be that Lessing is playing her own double agent? Are we meant to dislike these saintly "agents," meant to distrust their wisdom as they distrust our rhetoric, meant to question the "Necessity" they invoke as they dismiss our inadequate concepts of virtue, freedom, justice, compassion? Are we expected to protest the Orders from Above that everyone in the book obeys unprotesting (or if they don't they rue the day)? If so, Lessing is risking even more than I thought, and is undercutting her book as she writes it, in a fashion and to an extent that few fancy critics of formal preciosities or *auteurs* of self-deconstructed anti-novels would dare contemplate. But then she is asking too much of her readers, to carry on so strained a duplicity in book after book.

It's time the people from Canopus stopped looking down from the heights, all head, no body. Any redneck preacher or hard-line Freudian can spout this stuff about subduing our "animal" nature and the "beast" in us (as if it were *animals* that made the mess we're

in!). Surely Canopus, or Lessing, can do better than that? We don't
need the soppy pseudo-reassurances of an *E.T.*—but neither do we
need condemnations, preachifyings, and mystifications in the name
of Reason. If Canopus knows what it is we do need, in the mess
we've made, it's time they spoke. Put up or shut up, Johor!

DIFFICULT LOVES
by Italo Calvino
(1984)

Jorge Luis Borges gets the Nobel Prize in literature, only twenty-five
or thirty years overdue, and then the next year they give it to Italo
Calvino. . . . So much for daydreams. Meanwhile, here's a selection
of Calvino's short stories from 1945 to 1960, felicitously translated
by William Weaver, Archibald Colquhoun, and Peggy Wright.

A kitchen full of wild animals: frogs on the plates, snakes in the
saucepans, lizards in the soup, toads on the tiles— A forest full of
tame animals: lambs in caves, pigs in bushes, cows in clearings, a
chicken here, a guinea pig there— A pastry shop full of thieves,
ignoring the cash register to wallow in cream puffs and jelly rolls—
A furrier's shop invaded by a naked old beggar who robes himself
in sable, beaver, and lamb's wool, and appears to a startled shopgirl
as "a gigantic human bear with its arms entwined in an astrakhan
muff. . . ." Her response is pure Calvino. "How lovely!" she says.

Calvino's early stories, exact, delicate, kind, dry, crazy, often follow this theme of invasion or interpenetration of animal life and
artificial life—a subversion of order by the strange. I can't come at
the distinction more precisely, for it is a complex one, not to be
pulled out of the stories as a mere idea. It is a political, a social, and a
psychological theme, and a fascinating one. Indeed, Calvino is such
an interesting writer intellectually that one tends to forget the powerful gift of narrative that has let him pull off such "anti-narrative"
stunts as *Invisible Cities* or *If on a winter's night a traveler.* In this
volume you can see the storyteller pure and simple in "Mine Field,"
a paradigm of suspense. Will he get blown up or won't he? I didn't
know I could hold my breath for seven pages.

The war stories, fearful and/or humorous, are brilliant. A deaf
old peasant rides his mule down the mountain to get help for his
starving village in 1945:

Italo Calvino, *Difficult Loves,* translated by William Weaver, Archibald Colquhoun,
and Peggy Wright (New York: Harcourt Brace Jovanovich, 1984).

. . . he had lived his life with mules, and his ideas were as few and as resigned as theirs; it had always been long and tiring to find his bread, bread for himself and bread for others, and now bread for the whole of Bevera. The world, this silent world which surrounded him, seemed to be trying to speak to him, too, with confused boomings that reached even his sleeping eardrums, and strange disturbances of the earth. He could see banks crumbling, clouds rising from the fields, stones flying, and red flashes appearing and disappearing on the hills; the world was trying to change its old face and show its underbelly of earth and roots. And the silence, the terrible silence of his old age, was ruffled by those distant sounds.

Calvino's stories from the forties have the mood of the great afterwar films of Rossellini and De Sica, with their strange clarity of feeling, a vernal power springing in release from the dead grip of fascist lying and bullying. These tales are loving and terrible, very tender, never truly hopeful.

The stories from the fifties might make you think of Fellini—the farce, the fantasy, the wit, delight, and vitality, and the marvelous gift of image. Where Fellini errs towards incoherence, Calvino over-controls, erring towards the cerebral—but seldom, and never fatally. He is far too intelligent to become really cerebral.

"The Adventure of a Bather" won't become a myth or byword like Andersen's "The Emperor's New Clothes," because it isn't quite simplistic enough. The plot is certainly simple: swimming alone at a big beach resort, she loses the bottom half of her swimsuit. Now, how can you make anything out of that but a wink, a snicker, a snigger? Calvino makes it a story worthy of Chekhov, a tiny comedy that touches the great chords. The smartass kid who says the Emperor has no clothes on speaks for the child in us, but Calvino's swimmer is an adult, and her peculiar problem is an adult problem, in fact you could say that her problem is that she is adult—that she is fully human.

Repeatedly in the later stories the metaphor of happiness is a man's sexual enjoyment of a woman. I found this tiresome. A male writer may expect a female reader to accept a description of sex from the man's point of view as a satisfactory representation of human sexual experience, but he can't ask her to agree that male pleasure defines human bliss. Not these days. Once upon a time "the nude" could stand for "beauty," but these days she's likely to be seen as a naked woman painted by a clothed man. There is nothing pornographic in Calvino, of course. His sensuality is free and real, as exact, mysterious, and enjoyable as everything in his writing. But the metaphor, repeated, trivializes. In the last story, a fine restatement of the major theme, the image of inexpressible joy is a woman swimming naked, watched by a man. Wretchedly poor fisherfolk, seen by the same man, represent equally inexpressible despair. The second image, which works, reveals the banality of the first. Very pretty, the nude swimmer, but prettiness isn't what Calvino is after. And what a bore she is compared to that other swimmer, ridiculous, terrified, respectable, who instead of taking off her bathing suit to please a man, loses it and so wins the heart of anybody reading her story, our story, all of us swimming anxiously around in the Sea of Life getting colder and colder, and not brave enough, not shameless enough, to come ashore alone. . . .

"FORSAKING KINGDOMS":
FIVE POETS
(1984)

While painting seems more the business of stockbrokers than of artists, while orchestras endlessly replay old symphonies and let living composers go unheard, poetry flourishes. Living way below the bottom line, unexploitable, it remains as threatened and ubiquitous as the trees and the wild grass. Our very lack of a "great" poet may be a sign of the luxuriant vitality of the art. It's grand that the Brits had the sense to crown Ted Hughes's hard head with laurel, but in this wide country too much is going on for anybody to dominate the scene; and anyhow the mood, I think, isn't favorable to canons, cults, or hierarchies.

Of the five poets here reviewed the youngest is (as yet) the most self-limited, self-domesticated, unwild. A verbal confidence dazzling in itself, wit, control, precision mark Mary Jo Salter's work. In a Buddhist graveyard,

> Reading down,
> I felt as though the ashes of someone
> whose name ran vertically might lie
> differently, somehow, in the earth.
> Such a small note seemed everything. . . .

The oldest of the five poets was born in 1902. The early poems in Eve Triem's retrospective volume are often similarly crisp and controlled, but by the end she is passionate and incautious. Early on, she makes a lovely Taoist print—

Mary Jo Salter, *Henry Purcell in Japan* (New York: Alfred A. Knopf, 1985); Eve Triem, *New as a Wave: A Retrospective, 1937–1983* (Seattle: Dragon Gate Press, 1984); May Sarton, *Letters from Maine* (New York: W. W. Norton, 1984); Denise Levertov, *Oblique Prayers* (New York: New Directions, 1984); Carolyn Kizer, *Yin* (Brockport, N.Y.: Boa Editions, 1984); Carolyn Kizer, *Mermaids in the Basement: Poems for Women* (Port Townsend, Wash.: Copper Canyon Press, 1984).

moon-rim, a falling wave, a lifted cloud . . .

—but grown old she is a prophetess, a shaman, incantatory:

> The lake-sunk stars were ringing:
>
> "Nine times the nine white heavens
> call the things that creep, run, fly.
> Come to the fish-meal, eat from the tympani,
> drink from the clashing cymbals."
>
> I looked with all my faces.
> The houses rose, shine-drenched,
> the wolf ran at my side,
> through the Easter light of every morning.

Winner of the 1984 Western States Book Award, *New as a Wave* is a very readable book, various and lively; there are poems of homage to Morris Graves and to Jimi Hendrix, elegies, carols, songs, regional pieces. Through the deft lines moves a candid, elusive, rich personality, still growing strong at eighty. Her own woman, she shares life with us,

> (Not as the dead know—meek, learning by rote
> The riddling truths, myths, legends of the grave)
> Breathing and choosing in the jeweled world.
> Forsaking kingdoms. Becoming kings for love.

May Sarton is a mere septuagenarian, but count her title list with awe. This is a writer, this is what writers do: fourteen volumes of poetry, seventeen of fiction, two books for kids, and seven collections of essays. The newest of the lot, *Letters from Maine,* is mostly easy-going. The lines flow with facility and the grace of long usage, the rhymes are undemanding, one may be soothed by the conventionality . . . but look out. Sudden authority rings like sword steel, and the clear old voice says with awful honesty,

> The fact is I am whole and very well,
> Joyful, centered, not to be turned aside,
> Full of healing and self-healing.

Only the muse does not bid me cease,
Who does not listen and who cannot care,
Has never said "be quiet," uttered harm

She, the dark angel and the silent charm,
Is all of hope and nothing of despair,
And in her long withholding is my peace

In those lines is the power that is earned by a lifetime of using power
mindfully.

Denise Levertov's mastery—more than mastery, because she is
one of the originators—of contemporary poetic form, informed by
a fierce generous intelligence, can be frightening. This is the
charged, overloaded poetry of the age, demanding more of the
reader than most of us are mostly willing to give, so we don't read
poetry, we read a thriller or something, and oh, what dolts we are,
what wasters of our own brief time—to miss this tenderness, this
kind companion in hard times, not trying to sell us anything or
scare us or fool us, but going along with us,

All the long road
in chains, even if, after all,
we come to
death's ordinary door, with time
smiling its ordinary
long-ago smile.

Levertov is never "above the battle," never talks down, never shows
off. A poet's obscurity may be the inability of pain to speak clear,
but Levertov, hard disciplinarian of her own mind and soul, forces
pain to speak itself, and I take her words literally. The poem
"Thinking About El Salvador" begins this way, and this is the truth:

Because every day they chop heads off
I'm silent.
In each person's head they chopped off
was a tongue,
for each tongue they silence
a word in my mouth
unsays itself.

Courage is perhaps the keynote of Levertov's mind and art, but
never heroics; no standing tall in *Oblique Prayers*. This courage
permits simplicity and—though she says "oblique"—a prayer so

direct that it must say Thou, the old word of the soul, the poets' word.

> *To the Morton Bay Figtree, Australia,*
> *a Tree-God*
>
> Soul-brother of the majestic beechtree,
> thy sculpted buttresses only more sharp-angled,
> leaves darker, like the leaves of ilex—
>
> vast tree, named by fools who noticed only
> thy small hard fruit, the figlike shape of it, nothing else—
> not thy great girth and pallid sturdy bark,
> thy alert and faithful retinue of roots,
> the benign shade under the rule of thy crown:
>
> Arbor-Emperor, to perceive thy solemn lustre
> and not withhold due reverence—
> may it not be for this, one might discover,
> a lifetime led, after all?—not for
> those guilts and expiations the mind's clock ticks over,
> but to have sunk before thee in deep obeisance,
> spirits rising in weightless joy?

In *Women as Mythmakers*, Estella Lauter writes of "that emerging world-view of relationship between self and world which does not accept the categories that have enclosed our lives"—the category of Man versus Nature chief among them. Here that nonacceptance which is acceptance states itself gently, the movement which both bows and rises being timelessly that of a woman dancing.

Susan Griffin, in *The Roaring Inside Her,* writes of woman and nature, woman as animal, and warns rationalists of the danger of dissecting live lions. Carolyn Kizer doesn't keep the roaring inside her. She roars it. Her poetry is intensely, splendidly oral, wanting to be read aloud, best of all read or roared by the lion herself, golden at the waterhole over the remains of a disemboweled prig. Adherents of the buttoned-down school may confuse Kizer's flamboyance with carelessness, but lions have that casual look too.

> The room is sparsely furnished:
> A chair, a table, and a father.

Kizer is a marvelous poet of anger and laughter; also, increasingly, of measure and of grief. From "Afterthoughts of Donna Elvira":

True to your human kind
You seemed to me too cruel.
Now I am not a fool,
Now that I fear no scorn,

Now that I see, I see
What you have known within:
Whenever we love, we win,
Or else we have never been born.

A few poems from *Yin* are also in *Mermaids in the Basement;* the two books complement each other with little repetition, and together give a full view of the state of this poet's dark, brilliant, and sardonic art. "The wolf ran at my side," Eve Triem writes, and the wolf runs here too. The last poem in *Mermaids,* "A Muse of Water," states the rejection of a division between Man and Nature as women now perhaps must state it, not by speaking against Man "for Nature," but *as* nature, naturally, as flesh, as grass, as water, as woman. It is a deep, desolate, and beautiful poem. Let the theorists beware of reductionism; this matter of the woman-animal was never a simple one. The dissecter's knife twists in his hand, and as Kizer says in "Pro Femina,"

> . . . the role of pastoral heroine
> Is not permanent, Jack. We want to get back to the meeting.

But the meeting is a larger one than any held by corporations or governments. And if Jack kills the last wolf, Jill must become her.

THE MYTHOLOGY OF NORTH AMERICA
by John Bierhorst
(1985)

The oral literature of the American Indians, transcribed and translated, is a treasurehouse for all American readers and writers—the
only literature entirely rooted in this ground, the only words that,
like corn and sequoias, begin *here*. Instead of being treated as
"primitive" curiosities that only an anthropologist could love, Native
American prose and poetry are increasingly appreciated and rever-
enced by non-Indians, as a vital link to a lost past, of course, but
more importantly as a living literature. After all, most of it was
written down between 1850 and 1950. The plots, the forms, the
traditions may be ancient, but the actual pieces are no older than the
novels of Dickens or the poems of Yeats.

John Bierhorst, who has given us excellent selections of this oral
poetry and prose in *The Sacred Path* and other collections, presents
now a systematic overview of one type or branch of literature in *The
Mythology of North America*.

What makes a myth different from a legend, a folktale, a story?
Bierhorst has a notable gift for making such complex and much
argued distinctions clear by using the material to explain itself:

> In North America, where more than a hundred native lan-
> guages are still spoken and oral traditions once passed freely
> between cultures, storytellers have tended to divide narratives
> into two basic categories. Typically, the Eskimo used to speak of
> old stories and young stories. Among the Winnebago, stories
> were either *waikan* (sacred) or simply *worak* (narrated). To the
> Pawnee, the distinction was between true and false. The second
> of the two categories, which varies from tribe to tribe, can refer
> to fiction, nonfiction, or a mixture of both; mainly it sets up a

John Bierhorst, *The Mythology of North America* (New York: William Morrow, 1985).

contrast with the first category, which, whether defined as old, sacred, or true, corresponds to the English word "myth."

Later on Bierhorst mentions that among the Tlingit "there are two kinds of stories, *tlagu* (of the long ago) and *ch'kalnik* (it really happened)." What he is concerned with in this book are the *tlagu*, the old, sacred, true stories. Their truth is of that order which may be ranked above or even opposed to factuality. That they are old may mean that they are agelessly young and meaningful. As for their sacredness, it is not always of the kind monotheists easily or willingly recognize as such. From De Angulo, Bierhorst quotes an Achomawi tale-teller:

> What is this thing that the white people call God? They are always talking about it. It's goddam this and goddam that, and in the name of the god, and the god made the world. Who is that god? They say that Coyote is the Indian God, but if I say to them that God is Coyote, they get mad at me. Why?

For people willing to take that question seriously, those willing to take risks of the mind, the pleasure of these myths will often lie in the way they revalue the world, cleansing the doors of perception. Like all great works of art, the great myths change you. Anyone who has attentively read or heard such a story as Archie Phinney's "Coyote and the Shadow People" will know that the Greek myth of Orpheus is only one version of a deep and powerful human theme, and will have enriched their understanding of such matters as the landscape of the Western Plains, and married love, and death. Imagination is, after all, an intensely practical activity.

This Coyote story can be read in full in Phinney's *Nez Percé Texts*, and with commentary by Jarold Ramsay in *Traditional Literatures of the American Indian*, edited by Karl Kroeber, or in Ramsay's own recent *Reading the Fire*. Bierhorst gives almost no full texts or tellings; this is not a collection of myths but a survey, a guidebook to the mythologies of the whole continent, arranged first by region, second by theme. It is a formidable undertaking; the author's clear mind and style keep it from becoming a thicket of complications. The introduction provides a lucid short history of how and when and why and by whom these oral literatures were written down and translated. From Schoolcraft (our one-man Brothers Grimm) through the magnificent salvage work of Boas and his students and colleagues, both Indian and non-Indian, through the Benedictine school of myth as key to culture, Bierhorst brings us up to the recent studies of the performer and the performance—in other words, the artist and the art. Dell Hymes and others, by bringing sensitive and informed linguistic and literary criticism to bear on the "artless" and "formless" myths of the "savage," have revealed wonderful sophistications of structure and richness of meaning. Oddly, Bierhorst scarcely mentions the structuralist analysis of myth; I found the monumental volumes of Lévi-Strauss's *Mythologies* mentioned only once, in a back-of-the-booknote. (Does anybody else miss the lowly footnote? Does anybody else get tired of turning back and forth trying to find the notes to the chapter you're in the middle of, except you've forgotten the number of the chapter and lose your place looking for the notes in the back and it all ends up more like beating eggs with a whisk than reading a book?)

Bierhorst also chooses not to mention the secondary collections of Native American myths (those reworked from the originals, like Theodora Kroeber's *Inland Whale,* or gathered directly from the written sources, like Jarold Ramsay's *Coyote Was Going There,* or based immediately upon oral performance, like Dennis Tedlock's presentation of Zuñi tales in *Finding the Center*). The notes in the back refer only to chapter bibliographies listing the original sources. There is a courtesy in this towards the originators and true owners of the myths, in leaving out all "middlemen" as far as possible. But the paraphernalia of the notes is pretty formidable for the untrained reader. And the book, being a survey of a vast wealth of material, surely will often serve not only as an end in itself but as an introduction. Readers will want to go on from Bierhorst's synopses and descriptions of myths; but few will know how to cope with the great, grey-green volumes of the Bureau of American Ethnology or how to find the other primary sources, mostly available only in major libraries. A fuller bibliography, a descriptive or evaluative guide to the many secondary collections of Native American myths, would have added greatly to the value of the book. Bierhorst might even have begun steering us away from the silly and patronizing versions, the kind the newspapers dug up when Mount St. Helens erupted. We were told then how St. Helens, Mount Hood, and Mount Adams were "the beautiful maiden Loo-Wit" and "the braves Wy-East and Klick-It-Tat" who quarreled over her—the word "maiden" making it clear that this was quaint, the hyphens making it clear that Indians could not pronounce words of more than one syllable, and so forth. But now listen to a story being told the way

these stories were told (at night, in winter, and if you don't listen
Grandmother will pinch you):

> She saw a hair, she took it up, looked at it, looked at the hair, one
> hair, she looked at the hair she had found. "Whose hair? I want
> to know." She looked at it long, looked at the hair, one long hair.
> The woman thought, "Whose hair?" she thought.

That is a California story; things in California used to move at
their own sweet pace. Gertrude Stein grew up in California, too.
Bierhorst gives us only that passage, and few retellings would have
the courage to keep to that slow, oral rhythm. But there is a magic at
work there in the words, in the repetitions, the circling gait, which is
as essential as the plot (the fearful incest story of Loon Woman). In
giving us an overview of the mythologies of so many different
cultures, Bierhorst can usually give us only the plot, the gist, the
marrow without the bones, as it were. Even so, even in synopsis,
many of the stories are moving and fascinating; and Bierhorst's
descriptions of the background and history, the connections and
crossovers of the myths and mythologies, and his glimpses of the
world views of the various peoples and regions, are lucid and
thoughtful. *The Mythology of North America* may not be a landmark,
but it is a shapely and solid stepping-stone—perhaps a more valuable thing than a landmark, after all.

SILENT PARTNERS
by Eugene Linden
(1986)

> Taped to the front of their cages . . . were depictions of a number
> of Ameslan signs and their meanings. . . . "Oh, they sign all the
> time," he said. "That's why we put up the posters. The techni-
> cians kept seeing the chimps make these gestures, and they
> wanted to be able to respond."

Only in the Peaceable Kingdoms of art and Eden are the relationships between humans and animals innocent and harmonious; here
and now they are complex, uneasy, often cruel, and always profound. City dwellers, seeing only people plus an occasional Peke or
pigeon, can pretend that nothing on earth matters but us; but if we
want to eat or breathe, our dependence on nonhuman life is absolute and immediate, though mostly unexamined. When we *use* animals, as work partners, for food, or in laboratories, the ethics of the
relationship become both urgent and obscure. In the matter of the
use of animals in laboratory experiments, some extremists confuse
use with misuse and demand a total ban, while others justify means
by ends and demand that atrocities be condoned. Eugene Linden
has picked a particularly tangled but fascinating aspect of this
difficult topic to explore in his third book about the apes used in
language experiments.

In the seventies, when ecology was considered something more
than an obstacle to quick profits, experiments on the language
capacities of animals were, as Linden points out, an apt expression
of the generous and risk-taking temper of the times. They were
attempts to cross boundaries. And they were greeted with excite-

Eugene Linden, *Silent Partners: The Legacy of the Ape Language Experiments* (New
York: Times Books, 1986).

ment in part because they were conducted, not as manipulations of a "subject" by an "objective" experimenter, but as partnerships. Language is not one-way communication but essentially exchange, and to carry on the experiments, the individuals of two different species had to work together, to collaborate. Indeed, the teaching of language and the learning of it may go further than collaboration and require collusion:

> Ordinary discourse was characterized on our part by shameless cuing, outright prompting, and dubious interpretations of Gillian's gnomic, if not unintelligible, utterances. In fact, . . . Gillian began to demonstrate most of the behaviors critics have cited as evidence that apes cannot learn language: she interrupted, she repeated phrases incessantly, she responded inappropriately, and she jumbled her word order.

Gillian isn't a chimpanzee; she is Linden's then eighteen-month-old daughter. The point he is making is that normal human language acquisition is not a cool, methodical, detached affair but an intensely felt enterprise involved essentially with relationship. Chimpanzees and gorillas being sensitive creatures with notoriously strong emotional responses and attachments, it seems hardly surprising that "the interesting, if maddeningly inconclusive, results with regard to more complex uses of language came from experiments in which the ape had a relationship with the experimenter—experiments in which the use of the language was a natural part of the animal's day."

The experiments, and criticisms, based on the assumption that an animal is a kind of machine tried to eliminate emotional relationship and emotional reward from the attempt to find out if the ape brain could be programmed for language. Experiments such as the one that trained a chimp to express its wishes on a computer with food as reward for "correct" response have no more to do with language capacity than any animal circus act. But the temptation to use the stimulus-response machine model is strong, because the only model we have for language use is the human one: and it is a very dangerous one, for how is the experimenter to avoid anthropomorphizing, carrying the analogy too far? Such questions mine the whole terrain and make for exciting travel in it. Eugene Linden knows the minefield well and guides us through it with intelligence and unfailing good humor. This last is an achievement in itself, for as the passage just quoted continues,

> It was from such experiments that the most extravagant claims for ape language use came—experiments with the fewest controls and the most passionately committed experimenters. Thus we had a situation bred perfectly for the most vituperative type of debate.

And we got it! As he reports the vituperation, the increasing defensiveness of experimenters and bad faith of some critics, the sensationalism and sentimentalism of much media coverage, Linden's candor and fair-mindedness contrast wonderfully with the prejudice and paranoia he describes. He does not pretend, however, to stand above the battle; his concern is ethical and urgent. For, after all the claims and counterclaims, now that we no longer see photographs of long, thumbless, inhuman hands signing "friend" in the language of the deaf or read dismissive pronouncements from the lofty terraces of academic theory, now in the mid-eighties, what has become of the experimenters and their participants—Washoe, Lucy, Nim Chimpsky, Ally, Koko?

Linden's answers to that question are all to some degree painful and all extremely interesting, if only as tragicomic drama. Personality—both human and ape—is paramount from the first experiments to the last. *Silent Partners* is a great display of science as snake pit, and those who liked *The Double Helix* can get the same evil glee from it. But the cost of these experiments and their repression may have been more than intellectual.

> It may be that the language-using chimps are suffering the consequences of having shown themselves before the world was ready to see them, and the scientists who trained them, the disgrace of having a good idea before the world was ready for it.

Serious investigation of animal linguistic capacity has become almost impossible in the present climate; funding for such investigation was cut off years ago. But the animal participants in the experiments were not only emotionally responsive, highly intelligent, sensitive, but also temperamental, nondomesticable, formidable creatures, neither pet nor wild; rare; extremely valuable for medical experimentation; and expensive. So, when the experiments were closed down, what became of them?

In some cases the trainer has kept a relationship with the animal at the cost of career and even of normal human relationships. Janis Carter took the chimpanzee Lucy (raised as a "baby" by a couple who gave her to the training center) to an island in an African river, where the woman must live in a cage while two groups of chimpanzees roam free. Trying to rid Lucy of her human dependence, Janis Carter will not use sign language with her. Washoe and her trainer are keeping a low profile in the Pacific Northwest. Koko, the one gorilla involved in the first generation of language experiments, is still being zealously and jealously guarded by her trainer and interlocutor, Penny Patterson. The experiment is going on, but its results have been so selectively released that the most sympathetic scientist would have trouble defending Patterson's work against charges of incompetence or fraud. Without access to the evidence, it is easy to make such accusations and impossible to disprove them. This is an intellectual loss that may yet be made good; and at least Koko is as well off as she ever was. But Ally has vanished, nameless, into a maze of laboratories, Nim is in a kind of protective solitary confinement, and various lesser-known language-trained chimps are in the care of a tough-minded lab man, James Mahoney, of LEMSIP laboratories, who says, "Once you know that money is the determining factor, you know what is going to happen."

So these days the Centers for Disease Control can announce without excuse or comment that chimpanzees have been "successfully infected" with AIDS. From the point of view of these researchers the success is complete. Older laboratory animals, having been subjected to previous experiments (even if the experiments were intellectual not medical), are less valuable, hence appropriate for use in "terminal studies." Mahoney, asking for a kind of retirement colony for the older animals, is in a minority; most medical experimenters find "destruction" easier and cheaper (indeed, one is tempted to think they save their imagination for inventing euphemisms). Linden's discussion of such difficult issues is exemplary. Only a prejudiced mind will accuse this book of bias or naiveté. But probably some such accusations will be made, for some members of the scientific establishment react negatively to even the discussion of the possibility of language use by animals.

That language—genuine language including syntactics, jokes, lies, and disinterested or aesthetic observation—may prove to be a skill accessible in some degree to several species: this is an idea so distasteful to certain behaviorists and linguists that they attack not only the results of experiments but the investigation of the subject. Academic territorialism plays a part in this tabooing, but its basis seems to be a need to believe in human uniqueness, human supremacy. Critics of this kind of "speciesism" suggest that it is about as useful to science as a need to believe that the sun goes around the earth. (Linden may be unwise to call it "humanism," as he does in his last paragraph, for that word has become the shibboleth of religious fundamentalists, who, since they assert the God-ordained superiority of Man over Beast, would in this usage be humanists.)

The attitude of the human supremacist is expressed in a vocabulary very close to that of the male supremacist, and both positions probably rise from a terror of losing control of "nature" defined as an object of human exploitation. That animals might exist independently as subjects capable of cognition, emotion, pain—this perception so threatens some Alpha Males of our species that at any hint of it they go into full aggression display, baring their canines, beating their chests, ignoring the evidence. These displays are undeniably impressive, if unedifying. Meanwhile, one is left with the unforgettable images of an animal inside a cage saying, "Drink! Food! Hurry!" to a man outside the cage who doesn't know the language—and of a woman inside a cage refusing to talk to an animal outside the cage in the only language that animal knows. Such grotesque miseries bespeak a sickness of our times. Kind, quiet, and fair, Eugene Linden's book is both a diagnosis of and an antidote to the cruelty and confusion it describes. It is pleasant to hope that its success might be a sign of returning health.

Note: Professor H. S. Terrace sent me in October of 1986 a copy of a letter stating his strong opposition to *Silent Partners* and my review of it, and correcting two errors of fact. Professor Terrace says that "both David Premack and Duane Rumbaugh have reversed their originally positive assessments of an ape's grammatical competence. Yet both continue to be funded by significant federal grants," thus disproving my statement that "serious investigation of animal linguistic capacity has become almost impossible in the present climate; funding for such investigation was cut off years ago." (It does seem interesting that the continued funding is for two researchers whose "assessments of an ape's grammatical competence" are negative.) And Professor Terrace is justifiably annoyed at Linden's fail-

ure to check with him about Nim, who is not in "solitary confinement" as I, following Linden, reported; Professor Terrace reports
that "since 1983, Nim has been housed with Sally, his mate, in a
specially built, spacious home. I can attest personally that both
appear to be happy and in good health."

OUTSIDE THE GATES
by Molly Gloss
(1986)

Seeing fantasy trilogies tumble off the production lines as bright-colored and disposable as plastic toys, we curmudgeons hanker for the days when a fantasy novel was a rare, shy creature that lurked in the Mildew section of used bookstores and was usually by Mac-Donald, Dunsany, Eddison, or one Morris or another. As art it was both odd and considerable—the passionate expression of a truly unusual mind. Without in the least meaning to, Tolkien changed all that by the sheer force of his genius. To the publishing industry genius means profit. Sauron showed the industrialists where money was to be made, and so fantasy novels are now a modestly profitable industrial product, each one very like all the others.

The rare, odd, real stuff remains, of course, but has found new shadows to lurk in, far from the hype factories. "Young Adult" fiction can be such a place. Although the label is clearly that of a consumer item, although the prizes in the field can bring in real money, and although a YA book may have, over the years, an immense readership, still YA novels, like all "genre" fiction, remain unnoticed by the heavy advertisers and the powerful literary critics. YA means no more than quiche to the Real Men who control Real Books. So far even feminist criticism has done nothing to change this. We kiddilitters remain outsiders. Maybe that's a good thing. Maybe a book like *Outside the Gates* can only happen outside the gates.

The passionate expression of a truly unusual mind, Molly Gloss's first novel moves with the certainty of experience. Its fictional world is established without preamble or apology: this is the way it is here. The gates of human society, kinship, compassion, are shut upon the child gifted with uncommon power, whose "Shadow" is his truest strength. He must die in the wilderness or find there a new kinship,

Molly Gloss, *Outside the Gates* (New York: Atheneum Press, 1986).

a deeper compassion. Every adolescent knows this country outside the gates and is living there right now; adolescence is exile. Without using the heroic commonplace of One-defeats-Many, Gloss's story is that of the child alone in the world; it strikes upon deep, universal troubles and fears.

Beside the orphan Vren there are archetypal figures such as the Animal Helper familiar in folktales worldwide, here a loyal and engagingly wolfish wolf. Vren's "Shadow" is the power of mutual understanding with animals. Only when a perverted magic exaggerates this gift at cost of everything else in Vren's mind and body does it become the fairy-tale gift of the speech of the beasts—power *over* the animals. Such moral accuracy is characteristic of the book.

The sense of animal presence is strong throughout the story, mostly delightful, but when Vren obeys the perverse will of the Spellbinder, terrible. Human presence is even more vivid, though there are only four characters of any substance. Rusche, an older outcast who becomes father/brother/friend to Vren, a kind, timid, silent man, is so real a person that one accepts his ability to control the local weather as quite plausible. So, again, there is a sudden and terrific power in the climactic scene when the Spellbinder turns Rusche's mild magic into this:

> Rusche's face was dark and terrifying and unfamiliar. When he opened his mouth, he let out a great, terrible breath, a dark billowing cloud, oyster-colored and huge and angry. The thing rose from his mouth and, with a long, heavy thundering, spread itself under the overcast sky.

The single female character, an older woman, is both central and elusive. At the end of the book, Vren and Rusche are returning to her, but they don't reach her before the story ends; the gesture of reaching out, of embrace, is incomplete. There may be an element of incompleteness here in the book itself; but after all, Gloss is writing about loneliness and aloneness.

The Spellbinder, slave of his own power, is completely believable, a short, dark, bald-in-front, ordinary man whose banal spell catches the reader just as it does young Vren—before you know it. The chapter "Whispers," describing the effects of that spell, is extraordinary. Throughout the book the writing is skillful, the wording compact and exact, the tone quiet and, except for a few over-compressed phrases, musical. As in a well-made chair, each line is true, and counts.

The ethical concerns of the story are intense but unstated. No preachments. Nor is life here perceived as war, as "conflict," as it is in so much of our literature that critics have actually taken conflict to be the essential element of narrative. The guiding image of this narrative may be discovery: finding home, finding strength, finding one another. There is indeed a final struggle between power used well and power used ill; it is almost without physical violence, but the moral violence, the intensity of guilt, despair, rage, is almost unbearable when the Spellbinder forces friend to betray friend. Evil defeats itself, but at a high cost. There are no cheap victories. I find the book moving and valuable, and I think young readers will find it so, because in conception and narration it is emotionally honest—clear through.

GOLDEN DAYS
by Carolyn See
(1986)

A prepublication press release for *Golden Days* tells us that "against a sharply satirical background of the California life style," the heroine "comes to sun-and-fun country," where she meets "the end of everything." In its perfect obtuseness, this publisher's description shows what West Coast writers keep running up against: a wall—the wall Easterners build in their minds to separate Reality from California. When they come to live in California they leave the wall standing and float around in their swimming pool reading the *Wall Street Journal* and saying, "Man, this is unreal." Some of them have based whole novels on this insight.

The material of Carolyn See's novel is a lot more interesting than that, but I have to wonder if anybody east of Barstow is going to be willing to see it. The point is, she is writing as a Californian. The novel's narrator doesn't "come to sun-and-fun country," some Vacationland motel strip; she comes home. She was born there, it's where she lives, it's *her* country. And it's real. There's a lovely chapter, just before the nuclear war starts, about carless, careless teenage girls walking in Los Angeles in the fifties. (Nobody walks in Los Angeles, everybody in New York knows *that*.)

> Where did those girls walk? They walked for miles in the center of the city. . . . They walked northeast and down a long sweet incline to where Griffith Park Boulevard and Los Feliz and Fletcher Drive met. . . . They walked the old streets, Hyperion over to Vermont, stopping at the grocery store at . . . Sunset and Hollywood Boulevard . . . walking the width of the town they knew, over to La Brea, . . . and then another long, long walk home.

The streets are named for the love of saying their names. The girls walk in love.

Carolyn See, *Golden Days* (New York: McGraw-Hill, 1986).

300

There is a "sharply satirical" note in the book, all right, but it isn't for California; it's for Wall Street and D.C. and their "life style," for the corridors of power and the men who strut in them. "If women are opposite to men," Carolyn See proposes, "and California with its easy money and easy ways was opposite to the fierce, demanding East . . ."—and on this questioningly poised opposition she balances her extraordinary book.

> I had heard all my life that "California" was irrational. How could I dare say that it was not? But as a woman, and having seen, all my adult life, grim-lipped men jerking at their missiles . . . having seen their aimless horrid rage when the stuff dripped out of them: having *that,* as I say, designated by default as "rational," I suppose there was a conspiracy of brain cells on my part to say that maybe there was something else; death's opposite.

So she offers California as life; reality as "California." This is a soundly, sweetly anti-Puritan novel.

It is also quite funny, and takes incredible risks, and gets away with at least half of them. We are so well supplied at present with fiction that takes no risks at all, bone-dry minimalism, tough, lean, hard, all the euphemisms that mean "safe," that there may be readers yearning for some juice and pizzazz, some literary hang-gliding over Topanga Canyon. They'll like *Golden Days.* For all its glib wise-guy tone, this is a juicy, soft, and tender book; the strength of its feminism enables it to take the risk of being vulnerable. It isn't safe, but it's fearless.

A serious novel that has World War III about three-quarters of the way through its plot and lets the heroine live through its hideous afterdays *happily*—that book isn't playing safe.

Over the past forty years plenty of after-the-bomb stories have been written; the premise of many is that war purifies, radiation cleans, the tough survive. The lean, the hard, the minimalists, the real men, Puritans, safe and saved, rebuild Law 'n' Order on the glowing ruins after eliminating the eight-fingered gibbering Muties. Carolyn See takes this old sack of macho and dumps it.

"On the whole, they say, people got *what they expected,*" says the narrator. Not what they deserved—just what they expected. When the bombs fell,

> the generals and the military were very hard hit. A certain kind of women and children were devastated. . . . The ones I knew

who lived were the ones who had been making love, or napping,
or fixing dinner . . . the ones far out windsurfing who dove
beneath the waves and felt the whole Pacific turn warm . . .

Making love, not war. . . . A fairy tale? Of course! People get what
they expect. Those who expect to end crammed in a bomb shelter
shooting it out with the Commies, the Muties, or the Joneses, may do
so. That's their fairy tale. Carolyn See has the artist's right to endow
a greater expectation with the authority of imagination. Her vision
has a crazy majesty—the whole Pacific turning warm. It has a
stinging exactness—the word "devastated," the words "far out." If
her tale is that love, not hate, is what lives, this is a pretty good time
to be telling and hearing that tale.

The sophistication of thought in the novel is considerable, cool,
and Californian. The rigid European fixation of much East Coast
thinking doesn't encompass the real East at all. Concepts such as
satyagraha and *wu wei,* barely mentioned but structurally essential to
the book, may be invisible to readers to whom they're just foreign
words, something they do out West, or maybe in Selma. No harm in
that, unless it leaves the book underestimated by critics who should
know better. It's a fast, flip, funny read, a good summer book; it's
also something more, and deserves notice. Trying to write non-
violently about the ultimate act of violence, See bases her novel in
very old nonviolent traditions; writing as a woman about a "man's
world," she grounds her anger in feminine solidarity and human
kindness. On these firm foundations in the California earth, she has
built a Watts Tower of a book, fragile, brilliant, and surprising.

ACKNOWLEDGMENTS

"The Beginning Place" and "The Book of the Dun Cow" copyright © 1980 by Ursula K. Le Guin. First appeared in *Venom*, vol. 1, 1980.

"Freddy's Book and Vlemk the Box-Painter" copyright © 1980 by Ursula K. Le Guin. First appeared in *The Washington Post Book World*, March 23, 1980.

"The Marriages Between Zones Three, Four, and Five" copyright © 1980 by *The New Republic*. Reprinted by permission. First appeared in *The New Republic*, March 29, 1980.

"Kalila and Dimna" copyright © 1980 by Ursula K. Le Guin. First appeared in *The Washington Post Book World*, August 10, 1980.

"Unfinished Business" copyright © 1980 by Ursula K. Le Guin. First appeared in *The Washington Post Book World*, August 24, 1980.

"Italian Folktales" copyright © 1980 by *The New Republic*. Reprinted by permission. First appeared in *The New Republic*, September 27, 1980.

"Peake's Progress" copyright © 1981 by Ursula K. Le Guin. First appeared in *The Washington Post Book World*, September 27, 1981.

"The Sentimental Agents" copyright © 1983 by Ursula K. Le Guin. First appeared in *The Weekly* (Seattle), August 3, 1983.

"Difficult Loves" copyright © 1984 by Ursula K. Le Guin. First appeared in *The Washington Post Book World*, November 18, 1984.

" 'Forsaking Kingdoms': Five Poets" copyright © 1985 by Ursula K. Le Guin. First appeared in *The Washington Post Book World*, February 17, 1985.

"The Mythology of North America" copyright © 1985 by The New York Times Company. Reprinted by permission. First appeared in *The New York Times Book Review* under the title "Loon Woman in the Long Ago," September 1, 1985.

"Silent Partners" copyright © 1986 by The New York Times Company. Reprinted by permission. First appeared in *The New York Times Book Review* under the title "Apologies to the Primates," May 25, 1986.

"Outside the Gates" copyright © 1986 by Ursula K. Le Guin. First appeared in *The Five Owls*, November–December 1986.

"Golden Days" copyright © 1986 by Ursula K. Le Guin. First appeared in *The Washington Post Book World*, November 9, 1986.

Grateful acknowledgment is made to the following authors and publishers for permission to use quotations from copyrighted works: From the *Gododdin*, translated by Joseph P. Clancy, in his *The Earliest Welsh Poetry*. Copyright © 1970 by Joseph P. Clancy. Reprinted by permission of the translator. From Margaret Drabble, *The Millstone*. Copyright © 1965 by Margaret Drabble. Reprinted by permission of William Morrow & Company, Inc. From Terence Des Pres, *The Survivor: An Anatomy of Life in the Death Camps.* Copyright © 1976 by Terence Des Pres. Reprinted by permission of Oxford University Press. From Robert C. Elliott, *The Shape of Utopia.* Copyright © 1970 by Robert C. Elliott. Reprinted by permission of University of Chicago Press. "She Who," in *The Work of a Common Woman,* by Judy Grahn. Copyright © 1978 by Judy Grahn. Reprinted by permission of the author. "The Blanket Around Her," in *What Moon Drove Me to This?* by Joy Harjo. Copyright © 1980 by Joy Harjo. Reprinted by permission of the author and I. Reed Books. From "The Women Speaking," in *Daughters, I Love You,* by Linda Hogan. Copyright © 1981 by Linda Hogan. Reprinted by permission of the author. From *The Book of Laughter and Forgetting,* by Milan Kundera. Copyright © 1978 by Milan Kundera. English translation copyright © 1980 by Alfred A. Knopf, Inc. Reprinted by permission of Alfred A. Knopf, Inc. "Stepping Westward," in *Poems 1960–1967,* by Denise Levertov. Copyright © 1967 by Denise Levertov Goodman. Reprinted by permission of New Directions Publishing Corp. From "A Wild Surmise," in *Writing Like a Woman,* by Alicia Ostriker. Copyright © 1983 by Alicia Ostriker. Reprinted by permission of University of Michigan Press. From "The Parts of a Poet," in *Lost Copper,* by Wendy Rose. Copyright © 1980 by Wendy Rose. Reprinted by permission of the author and Malki Museum Press. From "Professions for Women," in *The Pargiters,* by Virginia Woolf, edited by Mitchell Leaska. Copyright © 1977 by Quentin Bell and Angelica Garnett. Reprinted by permission of Harcourt Brace Jovanovich, Inc. From *Islandia,* by Austin Tappan Wright. Copyright © 1942 by Austin Tappan Wright. Reprinted by permission of Alfred A. Knopf, Inc.